WHITEWATER RESCUES:
TRUE STORIES OF
SURVIVAL, BRAVERY,
AND QUICK THINKING

PRAISE FOR *WHITEWATER RESCUES*

"Over my career of taking first responder and rescue classes, some of the most valuable lessons I have learned came from the instructors' 'war stories' that detailed not just the technical information but also the human experience. Very often these tales have been based on situations that did not have desirable outcomes. This collection of success stories is such an interesting learning experience and helps give some insight into the ever-present question 'What would I do?'"

—Mike Mather, ACA Safety & Rescue ITE, Rescue 3 International Instructor Trainer, Higgins & Langley Award Recipient

"I've been reading Charlie's river accident reports for over 30 years, and his unflinching approach has helped develop my awareness of what goes wrong and why. This new collection provides a delightful counterpoint, offering stories of how quick thinking, strong teamwork, and ingenious solutions prevented the worst from happening. May this book inspire river runners to respond creatively to the inevitable challenges."

—Teresa Gryder, ND; safety chair, Lower Columbia Canoe Club (WA)

"Charlie's collection of whitewater accidents and successful results is a read worth your time. It underscores a clear meaning: that if we don't understand and analyze the mishaps and mistakes of those who have gone before us, we are most certainly going to repeat those occurrences and, without proper action and quick thinking, suffer the consequences. I believe Charlie has shared paddling experiences to guide us toward safer paddling."

—Virgil Chambers, National Safe Boating Council

WHITEWATER RESCUES: TRUE STORIES OF SURVIVAL, BRAVERY, AND QUICK THINKING

CHARLIE WALBRIDGE

MENASHA RIDGE PRESS
Your Guide to the Outdoors Since 1982
an imprint of AdventureKEEN

Whitewater Rescues: True Stories of Survival, Bravery, and Quick Thinking
Copyright © 2024 by Charlie Walbridge

Cataloging-in-Publication data is on file with the Library of Congress.
ISBN 978-1-63404-384-7 (pbk.) | ISBN 978-1-63404-385-4 (ebook)

 MENASHA RIDGE PRESS
An imprint of AdventureKEEN
2204 First Ave. S., Ste. 102
Birmingham, AL 35233
800-678-7006, fax 877-374-9016

Visit menasharidge.com for a complete listing of our books and for ordering information. Contact us at our website, at facebook.com/menasharidge, or at x.com/menasharidge with questions or comments. To find out more about who we are and what we're doing, visit blog.menasharidge.com.

Editor: Kate Johnson
Proofreader: Emily Beaumont
Editorial assistant: Jenna Barron
Indexer: Frances Lennie
Cover design: Jonathan Norberg
Art direction: Travis Bryant
Text design: Hilary Harkness

Cover photos: (front) Arcansel/Shutterstock; (back, top to bottom): Steve Barber and Yellowstone National Park/Flickr/Public Domain; (back, background) schankz/Shutterstock

Interior photos: **(page vi)** Will Fisher/Flickr/CC BY-SA 2.0 DEED (creativecommons.org/licenses /by-sa/2.0); **(page 6)** Densington86/Wikimedia Commons/CC BY-SA 4.0 DEED (creativecommons.org /licenses/by-sa/4.0/deed); **(page 42)** Ben Schumin/Flickr/CC BY-SA 2.0 (creativecommons.org/licenses /by-sa/2.0); **(page 100)** Bureau of Land Management/Public Domain; **(page 188)** West Virginia National Guard/Flickr/CC BY 2.0 (creativecommons.org/licenses/by/2.0); **(page 212)** Lars Plougmann/Flickr /CC BY-SA 2.0 DEED (creativecommons.org/licenses/by/2.0); **(page 254)** Yellowstone National Park /Flickr/Public Domain; **(page 287)** Jeff Souville/Flickr/CC BY-SA 2.0 (creativecommons.org/licenses /by-sa/2.0); **(page 298)** Ammit Jack/Shutterstock; **(page 330)** Steve Barber

Distributed by Publishers Group West
Printed in the United States of America

SAFETY NOTICE Neither the author nor the publisher is responsible for any loss, damage, injury, or inconvenience that may occur while using this book—you are responsible for your own safety and health on the water. The fact that a trip, activity, or technique is described in this book does not mean that it will be safe for you. Always check local conditions (which can change from day to day), know your own limitations, and consult a map.

TABLE of CONTENTS

INTRODUCTION

MOST WHITEWATER TRIPS ARE UNEVENTFUL, but when you mix people and moving water, accidents will happen. Most rescues are straightforward and routine. For experienced boaters, helping a swimmer get to shore, chasing down loose gear, or wading out to grab a lightly pinned boat is as normal as catching eddies or surfing: you respond quickly, chase the people first, then their paddles (because they're easiest to lose track of), and finally the boat. We do it so often that we forget how important it is. A surprising number of 911 calls are from inexperienced paddlers stuck on a midstream rock or island or caught on the wrong side of the river. Occasionally rescuers encounter a tricky situation or a difficult recovery that requires some planning, but rarely is it truly dangerous or scary. These rare life-threatening incidents are what we train for in our rescue classes.

Each season, a number of fatal whitewater accidents are reported to American Whitewater and recorded in the Accident Database. Individual paddlers can do a lot to reduce their chances of a serious

OPPOSITE: A kayaker navigates rapids on the Potomac River.

mishap, starting with having the right gear, developing their skills, and being ready to handle emergencies (see Appendixes). They can also improve their judgment by learning from their experiences and those of the whitewater community at large. Studying accident reports is a useful part of this process. I began reporting accidents 45 years ago because I wanted to learn what I needed to do to stay out of trouble. Today my goal is to help others stay safe by sharing these accounts.

In 1975, I was competing at the Icebreaker Slalom in southern New York, held on an easy Class II rapid below a dam. Taking a practice run, I looked downstream and saw that something was very wrong. At a small ledge underneath a highway bridge, a paddler was stuck underwater. Ropes were being thrown, and some very skilled paddlers and guides were there, but no one could help him. Finally, the water was turned off at the dam, and he was pulled free. His foot had been caught by a rock at the base of the drop, and the current pushed him underwater.

Although some were certain this was a freak accident, I wasn't so sure. Shaken, I talked to witnesses, and several reported that the man was trying to stand up as he washed over the ledge. As a summer-camp trip leader in the White Mountains, I'd learned a great deal from the Appalachian Mountain Club's accident reports. I assumed there was a source like this for whitewater paddlers. There wasn't.

After talking to a number of witnesses, I wrote an accident report that was shared among several Eastern paddling clubs. Several people responded with descriptions of similar accidents elsewhere. My report, published in the *American Whitewater Journal,* was the origin of the now-routine warning against standing up in fast-moving current. It also began a tradition of openly discussing river accidents and near misses. Rather than trying place blame, we try to learn as much as we can from each one and modify our paddling practices as needed.

American Whitewater has been helping paddlers learn from our mistakes since its founding, and the creation of the AW Safety Code in 1959 was the first important milestone. Accident reports in the *American Whitewater Journal* led to the creation of AW's online Accident Database, which today contains over 2,200 entries. Our goal, always, is to talk about what happened openly so we can all learn. I want to thank everyone who has contributed to the database. Whether you report an incident you were involved with or send in accounts that you found in newspapers or online, it all adds to our knowledge base and helps keep us safe. A special thanks to American Whitewater for keeping the information accessible. A portion of the proceeds from the sales of this book will be donated to American Whitewater to support its safety, education, and outreach programs.

Although reviewing fatality reports can be pretty depressing, I've also received many accounts of close calls and great rescues. Uplifting and inspiring, they spotlight the courage and ingenuity of whitewater paddlers. This book shares the most interesting and compelling accounts submitted to American Whitewater, edited as needed for length and clarity. There is much to learn from and admire in each of these stories, and I hope they will be useful to you.

—Charlie Walbridge
Bruceton Mills, West Virginia

1

THE EARLY YEARS: BETTER BOATS, RISKIER RUNS

ALTHOUGH PEOPLE HAVE BEEN PADDLING rapids for hundreds of years, boats used before World War II were easily damaged, and this made paddlers extremely conservative. Soon after the war, the first aluminum canoes arrived on the market. They were incredibly tough, which changed everything. People attempted steeper, rockier rivers and started developing better techniques. Over time, the sport drew a number of engineers and scientists who studied hydrology and developed new, dynamic river-running skills that form the basis of our sport.

The Europeans were years ahead of us, as American paddlers competing in the world championships in the 1960s quickly found out. Our guys may have finished at the bottom of the results, but they were fast learners. They brought home new designs and techniques that jump-started the sport. Several European experts who moved to the United States after the war helped teach and inspire a generation of paddlers.

Swiss slalom canoeist Eduard Kunz competes in a folding kayak in the 1949 ICF Canoe Slalom World Championships in Geneva.

I began paddling with a group of friends from college in the 1960s, a time when whitewater sport was small but growing. Almost all decked boats in the United States were homemade or built by small, one-man shops. Much of the gear was homemade as well. Paddling was usually done in Class II–III rapids, serious rescues were infrequent, and few paddlers carried ropes or other rescue gear. There was no real rescue training, and paddlers confronting a problem scratched their heads and developed their strategies on the spot. Here are accounts of a few rescues from that era.

BAD PIN ON LOYALSOCK CREEK

IN 1966, I WAS PART OF A GROUP of friends who started the Outing Club at Bucknell University in central Pennsylvania. My roommate was a counselor at a canoe camp and was very enthusiastic about whitewater. One trip down a local Class II creek in an open canoe and I was hooked! By April 1969, my buddy Jim Love and I were both kayakers. Thanks to the Penn State Outing Club pool sessions, we both had pretty good rolls. We'd run some Class II rapids and were looking for more excitement. We called our contact at the Penn State Outing Club and got invited on a trip down Loyalsock Creek, a Class III run in north-central Pennsylvania known for its frigid climate and icy water. In addition to our two kayaks, there were four tandem Grumman open canoes in our group. Putting in a few minutes behind us was a nationally known group of expert C-1 racers I'd met at Penn State's pool sessions.

All went according to plan until we reached the S-Turn rapid, one of the hardest on the run. I flipped and immediately executed my first-ever river roll in painfully cold water. I was whooping and hollering until I was suddenly confronted with a huge pour-over. As I went over, I saw that it was created by a pinned Grumman open canoe. One of the Penn State paddlers was caught under it. He was struggling for breath and in desperate trouble.

I eddied out but had no idea what to do. Several other guys were with me, looking at the pin from shore. Suddenly, like the cavalry in a grade B Western, four C-boaters paddled around the bend. John Sweet, Norm Holcombe, Tom Irwin, and Rick Rigg paddled into an eddy in a tight cluster. John grabbed a rope that was still in its original hardware-store packaging and unraveled it. Rick and Norm held the rope from upstream while John and Tom leaned back and waded out sideways toward the pinned canoe. Tom held the trapped paddler's head above water while John shoved his Norse paddle between the boat and the rock and rested it momentarily against his shoulder. He spoke quietly to Tom: "I'm going to lift the boat, but I can't hold it. I want you to move fast and pull him out." He then threw his weight into the paddle, and Tom pulled the man free. The whole maneuver took less than a minute.

Tom and John, using the rope, waded the victim to shore. He was so cold he could hardly stand. As they bundled him into the bottom of a canoe, they sent Jim and me for help. We got to the road and flagged down a motorist, who took the victim and his rescuers to Forksville, 5 miles downstream. A local family opened up their house to us; someone ran a lukewarm bath while others removed the victim's clothes. We made hot, sweetened tea. The victim said he'd been holding on to the back of his boat just as he'd been taught. The boat hit the rock, and the current pushed him down underneath it. He was right below the canoe when it pinned. An hour later, he was still shivering but able to get into dry clothes and ride home.

Jim and I went up the next week with a come-along and a length of climbing rope to try to rescue the canoe. We had no idea what we were doing and broke the rope twice. It snapped back wickedly past our heads both times. I decided if I was going to learn to paddle, I would need to learn to do better than that!

TOM YANOWSKI TO THE RESCUE AT STUBBLEFIELD FALLS

AFTER COLLEGE, I MOVED to the Washington, DC, area to enjoy the mighty Potomac River and the wonderful paddling community that surrounded it. Our relationship with the National Park Service at Great Falls was evolving slowly. Two incidents from the early 1970s are worthy of describing. The first is from the October 1972 issue of *Cruiser,* the newsletter of the Canoe Cruisers Association of Greater Washington, DC (CCA):

> *The high waters of October 7–8, which reached 9.7 feet, just short of the 10-foot flood-stage level on the Brookmont gauge, provided the Canoe Cruisers with our finest hour since Jamie McEwan's Olympic Bronze Medal.*
>
> *We bask in the reflected glory of the dramatic river rescue of two novice paddlers in the presence of the National Capital Park Police, the Glen Echo and Cabin John Volunteer Fire Departments, and the cameras of Channel 9 TV. (Note: One paddler told me there were so many flashing lights along MacArthur Boulevard it looked like Christmas!) Many CCA members also caught Tom Yanowski's post-rescue interview on the Saturday night news.*

Tom's account of the rescue is both simple and routine. He and other expert paddlers had been enjoying the heavy waters at Difficult Run and had decided to leave, as usual, at Old Angler's Inn. They met two boatloads of obvious novices about to take off downriver. Tom warned them that the river was rising—and dangerous—and, quite naturally (unfortunately), his advice was rejected, with thanks. It was some time later that Tom, who had been concerned that the novices would get into trouble, decided he had best paddle after them to provide help if needed.

The paddlers indeed were in trouble. Somewhere below Stubblefield Falls, both boats had flipped. While two paddlers made it to shore to spread the alarm, the other two landed on a midstream islet in the vicinity of Lock 8. It was slowly disappearing in the rising water. By the time Tom arrived on the scene, the land-based rescuers listed above had reached the point of frustrated desperation—they couldn't get a rope across to the islet—and had called in a helicopter.

Tom took the natural approach of an expert canoeist. He paddled his open Grumman up to the islet, took one paddler off and carried him to safety, returned to the islet, and rescued the second stranded canoeist the same way. Tom reports his only disappointment came in Channel 9's editing of his post-rescue comments: they cut out his plug for CCA and his plea that all beginning whitewater canoeists join canoeing organizations such as ours.

Back then, firefighters were not trained in river rescue and could not mount an effective response. Time and training changed that, and today the Cabin John Volunteer Fire Department and others have first-rate swiftwater rescue teams. North of DC, the Potomac goes through two states, four counties, and innumerable towns. This often led to large, uncoordinated responses to river emergencies like this one. In the next decade, the Park Service worked with area fire companies to assign responsibility for certain sections of river to each company so they didn't all respond to an accident. The second incident from the early 1970s is described below.

TWO PADDLERS PINNED ON DIFFICULT RUN

WHEN I WENT TO ONE OF THE MONTHLY MEETINGS of the Canoe Cruisers Association, I was surprised to find a broken kayak front and center and a person off to the side hobbling around on crutches. Both were the result of a close call on Difficult Run, a small tributary of the lower Potomac. The accident was discussed at length at the meeting, and it was the first account of a vertical (bow-first) pin that I had ever encountered.

On Saturday, February 26, 1972, four paddlers set out on Difficult Run. The paddling ended with two paddlers pinned in their boats halfway down a chute, with water pouring completely over them. One of the paddlers was freed after several minutes and then contributed to the eventual rescue of his companion, but it would be another agonizing hour before the rescue was accomplished. Following is the story of that trip, told by two of the people involved. It appeared as an insert in the November 1973 issue of CCA's "Cruiser" newsletter.

First is Frank Daspit's account, written on March 15, 1972:

Rain had brought Difficult Run up to 5.9 feet on the gauge, and this usually quiet trickle was a high, fast rush of water. Nick Cullander in his kayak, Chip Quietzsch running C-1, and Jean Goertner and I in a C-2 were there to see what could be run. From the parking lot on VA 193, it was an easy run to the first rapid, maybe a quarter of a mile down. From here on, it was scout and run, scout and portage. Nothing really bad, but tough enough not to mess with. Then another invisible drop came up, and again we got out to scout. This turned out to be a five-step, 20-foot drop stretched over about 50 yards. It was a beautiful sight but nothing to run. Below this series was a small, 2- to 3-foot drop with two passages. The approach was down the left bank, through an S-turn, then through a slot 4–5 feet wide with a clean sluice of water pouring through it.

In appearance, it was no different than many similar chutes we had run on other rivers, other than perhaps being cleaner. Both sides were smooth, vertical rocks with no projections, and probing with Nick's kayak paddle showed no rocks in the middle. After a little discussion, Jean and I decided to run the slot and, while we left the decision of which channel to use up to Nick and Chip, we felt they should have no trouble in either channel. Jean and I went first and had no problems at all, using only a light brace coming out. We took up station in an eddy about 20 feet down on the left and waited to help the boys if necessary. Nick came first in his kayak and made a good approach into the slot, and the next thing I knew, he was pinned halfway down the drop with water pouring over his head. All that was visible was a new, large hump in the chute with a vague figure occasionally visible in it. We shouted to Chip to stay back and started back up to help. Unfortunately, Chip was unable to hear what we were saying and could not see Nick, so he came ahead, spotting Nick's hard hat at the last minute and moving left just enough to avoid going down on top of him. Then he, too, became pinned, just to the left and somewhat higher than Nick. At this point we had two boats and paddlers underwater, and things did not look good.

By the time Jean and I got back up to the drop, it was evident that the water flowing over them was leaving air pockets, and they were able to breathe. Our first rescue attempt was to paddle in and have Jean pull on them while I backed. After several tries, it became obvious that we were getting nowhere. I got out into the eddy alongside the chute, intending to work my way over to the bottom of the chute and try working them out. I was unable to get a foothold or swim in the proper direction, so Jean pushed me over to the outside of the eddy, where I managed to climb out on the rock forming the outside wall of the chute. From here I found the stern of Chip's boat about 6 inches underwater near the top of the chute and, after some effort, managed to lift it up. The water then pushed under, and

Chip started out of the chute. About this time, I lost my footing and started down the chute myself. After hanging up for a short while halfway down, I washed through and floated down to the eddy below, where I found Chip standing in the water.

Chasing him out in front of me, I climbed out and headed back up the shore to see what was happening. When I got back up, Nick was all the way over against the rock on the right and a little farther down the chute. He was now out of water from the waist up and able to lean against the rock. Jean had extended a paddle out to him and was trying to pull him free that way, but without success. After some effort with one and two paddles and various sticks, it became apparent that Nick was not coming out that way, and that any further efforts would require somebody out on the rock again.

Chip had been carrying our only rope, which was now lost, and the paddles had pulled loose during one of the attempts to free Nick, so Chip and I looked for a stick. Chip found a good one, and I then sent him for help. Somehow or other, the stick and I got out to the rock. I know I swam. I think the stick was passed over by Jean. Using the stick, I tried to pull Nick free, without success. Finally, I asked Jean to come out on the rock, but she was about 2 inches short and washed down the chute. It then became a waiting game, trying desperately to think of something new to attempt and praying for help. Somewhere during this time, we decided there was no point in two of us doing nothing but wait, and Jean went to look for help also. After some time, Sam Huntington came in response to Chip's search for help, and things began to improve. My recollection of the rest is somewhat fragmented, and I'll defer to Sam's write-up.

Sam recorded his account on February 29, 1972:

About 4 p.m. on Saturday, February 26, I shoved off from Angler's Inn in my C-1 for an hour's paddle or so on the Potomac in, out, and around the Difficult Run rapids. I had expected to run into some other paddlers, but none were there, and I decided to go out alone. As the Little Falls gauge was about 5.5 feet, it took a little effort to get upstream. I had managed to ferry across the Maryland chute and was making my way over to the center rapids when I heard a muffled shout. Turning, I saw a figure halfway up the cliffs at the foot of the rapids. After running down to within shouting distance, the figure— who turned out to be Chip Quietzsch—informed me that there were some people in trouble up Difficult Run.

I paddled up Difficult Run as far as I could, picking up a canoe paddle and observing a C-2 and the remains of a C-1 lodged against a fallen tree on the way, and beached my boat. After scrambling up the shore, around a corner and over some rocks for about 200 yards, I recognized Frank Daspit crouched on a rock in the stream, separated from the shore by an 8-foot-wide strong current of water dropping sharply about 3 or

4 feet. Frank was holding onto one end of a short stick, and Nick Cullander—whom I did not know at the time— was clutching onto the other end, half-submerged at the foot of the drop. Nick's hands were quite red, and it was immediately apparent that he had been in the water for some time. Even though he was protected by a wetsuit, it was not clear how much longer he could hang on.

After a few words with Frank, I made a fast trip back to my boat for my 10-foot bowline and a canoe paddle. On returning, it soon became apparent that I could be of little use onshore since Nick was caught in his boat, which was wholly submerged at the bottom of the drop. Any attempt to pull him from shore would have dragged him into the main force of the current. At Frank's direction, I then jumped into the water some- what upstream of the rock and just reached the rock before being swept over the drop.

Once on the rock, we tied a large loop in the rope, which Nick was able to get over his head and under his arms. Frank and I then pulled on the rope for all we were worth, but without success. We then tied the rope around the handle of the paddle and laid the paddle on top of the rock so that only the handle was sticking out toward Nick. As the rope was taut, we could then hold Nick up by merely standing on the blade of the paddle. In other words, we were no longer dependent upon either Nick's or our own strength to keep him from slumping into the water.

For what then seemed ages but was probably about 20–25 minutes, we made several attempts to pry, jerk, or muscle Nick out of his boat using various sticks as levers—all with no success. Since during some of these attempts I was in the water actually standing on Nick's kayak and reaching into the boat to try to free his legs, I was able to judge fairly well the position of the boat. In coming over the drop, Nick was probably closer to the rock than the shore. The kayak's bow, with its low volume, must have plunged to the bottom and become solidly lodged against a rock. The substantial volume of water coming over the drop then forced the stern down into the drop so that the kayak was close to the rock Frank and I were standing on, pretty much in line with the stream but tilted downward somewhat, under about 1 foot of fast-moving water. The full force of that water was pressing against Nick's back, thus holding him firmly in the boat. When Frank and I pulled from the rock standing above him (which was the only place we could stand), we were actually pulling him against the forward deck of the kayak and were not directly counter-acting the force of the water holding him in place. In retrospect, I might have had more success trying to dislodge the bow of the boat than trying to pry Nick free.

As a later examination disclosed, Nick's kayak suffered relatively little damage. The stern seam between deck and bottom separated in several places, there were one or two tears in the bottom, and the front of the cockpit rim was broken. There was no evidence, however, that the boat had been doubled over in any way.

Eventually, the Fairfax County Rescue Squad, alerted by Chip, arrived about 10 strong—others arrived later. They tossed me a heavy nylon rope, which I tied around Nick under his arms. Again, it was apparent that a direct pull from shore would merely pull Nick into the current. But with Frank and I pulling laterally on the line and several members of the rescue squad pulling from a point somewhat upstream of the rock, Nick finally came loose. Frank and I were able to pull him up on the rock, which fortunately was large enough so that he could lie down. Some 10–15 minutes later, a wire litter arrived and was passed out to us. I tied one end of a heavy nylon rope around a projection of the rock. By passing it through the ends of the litter and having several men pull hard onshore, we had an overhead cable, and Nick, strapped securely in the litter, was safely pulled to shore. Frank and I followed, hand-traversing on the same rope.

Perhaps the most remarkable aspect of the entire operation was Nick's attitude. Without panicking and in extreme discomfort—both from the cold and the fact that, as it later turned out, he had two broken legs—Nick hung on, determined to survive the ordeal. How much longer he could have lasted had the rescue squad not come when it did is only a matter of conjecture; to hang on as long as he had to—which I would guess was in excess of an hour—took an incredible exercise of willpower.

*Frank also was called upon for a supreme effort, as
he did not have a wetsuit and had been fully submerged
in the water several times before getting onto the rock
where he was when I arrived. How he had the strength
he did, shivering all the while, I will never know.*

*Once onshore, the Rescue Squad carried Nick up the
Difficult Run trail to an ambulance. Frank, Chip, and Jean—
who had been with Frank in the C-2 and had also gone for
help—went with Nick. I rounded up the C-2 and Nick's kayak,
which had come free after we pulled Nick out, and towed
them back to Angler's Inn, arriving there about 6:30 p.m.*

TRAPPED AT GATE 23

IN THE 1970S, SLALOM RACING was a vital part of Eastern whitewater sport. There were very few kayak schools or clinics, and the
best way to improve your skills was to race. It was also a great way to
meet people. You could watch the top competitors tackle the course,
check out the newest boats and gear, and maybe run a nearby river
after the race. The boats were almost all homemade. Top racers
brought the latest designs from Europe, made molds from them, and,
after producing boats for themselves, would rent the molds to others.
Molds were often transferred at races, along with resin, cloth, and
other boat-building components.

Many racers back then liked their canoes and kayaks to fit very
tightly, and getting caught inside a pinned boat was a real possibility,
especially with borrowed boats. The following entrapment happened
at a major race and involved several elite slalom racers. The article
was written by OK Goodwin, longtime American Whitewater safety

chair and leader of the safety teams at many Savage River races. It appeared in the November/December 1976 issue of *American White-water Journal*.

Savage River International Slalom, Sunday, September 5, 1976: George Lhota (bow) and Mikki Piras (stern) in Boat No. 125 of the C-2M Class (first run) capsized at about Gate 16. Mikki bailed out and was helped in to shore by a heaving line at about Gate 21. George stayed with the boat, tried unsuccessfully to roll, and drifted downstream. The stern of the boat (a low-volume Hartung cut-down by Steve Draper) rode high, 1–2 feet out of water; George's end was underwater. The boat drifted almost broadside onto an exposed rock at about Gate 23. The bow (inshore) tried to negotiate a narrow 8-foot channel as most of the boat tried for the main channel. The boat lodged on a point about 18 inches aft of the bow cockpit, rolled slightly with the deck against the rock, and folded.

George did not come out, and it appeared that his legs were trapped in the boat. He was able to raise his head momentarily above the fast flow of water to breathe. But the boat settled, and water was diverted over the hull, making this more difficult. It seemed obvious that with any further collapse of the boat, George would be trapped with his head totally underwater.

Rescue efforts began even before the boat lodged. Safety personnel from Gate 21 and Gate 25 areas reached the site as the boat settled. Several competitors and spectators jumped into the water to try to reach

George but were swept downstream. The most effective action, however, was rendered by David Hearn (a competitor), who jumped the fast current to land in the eddy behind the rock on which the boat was pinned. (Note: Davey was wearing street clothes; no PFD or other gear.) Finding some footing in the current, he was able to support George's head above water. At about the same time, a heaving line was thrown to David to help him maintain his position. George, feeling the line, grabbed it too. Several people grabbed the line to haul George ashore, but he wasn't able to free himself from the boat, and the pulling turned to a steadying action. A second and third heaving line were thrown but did little good. (One did become entangled around George's neck.)

David had difficulty maintaining his footing but managed to be the key to a successful rescue. After what seemed an interminable few minutes, others released the stern end of the boat (the high end) from the rock by a relatively easy lift. George, boat and all, was hauled ashore, with him still in the cockpit.

The boat, already broken in several places, was literally torn apart to free George's feet and legs. He was checked over by EMT personnel from the Tri-Town Ambulance & Rescue Association that was on hand and, except for some numbness, scrapes, and bruises, appeared in good shape.

Mikki Piras, in the meantime, cold and fatigued from her swim, witnessed the attempts to rescue George. The shock caught up with her, as might have been expected. As it turned out, she probably suffered more in mental anguish than George suffered physically.

The accident might go on the books as having been "the result of a capsize in the Class IV rapids of this section of the Savage River," but there is obviously more to it than that. Several factors enter into the entrapment that, in themselves, do not seem critical:

- **George Lhota is a competent, self-assured paddler** *with the ability to roll a C-2 with his partner, or (as he has many times demonstrated) alone, after his partner has left the boat. He knows when to attempt a roll and will, when necessary, remain under a capsized boat until it drifts to calmer water before trying. Once upright, he is quite capable of maneuvering the waterlogged boat to shore. When all goes well, this is a relatively safe procedure.*

- **The outfitting in the particular C-2** *consists of what is called "machines." This is a particularly low seat thwart and two metal-strap thigh braces. Such outfitting results in a low center of gravity and a more "solid" feel of control in leaning the boat, but it is difficult to get into and, in circumstances such as those described, even more difficult to get out of.*

- **The point of impact of boat against rock** *determined whether the boat would hang there or pivot and slide around the rock to one side or the other. A matter of an inch or two either way and George might have rolled in the calmer water below.*

- **George was in no immediate danger** *when the boat was first pinned. Most paddlers recognize the potential of a boat collapsing and wrapping a rock even tighter and know that this is the time to leave the boat quickly. George (apparently) gambled that the boat would free itself or else he was unable to free himself in the brief moment before the boat did collapse.*

In retrospect, this accident had the potential of producing another fatality in whitewater. If any one thing was to be singled out as the factor that caused this "almost" fatality, it would have to be the tight outfitting. Many competitors use outfitting similar to that in George's boat. Low seat thwarts, rigid thigh braces, cramped legroom, extremely low decks; these are the components that make the bailing-out process difficult and, when conditions dictate, absolutely dangerous.

It must be added that George remained cool and calm through the entire sequence of events. After it was all over, someone remarked: "If such an ordeal had to happen, it's good that George Lhota was the one it happened to. No one could have handled it better." Amen.

And to David Hearn—the hero of the affair—must go the plaudits for quick thinking, quick and effective action, and total modesty.

David Hearn's account of the incident follows:

So, here is the story as I remember it: I was watching the slalom race at the Savage River between runs, about three-quarters of the way down the course. I saw Mikki Piras and George Lhota capsize upstream in the very busy section of the course. Mikki exited the boat, while George remained in the boat and rolled up. George was in the bow, and the Czech C-2 was a translucent, unpigmented racing layup. George used rigid non-adjustable sheet metal "machines" in lieu of knee straps.

The boat took on water and was low volume in the bow, making it a challenge to control, along with the fact that paddling even a dry end-hole boat from the bow is nearly impossible. So George's end of the boat was sinking, and he was trying to get to shore. The combination of those machines and the thwart seat made it hard to get out of the boat. Almost to shore, George lodged on a rock near river left, with a narrow but powerful flume of current separating the rock from the left bank. The boat's deck was against the rock, and George was shallowly underwater and struggling to breathe.

I looked at the situation for a brief time and mentally calculated that I could jump across the channel of rushing water into the eddy behind the rock to help George. Then I did it, and it worked well enough that I was not whisked downstream but was able to stand in the eddy and assist George by holding him up so he could breathe. But I couldn't do much more than that, since I needed both hands and arms to do it. At least two throw ropes were deployed toward George, but he did not really have the means to grab a rope, as he was plenty busy trying to breathe. Unfortunately, one of those

*ropes ended up looped around George's neck, so putting
any tension on it was contraindicated!*

*I was wearing a royal blue with yellow stripes
Adidas tracksuit jacket and pants, with an elastic waist,
over a purple-and-pink patterned Speedo, the latter of
which I normally wore in the boat while paddling in
those days. No life jacket, no helmet, but probably jelly
plastic sandals on my feet. Those Adidas pants were not
really staying up all that well with their waterlogged
weight pulling them down. So it probably lasted 5–10
minutes, and I was able to hold him up to breathe,
during which time some sort of tension was able to be
applied with a rope that was not around George's neck,
he in the boat was pulled to shore, and he was then able
to exit the boat upright onshore.*

*OK Goodwin, probably in charge of safety at the race,
along with being the ACA safety chair at the time for Slalom
and Wildwater, was upset at George for racing in an unsafe-
to-exit boat. I don't remember how I got back to shore.*

*A perusal of my first of many training logs finds
that this was on Sunday, September 5, 1976, at the third
and final race of the North American Cup. Jonquière,
Quebec, and Madawaska River in Ontario were the
venues for races 1 and 2.*

PIN ON THE CHEAT RIVER

FROM THE MID-1970s TO THE EARLY '80s I was a weekend safety
boater for a rafting outfitter on West Virginia's Cheat River. These

were the glory days of Cheat River rafting. For six weekends in April and May, my company, Mountain Streams and Trails, ran eight trips a day on Saturday and Sunday. Several other companies ran five to six trips daily, and over a dozen outfitters had a presence on the river. We all used the "guide assisted" format, where groups of 40 were accompanied by four guides, two in rafts and two in closed boats. The Cheat is a large river, with widely variable flows. This was Memorial Day weekend in 1977, and the water was low, under 1 foot on the Albright gauge. The rapids were picky Class III–IV. I'd volunteered to guide in a raft to spare my C-1. My friend Chip Quietzsch was boat-guiding as we entered Coliseum, which before the 1985 flood contained a nasty pinning boulder called Trap Rock at the bottom of a chute partway down. Chip's job was to sit in an eddy by the rock and help release any rafts that pinned. I'd seen several people caught over the years but nothing really serious.

Sitting in an upstream eddy, I heard Chip screaming for help. He's a pretty controlled guy and doesn't excite easily. I jumped onshore, grabbed a rescue bag, and sprinted toward his voice. About 30 yards downstream, a fairly large crowd of private boaters had gathered. Pushing my way to the front, I saw that a kayaker had wrapped completely around Trap Rock no more than 30 feet from shore. Chip was standing in the downstream eddy, shoulder-deep in the water, holding the guy's head up.

We shouted back and forth. Chip could support the guy but couldn't free him. One man in the crowd asked if he could help. I handed him my throw bag and swam out into the eddy. The kayaker was incoherent with pain. Chip and I talked for a minute, planning our next move. I signaled for the throw line and tied it to the far-side grab loop. Then, working together, we slowly peeled the boat off the rock. As we did this, Chip somehow got the guy out of his kayak and into the eddy. By this time, several other guides had arrived, and we used another throw line to swing ourselves and the kayaker to shore. I later learned that Chip had jumped out of his C-1 to make the rescue, letting it float downstream. We recovered it in an eddy a half mile below.

The kayak was trashed and the kayaker was hurting, so he rode out in one of the rafts. His legs were bruised, but nothing was broken. He was able to limp over to his car under his own power, dragging the remains of his boat behind him. He owed his life to Chip's quick thinking and to the fact that others on the scene were ready to help.

Will you be a spectator or a doer when trouble strikes? It's easy to freeze up in emergencies, but training and preparation give you the skills to draw on, and knowing what to do will help you respond quickly. Commercial guiding is a great way to develop group-management and rescue skills. As guides, Chip and I were expected to handle any problems we encountered.

VERTICAL PIN AT SWEET'S FALLS

CHRIS LEONARD IS AN EXPERT CANOEIST who devoted himself to river-rescue training after this scary incident. He was the driving force behind the James River safety symposium held in Richmond, Virginia, in 1982. That event introduced fire companies in the city and suburbs to the advantages of river-rescue training. His work was an important part of keeping the city's famous James River open to paddlers at high flows. Chris was paddling a 16-foot Blue Hole Canoe with airbags on the day of the incident. Here's his account, as published in the *Coastal CaNews,* the newsletter of the Richmond-based paddlesports organization Coastal Canoeists:

On September 3, 1978, a group of 21 boats from the Coastal Canoeists put in on the Gauley River immediately below Summersville Dam. It was 9:30 a.m., and a dam release was in progress. The Corps of Engineers was discharging slightly more than 1,000 cfs. As trip leader, this was the level I wanted.

Sweet's Falls drops 10 feet with little incline. Most of the water flows over the middle of this drop. There is a tongue in the middle of the drop. It flows down and into a very swift-moving pool below the falls. There is very little backwash here, no keeper; however, the pool is too deep and the current much too swift to stand in. This is where my trip ended in disaster.

Don Bowman and Jim Magurno both swamped at the foot of this rapid. I made the third attempt—I'm not sure why, but overconfidence was probably a factor. Rescue lines were out, there were boats and the water below me, and I was having a great day.

My entry into Sweet's Falls was too far to the left. Drawing right, I lost forward momentum. The bow of my boat planed out over the pool below, dropped, hit the riverbed with the impact of a sledge hammer, and stuck fast. I pitched forward hard. Somehow I got my right leg over the thwart in front of me. The thwart caught me in the crotch as my left leg slid under it. The Gauley River was now breaking over my back and head, pinning me to the thwart. To complicate things further, my boat collapsed partially under the force of the water—enough

*to assure that the thwart had a viselike grip across my
left thigh. I was trapped and I was scared.*

*Old Man River was doing his best to force my head
into the water, gathering in my boat and further collapsing it into the river below me. I gripped a thwart in front
of me to hold my head and upper torso erect—and the
water continued to pound away at me. After screaming
and blowing my whistle, I realized that the group was
aware of my predicament, and I settled down to await
help. Sure enough, a rescue line entered the current and
reached me. They had stretched a line across the river
and lowered it to me, hoping I could get my arm over it
and that they could thereby pull me from the boat. Not
a chance! My boat had to come out for me to come out.
Hoping they could tie a rope to my boat, I remembered
that my own rescue line was within reach. I grabbed
my throw bag and tied the rope to the thwart I was
braced against. It was a lot of work to tie that rope to
the thwart, and I realized that hypothermia was coming
on rapidly. (The Gauley, being dam-controlled, has cold
water even in the summer.) I threw the rope downstream
and waited for the rescuer to grab it.*

*Another half hour passed. Things didn't look too
good. I was not in a state of panic or shock. I was going
to die that afternoon. The cold water was beating me.
It was just a matter of time. I was mentally and emotionally prepared to die but determined not to give up.
There were 20 good men out there pulling for me. After
a while, I slumped forward, propping my head up on one*

hand. I rested, hoping to conserve energy. Time passed, and I got a second wind. I know I had been motionless for a long time and thought, Those guys think that I am dead! I sat erect, reached as high as I could, and felt my hand break the water. I later learned that this signal was extremely encouraging to my friends.

The number of rescuers had increased now by two more groups of paddlers arriving at Sweet's Falls. Between rest periods, I raised my left hand two more times. The Corps of Engineers had cut the release from Summersville Lake by 300 cfs at 1 p.m., so perhaps the water had dropped a little. Maybe the boat had shifted a little; perhaps the group had moved it slightly. Several men were now pulling my rescue rope from river right. No good! They were ready to have a line ferried to river left when Randy Perkins noticed that something had changed. He ran to the water's edge, waving and exhorting, "Pull!" And pull they did. My boat rolled free. This brought me around in a real hurry. I was able to kick and wiggle loose. My life jacket kept me afloat; when the group saw that I could hold my head up, all 20 men cried.

Two kayakers reached me in seconds. I didn't know them, but I'd never been happier to see anyone. They towed me into 6 inches of water, but I couldn't stand or walk; I was carried out. My appearance must have been frightening: face and lips blue, eyes recessed, joints swollen and aching. I was shivering uncontrollably. Dan Hix, Jon DeBoer, and Bill Edmundson were just return- ing. They had paddled and hiked out to a phone to have

the Corps bring the dam release to a halt and had notified the police and rescue squad. The time was 4:20 p.m.

One of the late arrivals, Carl Lundgren, took charge
of hypothermia treatment, bandaging, and splinting. We
were all thankful for his presence. Carl's knowledge of
emergency first aid treatment was most helpful. A litter
was improvised from my canoe, and nine men carried me
down the railroad tracks that led out of the gorge.

We reached a point where we expected an ambulance
to meet us. Wrong again. Soon two troopers showed up
on dirt bikes. One left to report our location and, after a
lengthy wait, a railroad company vehicle picked us up and
took us to the Peters Creek takeout, where the ambulance was waiting. We reached Summersville Hospital at
midnight, 10 hours after the ordeal had begun. I'm a very
fortunate young man. I suffered only muscle and tissue
damage to both legs, several stitches in my right ankle,
and crutches. I could have died.

The lessons we learned that day are numerous.
Without Carl, I would have suffered more. The emergency first aid training and experience of the other
participants on that trip was very limited. My group
tried everything possible, within and beyond reason, to
get me out of there, yet some of us feel that the rescue
operation needed a leader. I wasn't well prepared. Had
someone else been trapped, and had I needed to go for
help or notify the authorities, I didn't know a way out of
that gorge other than the Peters Creek takeout.

*My personal attitudes toward river paddling have
changed. I'll probably paddle the Gauley River again.
But on all rivers, I'll look at each rapid with a "What if
something goes wrong?" or "What can go wrong?"
attitude, as opposed to "I stand a real good chance,"
"HE ran (or swam) it; I can do it as well," "There are
good safety and rescue personnel out here today," or
"I've been having such a good day."*

FIRST RESPONDERS BLUNDER THROUGH A KAYAK RESCUE

IN 1980, VERY FEW RESCUE SQUADS WERE TRAINED in swift-water rescue. When called to assist skilled river runners, they often got in the way or actively interfered with rescue attempts. Local paddlers used the following incident as a catalyst to demonstrate their swiftwater rescue capabilities to first responders. Here's the report I wrote about the incident:

On May 18, 1980, during a routine run on the Kern River in California, Louis Nicklas, an experienced kayaker making his first run of the season, broached on a rock in a Class II rapid. The boat folded suddenly behind the cockpit, trapping him. Two-and-a-half hours later, he was pulled from the river by a Navy helicopter.

The Kern River above Bakersfield, California, is a powerful stream containing rapids of varying difficulty from Class I to VI. That day the river was flowing at 3,000 cfs, a medium-high but safe level. Both the victim and his companion were experienced, well-trained kayakers who had run more-difficult sections of the river before. The rapid in question is a long S-turn known as Mourner's Corner, a Class II on the six-point international scale, with many submerged rocks and small, choppy waves.

Nicklas and his partner were proceeding down the rapid when, about a third of the way down, Nicklas broached unexpectedly on a rock. His previous experience indicated that he could brace into the rock and pivot off, but his boat instead stuck fast and folded without warning. There was no time to exit, and he was essentially sitting sideways on the rock with his head upstream. He was able to keep his head above water with great difficulty by leaning toward the surface and holding on to the side of his kayak.

Nicklas screamed for help. A bystander heard him, grabbed a rope, and, with her husband, attempted to assist. The rope, about 75 feet long, came up short. She called the sheriff's office. Nicklas's friend, waiting "patiently" at the bottom of the drop, assumed his partner had capsized and was dumping his boat. It wasn't until he heard the sirens that he realized his friend might be in danger. This "waiting time" was about 30–40 minutes.

A deputy sheriff arrived promptly on the scene. He decided that rescue from shore was "too dangerous" and requested a helicopter from the Naval Weapons Station at China Lake at 4:25 p.m. He thought that it would take "about 15 minutes" to get the chopper. What he did not know was that it would take 25 minutes to get the necessary clearances and 35 minutes to scramble the crew before the 15-minute flight could commence. Since the chopper's radio was on a military frequency, it could not contact the sheriff directly, so the deputy had no way of knowing about this delay.

A few minutes after the request had been put in, a commercial rafting party under the leadership of Gary Peebles arrived at the scene. Seeing that many rescuers were on the scene with ropes yet not attempting the rescue, he sought out the deputy in charge and offered his services. His help was refused; he was also warned that he would be held legally responsible if he attempted to help and the rescue failed. The deputy also told him that the helicopter was due "at any minute." Realizing that the victim was in serious trouble due to cold and fatigue (not to mention the frustration of seeing dozens of people on the bank doing nothing), Gary began to organize a rescue. The deputy then threatened to revoke his commercial rafting permit if he "interfered with the rescue."

Gary, threatened with the loss of his livelihood, fired one of his employees, who, now acting as a private citizen, swam out to the victim to hold his head out of the water and to give him hope. Soon after, another kayaker joined Nicklas and told him how he himself had been pinned for over an hour the previous year on a tree. These actions saved the victim's life, since he had nearly given up hope and considered drowning himself to end the agony.

Another group of private rafts arrived. As they were debating how to organize a rescue, the helicopter arrived. The time was 6 p.m., 2.5 hours after the accident and 1.5 hours after the request for the chopper was first put in. A rescue collar was lowered to the victim, who, assisted by the two men helping him, put it on. The people in the helicopter had no idea how much water was in the kayak or if they had enough lift to do the job, much less if this could be done without injuring the victim. The helicopter lifted both the victim and his boat clear of the rock, lost lift, and dropped the kayak back into the river. For one awful minute, a crash seemed imminent as the current started to pull on the chopper. Fortunately, the helicopter regained its lift and brought the victim to shore, where he was removed from his kayak.

Onshore, the incompetence continued. Nicklas was placed in the back of an open pickup and transported to the helicopter landing area. No attempt was made to cover, much less warm him, despite the efforts of the boaters on the scene to do so. After being transferred to the hospital via the helicopter, the victim was rewarmed and found to have no broken bones, only bruises. Amazingly, no X-rays were taken. The attitude of the hospital staff seemed to be "anyone who is crazy enough to be on that river deserves what they get."

This incident points out the sorry state of readiness among first responders charged with river rescue back then. Since that time, California has become a leader in the field. But despite vast improvements in gear and training nationwide, gaps in readiness still exist, and response time can be slow. Therefore, it's extremely important for all boating parties to be ready and able to perform their own rescues.

Demonstration by Tom Johnson

After the above accident, the late Tom Johnson, a former firefighter, US Whitewater Team paddler, Olympic whitewater coach, and boat designer from nearby Kernville, California, pulled together a meeting between the U.S. Forest Service (USFS), the Bureau of Land Management (BLM), the local fire department, and other agencies with interests on the Kern. He had prepared a demonstration for these agencies with the help of four out of the five outfitters on the river, as well as a group of local kayakers. The intentions were two-fold: first, to convince them that organized paddlers are a safety-conscious lot, and second, to demonstrate the effectiveness of their skills and equipment in making rescues. The steps in the demonstration were as follows:

1. Five swimmers started in a pool above a drop and landed on a midstream boulder.

2. An 80-foot throw line was heaved to the "stranded victims," and a PFD was fastened to the line by a carabiner and slid out to them to model the techniques.

3. One of the victims showed how to "swim for shore," making it after being carried downstream 200 yards.

4. One swimmer was pulled into an eddy using the throw line.

5. A rowing raft came down to the rock and picked up one victim, then a paddle raft picked up the last two.

6. A demonstration was given of taking a line across the river by kayak.

The demonstration impressed those present. The Kern is a dangerous river, close to Los Angeles, and has an average of five drownings each year. The rescue squads already possess considerable land-based expertise. This, combined with new skills and a spirit of cooperation with the paddling community, should lead to more effective rescues in the future.

CHARLIE'S INSIGHTS:
Several Important Lessons

Nicklas's partner was not prepared to assist him. Anyone who "waits patiently" for over half an hour at the bottom of a drop simply isn't keeping the kind of close tabs on one's partner that whitewater requires. In a two-person party, you should not let your partner out of your sight for long. Had the partner been more alert and ready to assist the passerby who sounded the alarm, Nicklas would have been a lot more comfortable, and, with this assistance, the rescue might have been made without involving first responders.

No mention is made of whether Nicklas and his partner were carrying ropes. Many Western boaters of that era did not, and this incident underscores the importance of doing so. If the other members of a party are not alert or trained, ropes do no good. But in this case, combined with the assistance from bystanders, two ropes and three people under competent leadership should have been enough.

The action of the deputy is understandable—he felt that the helicopter's arrival was imminent and was too unfamiliar with the river to organize a shore-based rescue. This does not, however, excuse him. River rescues are not like other kinds. Time works against you, and a helicopter is, at best, a backup. The sheriff was not trained and did not know where competent help (like former Olympic Coach Tom Johnson of Kernville, who has worked as a firefighter) could be found, and yet he felt competent to discourage professional river guides from assisting him. This kind of ignorance is both unprofessional and inexcusable.

The boat folded behind the seat, ahead of the rear foam wall, compressing the cockpit area and causing the entrapment. From all accounts, the boat was properly braced, and the trouble was not due to a slippage or failure of the walls.

With the increasing number of rotomolded kayaks being made and used in whitewater, it is becoming evident that entrapment is a real problem. A fiberglass boat would probably have either been able to pivot free because of its rigidity or broken in half; rotomolded plastic boats are much more flexible and almost unbreakable. Manufacturers must do the research and development needed to minimize this danger to avoid further accidents.

When rescuing a pinned victim, you free him or her by pulling on the boat. Ropes to the body are used only in the most desperate situations, when they are needed to keep the head above water, and even then, the force of the pull should be on the boat. A rescuer should be stationed with the victim both to coordinate activities onshore and to go into the water and free the victim from the boat once it is pulled free. The shore party can assist by pulling in the boat quickly. Because of potential entanglement problems, the rescuer must have a knife available to cut the rope if needed.

River rescues are not like other kinds.
Time works against you, and a helicopter is,
at best, a backup.

2

BAD SWIMS AND NEAR DROWNINGS

WE KNOW THAT WHITEWATER RAFTERS take a swim from time to time—it's part of the sport. That's why paddlers wear life vests and wetsuits. But although some swims can be easy and even fun, some are truly horrible. You can be thrown against rocks, pulled under by countercurrents, recirculated by holes, or just pummeled by breaking waves that go on and on and on. The risk of flush drowning, a whitewater death that occurs despite the use of a PFD, is real. Many paddlers have experienced swims that took them to the limits of their endurance. Experienced boaters know how to swim in rapids. They roll over on their back and assume a feet-first position. They relax when they are being pummeled, trusting their PFD to pull them to the surface. They are prepared to swim into an eddy at the first opportunity. Novices are often frightened, and this makes even a routine swim seem like a near-death experience.

Here are some reports of bad swims that could have been worse.

View of Great Falls on the Potomac

BAD SWIM ON THE LOWER YOUGHIOGHENY

THIS ACCOUNT OF A SWIM THAT HAPPENED on Pennsylvania's Lower Youghiogheny (pronounced "yocka-gain-ee") River describes a pretty routine incident; the swimmer was quickly rescued by her own group. This account is included not because the swim was a true near miss but to remind all of us who deal with novices how traumatic a swim can be. Furthermore, since even a simple incident like this can be quite strenuous, it underscores the need for participants to be in good physical condition. The following letter to the editor was submitted by Joan B. and published in the *Pittsburgh Press* on August 15, 1987:

> *Several years ago, my husband and I went on a guided raft tour at Ohiopyle. It was Memorial Day and the river was running high due to spring rains.*
>
> *Before the beginning of the trip, we were all given life jackets and told what to do. We were told that if*

we fell in the water we should lie on our backs, feet up and pointing downstream. In the calm water before we approached each set of rapids, the guide would tell the group how best to approach and paddle through the rapids. We were apprehensive as we approached the first rapids. It seemed more like a waterfall to us, there being quite a drop. We made it through, though. It was fun and exhilarating. I remember saying to my husband, "This is great! We'll have to bring the girls next time." (We had two teenagers still at home at the time.)

The second half of our journey went well until we hit the Double Hydraulic Falls. One minute I was in the raft, the next I was flipped into the rapids and went underwater. With my eyes open, I could see the huge boulders all around me and the swirling waters. I was never so terrified in my whole life.

When I surfaced, I tried to lie on my back, but I couldn't! The churning, swirling, foaming water made it impossible. One of the guides in a kayak came alongside me. I tried to grab on but my hand slipped off, and I went under again. The water was so cold, and I was so scared! I thought I was going to die. When I finally surfaced again, I was able to grab onto our raft and was pulled back in.

Somehow we finished the river. I don't remember much . . . I think I was in shock. I am writing this to make people aware of how dangerous this activity can be.

FLOOD-STAGE CHAOS ON THE UPPER WATAUGA

VERY HIGH WATER IS OFTEN UNDERESTIMATED, but it can overpower the most experienced paddlers. This incident occurred above the Watauga Gorge, near Banner Elk, North Carolina, and brings to mind the saying "Sometimes it's better to be lucky than good." Here is Fred Seifer's account:

> *Dave Jordan and Bruce Hayes had dropped in on the evening of Monday, July 3, 1989, after spending four days paddling in West Virginia. I had not planned on paddling on July 4, but I was juiced up with the arrival of Dave and Bruce. On our way to the Watauga, we checked the Doe Gorge, which proved to be too low to run: estimated level was approximately 300 cfs. When we crossed the Elk River, we knew that the Watauga would be cooking, as the Elk was screaming out of its banks. The bridge to the put-in for the Watauga was completely submerged. The river was well into the trees—flood stage.*
>
> *Obviously, the Watauga Gorge was out of the question. Leon then suggested running the upper section, above the gorge, stating that it would be "a quick flush." I wasn't too excited about a quick flush, as it didn't seem much like a challenge. I did, however, decide that I might as well paddle, as I had driven all that way and wanted to wet my boat. The water was typical flood stage: fast, and muddy brown.*
>
> *We all hit the river with hopeful anticipation. Bruce took the lead, with Dave and I approximately 30 yards*

*behind and Leon and RB bringing up the rear. I kept
a watchful eye upstream, spying for floating trees and
other flotsam. After approximately 5 minutes on the
river, things started getting interesting (i.e., big water,
8- to 10-foot waves, and pushy crosscurrents). I thought,
"This is no flush." Then we encountered two big holes,
back-to-back, which we all managed to maneuver
through safely. The adrenaline was pumping, as was the
anxiety level.*

*At this point, I realized that this was, in fact, no
flush, but rather a locomotive out of control, a train I no
longer wished to be riding. Unfortunately, there was no
way off. The water was moving at approximately 10–20
miles per hour (it seemed like 100), and before I could
eddy out (where were the eddies?), I saw Bruce drop into
the ugliest hole I had ever seen. He just disappeared. I
took a half dozen quick back sweeps to alter my point
of impact to approximately 10 feet to the left of Bruce's
line, to avoid the heart of the hole. I was back-ended and
flipped. I went into a tight tuck to protect myself, waiting
to get oriented and to roll. The problem was that I never
surfaced—that is, I was doing a mystery move upside
down in my Dancer XT. After waiting approximately
5 seconds, I started to think about punching out, but
I never had a chance. Suddenly, I was being slammed
from all sides by the most turbulent, powerful water that
I had ever experienced. I was ripped from my boat.*

*I opened my eyes, expecting to see the light of
day; instead, I encountered nothing but silent brown*

darkness. I think I still had my paddle in my right hand (though I'm not sure), but at that point, I just started dog-paddling (I think I was also kicking). My eyes were darting around, searching for signs of light to help me orient myself. Nothing but brown darkness everywhere. I couldn't even see my hands. Only once, for a second or two, did I think I was going to die. After dog-paddling for what seemed an eternity (but was probably no more than 10 seconds), I thought, "Maybe I'm paddling in the wrong direction. Maybe I should dive for the bottom" (that is, if I knew where the bottom was). I didn't have any sensation that I was making any progress. I felt suspended in time, in brown darkness. Just then, my head broke the surface, without warning. I went straight from darkness into the beautiful light. I don't remember that first breath. I don't remember gasping for air. What I remember thinking was, "I've got to get out of this wave train. I've got to get to the shore."

As I paddled to the shore, I noticed that my life vest (an Extrasport Rogue) had been completely unzipped while I was submerged. The only thing that had kept it on were the waist ties at the bottom. I thought, "Should I take time to rezip the vest or just swim like hell to get off the river?" I kept swimming and entered the treeline— trees everywhere, with water flushing through, carrying me along. I was headed right for a small tree—a nice clean tree trunk. At first, my instinct was to grab the tree, but then William Nealy cartoons started flashing in my brain—pictures of kayakers eating tree trunks in flood-stage rivers, followed by the image of a kayaker pitoning on a tree with his feet. Resisting the strong urge to grab the tree, I quickly brought my feet up to meet the trunk. With a hard push, I directed myself toward the river-right bank, out of harm's way. I managed to stand up in still water and climb up to the bank. I stood there, stunned, scanning my body to make sure I was all there, in one piece.

I could see RB and Bruce working their way out of the water on river left. Then I heard moaning and turned to my left, behind me, to see Dave crawling out of the water, 20 yards upstream of me. Gasping for air, he asked if I was OK. Still bending over, he made the sign of the cross on his chest. We closed the distance between us and hugged each other, glad to both be alive.

Everyone was now accounted for except for Leon. Where was Leon? Dave and I started bushwhacking downriver. We found Leon's yellow Dancer approximately 100 yards downstream, wrapped end to end at the level of the cockpit, which was facing downstream. At first, we thought Leon was still in his boat. Realizing that was not the case, we continued searching for the missing boater. Without success, we decided to walk out, back to the put-in, a mile or so upstream, hoping that Leon would turn up. On the way back, we spotted RB's blue Reflex floating in a thicket, upright and intact. We grabbed the boat and carried it out. When we arrived back at the put-in, no one was there. Hitching a ride with a bystander who happened to witness the river carnage, we proceeded downriver again, this time along US 321, paralleling the Watauga. To our collective relief, Leon was with Bruce and RB. He had stayed with his boat and was unable to break out of the wave train until he finally decided to swim for shore, abandoning his boat to the current and trees.

Everything everyone was saying entered my mind in a staccato fashion, piecemeal. Leon had dislocated his left shoulder. RB had hyperextended his legs. For the most part, there was quiet; few words were actually spoken, just a lot of long, somewhat empty stares. Everyone seemed to be off in their own little world, reliving and reflecting on their own unique experiences.

How could five experienced Class IV–V boaters be so cavalier as to get on a flood-stage river that no one really knew, especially at that level, which probably was an all-time high, with only the one simple statement: "It will be a flush"? Speaking only for myself, in retrospect, I guess I had an attitude (though I never would have admitted it to myself or expressed it to others openly) that I "couldn't be touched." I had a bombproof roll (onside and offside), a solid combat hands roll, plenty of nasty hole experiences with good hole-escape techniques, and experience on both tight technical and big Class IV–V water, with competence. This near miss has definitely put things in proper prospective. No more brown-water runs on unfamiliar streams that can't be scouted. No more leaping without looking. I hope to be a much more cautious boater in the future.

Epilogue: As of July 7, 1989, three days after the event, four boats and two paddles have been recovered, three of the boats, including my own, having been wrapped on trees.

MIRACULOUS SAVE ON THE ARKANSAS

THE TITLE SAYS IT ALL! Here's a fantastic rescue story by Tom Karnuta, then chief instructor at the Rocky Mountain Outdoor Center.

June 7, 1990: Four expert local paddlers—myself, Greg, Tim, and Lincoln—were running a section of the Arkansas River in Colorado known as the Numbers. The run was fast; continuous; and, at a gauge reading of 4.7 feet, solid Class IV. All paddlers put boating at the top of their life's priorities, boating in excess of 150 days per year. They had just completed rapid number five and were within a quarter mile of our takeout when a lone boat came past. Looking back upstream, we noticed the boater was onshore and OK.

The river at this point was very continuous, and as the four of us took off after the kayak, we knew we could be in for a long chase. As we chased the boat, we all noticed that a throw rope (a large, 70-foot type) was attached behind the seat of the kayak. A small piece of rope ran through the rear wall of the boat, attached directly to a carabiner that was connected to a small D ring attached to the rope bag (very common on most commercial throw bags).

CHARLIE'S INSIGHTS:
Knowing Your Limits

The decision to run a rapid can be a difficult one. Trying to progress as a whitewater paddler means pushing your limits, which might motivate anyone to move too far too fast. Even very experienced paddlers can get pulled into a run that is too challenging for them. Plus, everyone wants to be respected and admired by their peers. Sometimes there is real pressure to fit in, or just to show that you can keep up. Some groups resort to teasing and shaming cautious paddlers. They might even encourage them to get in over their head for the "entertainment value." Stay away from these people! People who watch out for others are respected.

Crowds can also affect your judgment on some popular runs. At scheduled releases, people often line up and wait their turn to run very difficult drops without scouting or setting safety. Just because a lot of people are doing it doesn't mean you should.

Beware of talking yourself into running a river that's too high or too cold because you've driven for hours and don't want to turn around empty-handed.

During the chase, the knotted end of this rope came
loose from the bag, and all 70 feet of rope was trailing
in the river, still attached to the kayak. Several facts are
important to note at this point:

1. The loose end of the rope had a large loop knot in it.
2. The bag end of the rope was still attached within the kayak.
3. All 70 feet of the rope had paid out from the bag.
4. All four of us were aware of the above situation.

We chased the boat through very continuous Class III+
water, with virtually no eddies for about half a mile. At
this point, Greg and I were ahead of the boat and eddied
out in a large eddy on river right. Looking upstream
from this eddy, we could see Tim and Lincoln moving
with the boat toward our location. At our position in the
eddy, the river constricted a bit, forming several large
waves in the main current.

Just above this location, the boat got away from
Lincoln and moved out into these waves. Lincoln quickly
made a move back toward the boat, which was in the
center of the river, directly across from Greg and I in
the eddy. At this point, Greg and I were both in the
process of peeling out of the eddy, and Tim was slightly
upstream. Lincoln, moving very quickly and precisely,
was about to make contact with the loose kayak with the
bow of his boat. As Lincoln positioned his bow against
the kayak, the front of his boat (a fiberglass race boat)
passed under the rope from the throw bag.

The rope was totally invisible to all of us at this time. (The knot of the rope lodged in a rock somewhere upstream very close to its maximum length.) As Lincoln paddled into the unseen rope, it tangled in his paddle and around his upper right arm.

Lincoln gave a short yell as the rope quickly extended to maximum length, pulling him and his boat underwater. It is important to visualize Lincoln's position at this time:

1. His body was completely submerged.

2. The rope was around his right biceps and the paddle shaft.

3. He was facing the current, allowing his life jacket to remain in place.

4. He was positioned in the center of the river, directly in a large, violent wave.

Quick action was taken by the boating party to extend a throw rope across the river, in an attempt to snag Lincoln. We had just finished running gates upstream and only had one throw rope, a 50-foot kayak bag. Unfortunately, this rope was not long enough to extend across the river.

Lincoln's paddle (wood), attached to his arm, was violently being snapped up and down with the pulsating wave. By some stroke of luck, the paddle shaft broke in half, allowing Lincoln to slide free of the rope. We noticed his blue life jacket some 15 yards downstream and quickly set off in pursuit. (Approximate time elapsed at this point was 4–6 minutes.) As I quickly approached,

I thought it was only the life jacket, but upon reaching it I found Lincoln was still in it, face down, on his stomach, extremely cyanotic. I held Lincoln's head up out of the water in an attempt to reopen his airway and, with great effort by Greg, moved Lincoln through extremely continuous Class III water toward shore.

Tim and I immediately started CPR. Greg went to call the ambulance. It is important to remember that the water was runoff (cold). We kept Lincoln's body close to the water the entire time CPR was administered (approximately 45–50 minutes) while waiting for the ambulance. Lincoln regained a weak pulse and started breathing on his own just as the EMTs arrived. Oxygen was immediately administered, and Lincoln was transported to Salida Hospital and then airlifted to Colorado Springs. There, he made a complete recovery over the course of several weeks, and he's back on the water as I write.

Special thanks must be given to Al Johnson, whose fantastic high energy and enthusiasm were instrumental in keeping us all going, and to the guides of Crested Butte Rafting, who were on the scene and were also instrumental in providing excellent CPR and support.

NEAR MISS AT A LOW-HEAD DAM

THE DANGER OF RUNNING LOW-HEAD DAMS is well-known, but the risk of being pulled in from downstream is much less apparent. Here is a rare instance of rescue and survival, based on a report in the *Louisville-Courier Journal:*

In June of 1996, Tom Poirier, 57, and his 12-year-old son, Jim, were paddling with Scout Troop 327 on North Elkhorn Creek in central Kentucky. The group stopped beside a dam for lunch, then portaged their canoes around it. After getting back in, the Poiriers' canoe was pulled into the dam backwash from downstream. Their canoe overturned, and father and son struggled to get out from under it. Tom finally burst to the surface, but when he didn't see his son, he went under again. He grabbed his son's shirt and pulled him to the surface, but they were still in grave danger. Tom Hagman, another father in the group, saw the trouble and dove in. But he, too, was sucked into the hydraulic and nearly drowned.

Jim was washed free and floated downstream. His father, meanwhile, passed out and was pulled underwater. Hagman and Jim managed to get to the bank of the river. While Hagman lay gasping for air, Jim saw his unconscious father being carried downstream toward him. Jim reached out, grabbed his father, dragged him to shore, and began CPR, which he'd learned the previous summer for his first aid merit badge. Two adults finally made it across the steep, muddy bank and took over CPR.

Meanwhile, an older Scout went to find help. He found a farmer, who rushed home and dialed 911. As Tom came to, volunteer firefighters and emergency medical technicians arrived at the scene. Tom was evacuated to a local hospital, where he received antibiotics intended to prevent a lung infection from inhaling dirty creek water.

This incident shows the danger of getting too close to a hydraulic on the downstream side. The hardest thing for a rescuer to do when making dam rescues is to stay clear of the hydraulic; in this instance the rescuers did not. Their survival is attributed to their PFDs.

BODY PIN AT SNAGGLETOOTH ON THE LOWER YOUGHIOGHENY

THIS INCIDENT, REPORTED BY BILL ROBERTSON, appeared in the Three Rivers Paddling Club's newsletter.

On July 19, 1997, Michael Stein and I paddled the Lower Youghiogheny (pronounced "yocka-gain-ee") River in Western Pennsylvania. As we approached River's End rapids, two people on river left frantically gestured for us to hurry. We eddied out behind Whale Rock and saw a girl wedged between Snaggletooth Rock and the adjacent boulder. She was pinned facing downstream, wedged at the hips. The current was pushing at her back and she was struggling to keep her head above water. Her boyfriend stood in the downstream eddy but was not close enough to help. Later we learned that her name was Lisa; she, her boyfriend, and another couple were inexperienced rental rafters.

The best spot for rescue was on the rocks to Lisa's right. I headed into an eddy below her and exited my kayak. I removed my throw bag and started up the boulders. After leaping onto the second boulder's steep surface, I slipped, dropping the throw bag into the water. Michael retrieved the bag and tossed it back to me. I found a better route to climb the second boulder, then jumped to the next one. My final destination was the boulder nearer Lisa, but it was too far to jump and too steep to climb to it. The boulder I was on, however, was close enough to get a rope to her. My throw was good:

the rope landed upstream of Snaggletooth and drifted down to Lisa. I belayed the rope and sat down to wait.

Michael was in the eddy encouraging Lisa to hold on, assuring her that help was coming. She had been pinned for several minutes and was exhausted from using her arms to hold her head above water. She was crying and telling Michael that she couldn't hold on much longer. When the rope arrived, he shouted directions in such a positive manner that she abandoned her fear of letting go of the rocks to grab hold of the rope with one hand. More commands by Michael and she put two hands on the rope. More commands and she pulled.

Sitting high on the boulder, I couldn't see Lisa or Michael. It seemed like an eternity before I felt pressure on the rope. Then a strong pull came, lasting 3 or 4 minutes, then weakening. The rope went slack, but there were no reports of success, and I worried that Lisa might have been too weak to free herself. A couple of minutes later, some weak pressure came back, then slack, then a rather strong pull, and again, slack. I heard someone yell that Lisa was free. Michael told me that when Lisa finally got loose, she let go of the rope and passed over the drop. She disappeared under the water for several seconds, then reached up from the depths to grab his bow.

When I came down off the rocks, I saw Lisa in her friend's arms. Both were very cold and weak. A guided raft group was descending, and we tried to get someone to help them off the river. A ducky finally approached and got Lisa to shore. We took her to the sunny side

of the river to shake off the cold. Her legs were badly
bruised from knees to hips. But once she warmed up,
she assured us that she could continue to paddle to the
takeout. Since the rafters were all inexperienced and
badly shaken, Michael and I guided them the rest of the
way. As we parted at Bruner Run, Lisa thanked me. I
admonished her group that if they returned, they needed
to go with a guided trip.

BAD SWIM AT BIG SPLAT ON THE BIG SANDY

BIG SPLAT ON WEST VIRGINIA'S BIG SANDY is a steep Class V+
drop with a boulder in the middle of the chute. This drop, roughly
15 feet high, has been the scene of one fatality and several narrow
escapes. This report by Dag Grada first appeared in Colorado Whitewater's newsletter.

Our group of three was running Big Sandy near Bruce-
ton Mills, West Virginia, on July 9, 1998. At Big Splat,
one paddler ran the drop, while the other elected to
portage. Nick Lipkowski had run Big Splat before under
similar conditions (5.4 feet at Rockville). I asked Nick if
he wanted me to set up a rope, but he replied that he was
not going to run.

Sometime during my carry, Nick changed his mind.
He signaled that he intended to run and started down
before safety was in place. He cleared the opening
drop and made the left eddy. Then he peeled out with
too much momentum and struck the river-right wall.
Attempting to correct, he caught an edge and flipped.

He blew two roll attempts, panicked, and punched out just above the lip. He washed over the drop river right behind Splat Rock.

As I completed the portage, I looked back upstream to see Nick's kayak emerging from the base of the falls. I shouted and started moving upriver. My other friend scanned the area above the falls, then started to throw his rope into the backwash. It was 1–2 minutes before I spotted Nick downstream, weakly swimming toward shore on the left below the drop. My relief upon seeing him alive was swiftly tempered by his appearance as I approached. The force of the water had torn off his PFD, sports glasses, boating shoes, and neoprene socks. There was probably not a spot on him larger than a pair of open hands that did not contain a laceration or bruise. His lower leg had a large laceration that cut to the bone.

One of our group, Eric, is a resident physician at a hospital in Morgantown. He examined Nick's injuries. The leg injury had been caused by a fairly blunt object, and the flesh was torn rather than cut. No major blood vessels had been severed. Other surface wounds were comparatively minor. But when we attempted to move Nick, his leg collapsed under him. He stated that he thought it was broken. We later found out that the bone was intact, but several ligaments around the knee had been torn.

Eric fashioned an air splint from a stern float bag, a PFD, and a throw rope. We ferried Nick over to river right and began to carry him out. He was in pain, but his condition was stable. The cavalry arrived just before we began moving him up a steep slope to the old railway grade that follows the river. Several parties of boaters arrived at Big Splat, and we flagged them down. I cannot thank these people enough for taking time out to assist us.

One boater blitzed the remainder of the run to call an ambulance and arrange for a four-wheel-drive vehicle to meet us at Wonder Falls. Another individual allowed us to use his inflatable kayak (IK) as a stretcher. Nick was covered with a space blanket and lashed to the IK with a throw rope. Several NRS Straps became carrying handles as we carried Nick out. Even with eight people carrying and several others clearing the path and relieving the carriers, it took at least 90 minutes to reach Wonder Falls, a distance of less than 2 miles.

We were met partway by firefighters and paramedics from Bruceton Mills. They reassessed Nick's condition and helped us complete the carry. We were told that a medevac would meet us at Wonder Falls. The pilot executed a beautiful landing on the rock shelf, and Nick was taken to Ruby Memorial Hospital in Morgantown. He has since made a complete recovery and is boating again.

I will refrain from commenting on Nick's decision to run, as I am sure that many others will be glad to do so. Nick is painfully aware (and will be for some time) of the consequences of his decision. I'm glad that he lived to tell the tale. But there are two things that I will comment on:

*First, EMS was confused as to the location of the
accident, a not uncommon problem on rivers. For future
reference (filed as: hope it's not necessary), Wonder
Falls is known to the locals as Big Falls; Big Splat is
known as Little Falls.*

*The second point is something that I am guilty of.
For many years, I carried a first aid kit, a breakdown
paddle, and a dry bag full of rescue gear. Many times,
I was the only one in a group lugging this extra weight
around. That day on the Big Sandy, I was running without it. I am thankful that my negligence did not cause
the loss of a friend. I am thankful that other individuals
had this "extra weight" along, and I will be restocking
my boat.*

A BRUTAL COLD-WATER SWIM

HEIDI DOMEICIN IS AN UNUSUALLY FIT and capable paddler. Her
report is a remarkably vivid description of what it feels like to escape
from a cold-water flush drowning.

*I was on the Cold River in Massachusetts at 7 feet on
November 30, 1999. Four feet is pretty high; it's a steep,
solid Class IV run. The ice had just broken, and the river
was brown with silt. The first rapid is Class V. I flipped
and tried to roll but hit icebergs while sweeping. I came
up on my second roll too exhausted to stay upright. On
my third try, I was loose in the boat, and my roll just
rolled me out into the river. I was very conscious of the
seriousness of my situation—absolutely no one could*

help me. I held onto my paddle and boat for a short
time. The holes kept endering my boat (tossing it end
over end) and nearly ripped off my wrist, so I had to let
the boat go.

    I dropped into one hole after another, concentrating
on clearing my airway and breathing in before the next
one came. I used my paddle to try and ferry my body
to shore, but it was only slightly effective. Although my
brain knew what was happening, I could feel my body
shutting down. I felt very calm; I was too tired to panic.
I got over to the river-left shore, where the current
wasn't too strong, and tried to grab some bushes, but I
couldn't open or close my hand. "You've got to do it," I
thought, but my body wouldn't react. Then my legs went
over a pour-over, and the water stood me up. I guess I
was pretty stiff from the cold water. I aimed for shore as
I toppled over, then rolled onto the bank and somehow
stayed. I still had gross motor control of my legs and
arms. I had a splitting headache. My breathing required
a major conscious effort. My diaphragm wasn't con-
tracting on its own, so I was forcing air in and out by
working the abdominal muscles.

    After a time, my breathing became easier and my
headache went away. The shuttle bunny saw my gear
floating by and drove upstream to help, but I was on
the wrong side of the river and had to walk upstream
to a bridge. After about 15 minutes, I could get my
legs coordinated well enough to walk along the steep
embankment to a bridge. The group retrieved my gear

and regrouped. We paddled a Class III river later in the day. I can't believe I tried another river after getting so badly spanked!"

LAKE SUPERIOR NEAR MISS

THE MOUTHS OF RIVERS often have tricky currents, and when they empty into large bodies of water, a capsized paddler may be carried some distance from shore. In a previous accident, two boys capsized a canoe at the mouth of the Brule River. They were swept out into Lake Superior, where they died of hypothermia. In this case, the presence of other skilled paddlers prevented a tragedy. Fred Young describes what happened:

This incident, which occurred on May 11, 1999, involved a group of 12 whitewater paddlers from the Wisconsin area. They had finished running the Baptism, a Class IV+ run, and decided to end the day with a surf on Lake Superior. The mouth of the river was about 30 feet wide, with a gravel bar on the left and a sheer wall on the right. There was a strong onshore wind, and the waves were 4–6 feet high.

Three members of the party were surfing across the mouth of the river and were forced against the rock wall by the current, where they capsized. They were able to work their way away from the wall, only to be pushed far out into the lake by the river's current. Lake Superior is always extremely cold, and the victims were in grave danger from hypothermia despite their wetsuits. Prompt mobilization of the party allowed all hands and their

gear to be rescued by ferrying them out of the path of the
current, then to shore.

A DEFIBRILLATOR SAVES A YOUNG KAYAKER IN MEXICO

THIS LETTER FROM WAYNE SCOTT, father of Jordon and Joel Scott, was published in the cboats.net forum. In sharing their experience, the Scotts wish to increase awareness of the value of automated external defibrillators (AEDs).

This past September, two of my sons enrolled in a
three-month program called WILD, learning whitewater
rescue, wilderness first aid, and EMT training with an
outdoor adventure company called Esprit, based on
the Ottawa River by Davidson, Quebec. Their program
started in northern Quebec, continuing through the
United States and working south to Mexico. They were
in Mexico from mid-October to the end of November.

On Tuesday, November 18, 2008, I received a frantic
call from my son Jordon (age 21), who told me my son
Joel (age 25) was in an intensive care unit in a Mexican
hospital on life support. We received the call around
2:30 p.m. our time. I found out that he was in a kayak
going through Class II whitewater and that suddenly his
kayak overturned and he did not right it immediately.
Jordon saw this and went back upstream and got Joel out
of the kayak and to shore and immediately started CPR.

Miraculously, there was a raft right there that had
an AED on it, and another young person, Caleb, put the
machine on Joel. He activated it twice, starting Joel's

*heart. They called the Esprit base for transport and
got him in a van—it was another miracle that one was
nearby in remote Mexico. The adventure company staff
and WILD students continued CPR and drove Joel to a
hospital in Xalapa, Mexico.*

*My wife and I could not get a flight to Mexico until
8 a.m. Working out the logistics of the travel was quite
overwhelming. It seemed like* The Amazing Race, *only
the Scott family travel purpose was much more important than anything monetary. My wife and I arrived
in Mexico at 1 p.m. and got to Veracruz at 4 p.m. We
were met by Esprit staff and drove 2 hours to Xalapa.
Arrangements were made for us to see Joel at 7 p.m.*

*Prior to going into the hospital, my wife and I were
met by all the WILD students and Esprit staff with flowers
and cards to show their support for Joel and our family
(most of the students and staff slept on the hospital lawn
to see Joel off). We met with the ICU doctor and then went
in to see Joel. Arrangements were made for a medevac
flight from Veracruz at 6 a.m. At 5 a.m., we followed the
ambulance to the airport, where we met the Canadian
medevac crew. It took the crew 2 hours to stabilize Joel
for the flight on the Learjet to London, Ontario.*

*My wife and I got on a plane at 8 a.m. In the airport
we met two friends who had some good news for us:
Joel was now conscious, the tubes were out, and he was
breathing on his own and asking where his brother
Jordon was. There were a few tears at this time.*

Back in Canada, we drove to the London Health Sciences Centre, where Joel was in the cardiac care unit. Hospital staff allowed us to go in, two at a time, and see him. He was sitting up in bed smiling and quite giddy from all the drugs in his system and was amazed he was in London. I was told by a nurse that a cardiologist and some interns went to see Joel. The doctor told the interns that this boy not only was revived from a stopped heart but also had drowned and was revived without any brain damage; apparently the word miracle was used. Joel had a defibrillator implanted on November 27, 2008, and was discharged from the hospital later that day.

The above is an overview of what happened, and there are many more astounding details to this story. We would like to convey to the world that CPR training and AEDs do save people. The hospital staff were astounded that the adventure company had an AED and knew how to use it. I heard from the WILD students that Esprit was the only adventure company they knew of that carried one. I hope that more groups have them in the future, so there may be more good news stories.

Sincerely,

Wayne Scott

P.S. Joel had previously been diagnosed with a heart condition called hypertrophic cardiomyopathy, which in short means "an enlarged heart." This is the same condition you hear about when athletes suddenly drop on the playing field. Although he had been cleared

*medically to participate in WILD, we suspect (but do not
know for sure) that this was related to his capsize.*

*It is not uncommon for people with heart-related
conditions to live an active and adventurous life, but
medically we are all "an experiment of one," and suddenly Joel was upside down. There is a lot of learning
from this story and many steps along the way that contributed to Joel's successful recovery, the first of which
were having a satellite phone and AED on hand to make
the save and evacuation happen quickly.*

NEAR DROWNING ON WEST VIRGINIA'S NEW RIVER

THIS IS THE STORY OF A ROUTINE SWIM that turned ugly. It took
place on September 28, 2009, on the Dries, the lowest section of West
Virginia's New River. When the group arrived at the river that day,
they saw that it was running low, but they put on anyway, encounter-
ing mostly Class III waters. Above Mile-Long rapids, they stopped at
a small play wave where Gisela, the victim, flipped. She tried to roll
three times. After the second attempt, two paddlers started to chase
her down. After the third attempt, she pulled her skirt and stayed in
the middle of the river with her boat. Her group wrote what happened
next.

*We attempted to get the boat to the side. Gisela then
went to grab my stern, and I gave a few paddles to shore
and looked back to see she had let go. She seemed really
exhausted at this point. We passed a few large eddies
that she did not try to swim into. We went into a small,
benign-looking ledge hole 2–3 feet high. Three paddlers*

had already swept through, while one was still above. The hole was toward the center right of the river. Gisela dropped in and started to get recirculated.

The one paddler above immediately got out a throw bag, but Gisela was unable to grab it. We tried to paddle into the hole. One paddler made it within 2 feet of her, but she was already unconscious and he couldn't grab her. Another paddler left his boat, ran the shore, entered the water above, and swam into the hole, grabbed Gisela, and pushed her out. He got recirculated a few times and then was able to get out himself. The paddler and swimmer then grabbed Gisela downstream and got her to a large boulder onshore. She had been underwater and unconscious for 3–4 minutes.

Gisela was blue, and there was no pulse. CPR began immediately, and two paddlers continued downstream as fast as they could to get help. At that point, there was no easy exit; we were in a roadless canyon. After 15–20 minutes of CPR, we felt a slight pulse and extremely shallow breathing. Her color had improved. Rescue breaths continued for the next 10 minutes to assist her breathing.

Gisela slowly gained consciousness but for 10 minutes was incoherent. After that, she was able to communicate her name, and a pain in her chest from the ribs I broke doing CPR. She would become more alert when she heard the whistle we kept blowing. She had no memory of even kayaking. All she knew was her name, that she was born in Germany, and that she had a husband, Chris, and four kids.

Rescuers took about an hour and a half to get to us, using the railroad track. Gauley Bridge and Smithers volunteer firefighters walked the 2–3 miles in on the tracks. They then descended to us through the briars and over large boulders to carry Gisela to the railroad tracks. People showed up on four-wheelers, dirt bikes, walking, whatever they could. High school kids stood grabbing trees with one hand while pulling people up with their other hand, all while getting torn up by the thorns. Gisela still at this point was really only able to communicate a pain in her chest.

According to the Beckley, West Virginia, *Register-Herald*, Gisela was loaded onto a CSX high-rail truck, which took her then to a waiting ambulance. A helicopter landed on the Cotton Hill Bridge, and then she was taken to a Charleston, West Virginia, hospital. She was in intensive care several days with broken ribs and a punctured lung caused by the 15 or 20 minutes of CPR, which revived her.

BIG SWIM ON A FLOODED POTOMAC

FROM THE POTOMAC RIVER PADDLERS GROUP:

On March 6, 2010, Scott, a solo kayaker from West Virginia, was rescued from the Potomac River. He capsized, his paddle broke at the shaft, and he bailed out and swam. He lost his boat and was swept away by the raging river. He thought he was going to die. The river kept pushing him to the middle as he tried to swim to safety, and he couldn't make it to shore. He grabbed hold of a submerged tree. Then the sun set.

The rescue occurred just south of the US 340 Bridge in Sandy Hook. At the time of the rescue, the river was running high and water temperatures were around 50°F. A Sandy Hook resident along the river heard a man calling for help and blowing a whistle just after 7:30 p.m. Fire and rescue units from Frederick and Washington Counties dispatched five boats and two ambulances, as well as two Maryland State Police helicopters (Trooper 2 and Trooper 3). Due to the extremely high and dangerous water and difficulties accessing the search area, the rescue crews coordinated with the crew of Trooper 3 and decided to wait for them to assess the situation before putting rescue personnel into the high water.

It was too dangerous to put any rescue boats in the water. Trooper 3, based out of Frederick Municipal Airport, arrived on the scene at 7:57 p.m. ready for a hoist operation. Its crew began searching the river, islands, and small pockets of trees that protruded up through the high water with both the searchlight and night vision goggles. The victim was located with night vision goggles, clinging to a small group of trees that were partially submerged. He was able to climb into one of the trees and stand on a branch, elevating most of his body out of the frigid, rushing water. Trooper 2, based out of Andrews Air Force Base, arrived on the scene at 8:17 p.m., just in time to assist Trooper 3 by providing additional lighting and clearing hazards. Trooper 3

CHARLIE'S INSIGHTS:
Group Size

Two paddlers are good; three give you more options in emergencies. Once group size increases beyond five or six boats, the group will move more slowly, and keeping track of everyone becomes a hassle. With really large groups, it makes sense to buddy up with another paddler and keep track of each other between head counts. Solo paddlers have no backup, adding to the risks. Several paddlers in a single boat are not that much better off; when they flip, there is no backup! If you like to go by yourself from time to time, it's wise to mitigate the risks by choosing a river well below your skill level, making sure your equipment is in good order, and being certain that weather and water levels are reasonable.

Remember: one is a victim, two is a witness, three is a rescue.

*executed the extremely difficult night hoist over rushing
water from approximately 50 feet; the crew lowered a
rescue basket down to the water beside the trees where
the kayaker was stranded. He was able to climb into the
basket and was hoisted into the hovering aircraft.*

*Scott was then flown to a waiting ambulance on
Keep Tryst Road for further evaluation. Washington
County Advanced Life Support units assessed the victim,
who ultimately refused transport. The rescue was an
overwhelming success and well coordinated with all of
the involved agencies.*

*The paddler was very lucky! Remember: one is a
victim, two is a witness, three is a rescue. Never paddle
alone, especially on a big, flooded river at sunset!*

NEAR MISS ON THE MOOSE RIVER AT CRYSTAL RAPID

THIS ACCOUNT SHOWS GREAT TEAMWORK in the middle of
a Class V rapid on the Moose River in upstate New York during a scheduled water release. It was written by Catherine Blanchette, a friend of
the victim and the one who held onto him in the water that day.

*The rapid where all this started is between Powerline
and Crystal Falls. At that place, the river splits in two:
the left side is just water, while the right side shows one
drop, small and not that dangerous-looking.*

*Three of my friends went first without any problem,
and so did I. The paddler who was following me did a
different line and got stuck in the hydraulic at the bottom*

of the drop. We raised paddles to send a "no" sign for paddlers upstream, but the last member of our party was too close and couldn't stop. He paddled backward to allow the stuck kayaker to work himself out of the hydraulic, but it was not enough. They collided. The first paddler got to shore, but my friend stayed stuck.

I was 20 feet downstream. I could see the boat in the hydraulic but not the paddler. When I realized he was still there, 30 seconds had passed. There were two kayakers right beside the drop, waiting in small eddies, but the configuration of the drop and its shores did not allow them to get out of their boats easily. The person on right shore got out of his boat and threw a rope, but the rope came back empty.

My friend stayed in the water for 60–90 seconds before being released, not moving, head down. Two kayakers paddled up to him and grabbed him to lift his head up. Unfortunately, they hit a big rock, and both lost hold of the victim. The victim sank, and when he came back to the surface, he was right in front of me. I took him by his PFD and looked at his face. He was white, with deep-blue lips and eyes completely out of their orbits.

I started paddling to the right shore through the rapid as best I could, but I just had one hand, so I did not have much power. I did not know what to do. I yelled for help, but I was not in a good position to be helped, with Crystal Falls coming. Another friend was paddling behind me, but he decided to reach the shore instead of following me. He did not know the river, and he did not want to be the second victim. He made the best choice.

I could not see well what was going on. I was paddling when I saw a rope land on my skirt, from one side all the way down to the other. It took me a second or two to understand what it was and to release my paddle to grab the rope. Unfortunately, the weight of two people and one kayak was too much. I chose the victim instead of the rope, which I released.

I found my paddle and continued to work toward shore. The very high water level had opened a new way on the extreme right shore, where I was able to bring both of us. I did a final drop (around 6 feet), below which someone jumped in the water and caught the victim.

When I did the final drop, I heard him groaning for the first time, and I thought, "He is breathing!" During all the time I was holding onto him in the water, I was afraid I would have to do CPR. Hearing him groaning was a big relief. So when we reached the shore and got him out of the water, we put him on his back to open his airway. I placed myself at his head because I wanted him to hear a known voice, in his mother tongue (French).

We took off his PFD and helmet and cut down his drysuit. He was groaning more and more and then started to react to his environment and to move slowly. Liquid started to bubble out of his mouth, and we turned him on his side to allow it to drain. At that time, he really came back to our world and wanted to sit down.

He did not remember what had happened; in his mind,
he had just gotten out of the hydraulic.

Since he was quite alert and breathing well, he
got back on his feet. He walked around 150 feet before
sitting down, exhausted. The ambulance had been
advised, and the first responders reached us there. We
gave him oxygen and he stayed there a couple of min-
utes, lying on his back. Then he began to throw up. The
liquid was red, so we began worrying about internal
injuries. We asked him about it, and he answered that
he had drunk a lot of red Gatorade on the river. We
laughed a lot—quite a relief for us!

He finally did the whole walk back to the ambu-
lance by himself. First tests in the ambulance showed
he was in "perfect" shape. He was completely alert and
conscious, knew the day, the hour, his address and phone
number. No respiratory distress, no wound, injury, aches.
As we all were from Quebec, going to an American hos-
pital would have cost him a lot of money. And as he was
stable and in relatively good shape, we decided to drive
him to the border and visit the first hospital door when
we arrived in Canada.

Today, my friend doesn't have any consequences of
that accident. No water in his lungs, perfect blood tests,
and he is not traumatized either. As for the "dead body"
I had been holding onto in the water, I may say that he is
a survivor, nothing less.

Here are some thoughts I had after that rescue:

- **Keep your equipment close and easy to reach.** *My whistle was right in front of me, but the panic made it impossible to reach, so I kept yelling. If your equipment is not easy to reach, you will never find it in an emergency.*

- **In a different river configuration** *(less water, less-dangerous rapids), I could have done things differently. I could have attached the victim to my tow rope and used both hands to paddle hard to the shore (making sure to keep his head up). As my other friend was paddling close to me, I could also have held onto his tow rope, allowing him to tow us to shore while I held onto the victim.*

- **Although his drysuit full of air and his PFD** *may have contributed to keeping him stuck in the hydraulic, they also made him float more, which allowed me to keep his head up more easily.*

Someone told me that the short moment I grasped the thrown rope is what prevented us from moving up to the worst part of Crystal Falls. I cannot say yes or no to this, but what I can say is that every single action contributed to saving my friend's life.

And the most important is coming.

As the one who held onto the victim on the water and brought him to shore, I may be remembered as the one who saved his life. But we were a group of five that day. The victim was our friend, and all of us four did what we could to save his life. And other paddlers helped us too— the one who threw the rope in the hydraulic; the one who first grabbed the victim with my other friend; the one who made the perfect hit while throwing me a rope; the one who jumped in the water to catch the victim; the ones who reached us at the shore, ready to do CPR, and helped cut the clothes and secure the victim; the volunteers and first responders; and all the others who were there, ready to give any help possible. We all made that rescue a success, and we all saved my friend's life.

Paddle with people on whom you rely, because they could save your life someday.

Here are the victim's comments:

This emergency situation happened even though I had taken lots of water safety classes, had good risk management knowledge, and am a guide on other rivers. Nobody is fully protected against an accident. Mistakes that caused that accident are easy to avoid.

- **The water level was way higher than I thought it would be** *(5.5 feet vs. 3.5). But as I had traveled there to do it, I decided to do it.*

- **I was paddling with better kayakers than me.** *I was afraid to slow them down, and I did not tell them my fear. I am used to scouting the harder rapids before doing them. But that day, I did most of them without scouting first, hoping nothing would happen to me while doing them. The high quantity of paddlers on the river that day made me think I was invincible. Even though the drop was easy to do, I underestimated the consequences of swimming it.*

- **Upstream of the drop, a group of kayakers was arriving.**
  *I decided to go, even though I did not receive the "Go"
  sign from my friends. By the time I received the "No"
  sign, it was too late for me to stop myself. I succeeded
  in avoiding the stuck kayaker, but I did not have enough
  speed to punch the hole, so I flipped over and got stuck
  too. If people had waited their turn before going through
  the drop and if the communication had been better
  between me and the others, such a situation would never
  have happened.*

- **I needed speed to succeed in that drop.** *In order not to
  hurt the paddler, I slowed down and got stuck. (If I had
  accelerated, I could have hurt the paddler and created
  another emergency situation.)*

- **I got in a panic, so I lost my breath faster.**

- **There was nobody onshore with a throw rope,**
  *ready to assist immediately. By the time the one paddler
  succeeded in standing up and throwing the rope, it was
  too late.*

  *Here are the strengths that made that rescue a suc-
  cess and that saved my life:*

- **We were paddling in a group of five all day long.** *I was
  never alone, and someone was waiting in his boat, in an
  eddy close to the hydraulic, ready to help. The others
  were farther down, ready too.*

- **We all were experienced and trained in wildwater
  safety** *and first aid, so we had the knowledge of how to
  react in such a situation. My drysuit kept me warm, and*

the air inside it helped to keep my head out of water, as did my PFD.

Even though that experience was crazy, I am happy to be safe and not have any consequences. I now know that drowning can be really fast. Don't make the same mistakes I made! Wild water is a passion for me. I am not traumatized, and I will continue to paddle. Stupid mistakes almost cost me my life. Let's all learn from my mistakes.

NOC SHUTTLE DRIVER MAKES TIMELY UPPER NANTAHALA RESCUE

THE UPPER NANTAHALA IN NORTH CAROLINA is a fast-moving, continuous Class IV run. This rescue occurred during a scheduled release; Rob Kelly, a very experienced riverman, was working as a shuttle driver for the Nantahala Outdoor Center (NOC) during this event. He was wearing street clothes when he made the rescue! He writes:

Here's a quick run-through of the incident that happened on Saturday, September 29, 2012, during the Upper Nantahala release. At approximately 1:15 p.m., while driving upstream, I saw a paddler pushed under a tree that had caused some problems for a number of other people that day. I saw this as I was looking upstream while crossing a bridge in my van, driving upstream. I grabbed my throw rope and rushed down to the river. Neither she nor her boat was visible, but a bystander confirmed she was under the tree.

*A paddler on river right, below the tree, was trying
to traverse upstream to help. I threw him a rope to try to
assist him. This proved futile. A boater to my side had a
rescue vest on, and another person had a rope farther
upstream. My mind started to do the timeline at about
3 minutes, and I needed to move more quickly. I decided to
wade out in the shallow water by the river-left bank where
I was. It seemed prudent and controlled at that point, even
though I was not wearing a vest or helmet.*

*Reassessing the situation, time, and options at hand, it
seemed safe enough to continue. My footing was good, and
the rapid below was not too aggressive if I had to swim.
People were starting to gather at the bridge, with boats
and ropes. I waded downstream to the tree, heading into
deeper, swifter current. If it had been lateral, or upstream,
it would have been difficult to approach while maintaining
my balance and footing. At the very last part of the walk,
my footing was poor, but I made it.*

*When I arrived at the tree, I saw the victim's boat. The
stern tip was about a foot underwater and was difficult to
make out. I reached along it and felt the tree contact, and
continued until I felt the victim. I was able to swing her
torso around the tree and bring her head to the surface but
could not free her. I let go, reset with my body against the
log (making sure to keep my hips above the water line).
This time I was able to bring her up to the surface (still
in the kayak). From my initial assessment, I thought there
was little chance of a rescue. Training, instinct, and hope*

all made it a no-brainer to give two to four rescue breaths before going back to getting her free.

At that point, it seemed that pulling upward was not going to free the victim. The tree was like a cantilevered leaf spring, with water and the victim's surface area pushing up and the tree pushing down. I had to push her down and under the tree to get her out. Finally, she drifted under and out, still in the boat. I looked up and saw that people were ready below and signaled and shouted to them that she was floating downstream. They quickly got her to shore.

The next part is relayed from others involved. They began with compressions and breaths in a less than ideal position. They then carried her to the road and had better access and positioning to administer two-person CPR. Two respondents, maybe more, were medical professionals with an IV bag and other equipment. I took to scene management and let them be primary. I made sure a paddler was driving downstream to cell coverage to call EMS and rangers. Traffic was the next issue, and then getting space around the victim. By this point she had been gurgling, then coughing, progressing to moaning. Slowly she was regaining awareness.

With the scene stable and EMS en route, I realized that my other guests and bus were more in the way than helpful. I handed the scene over and drove my guests upstream out of the way. Timeline summary: roughly 4 minutes from head down to rescue breaths, and 8 minutes from head down to compressions.

First-person account from the rescued kayaker:

I was having a ball on the river before the incident. This was my first time down the Upper Nanty. It reminded me of a condensed version of the Middle Ocoee—tighter and more technical, but not above my skill level. I have done section 4 of the Chattooga, and Ocoee, and did not feel uncomfortable at all on the Upper Nanty. Kim, one of my fellow paddlers, was sweep and was faithful in being sweep the entire run. If he had not been behind me to hold me up when I got pinned, I would not be here. He certainly did his part and did it well.

Anyway, we did well the entire run until this incident. It was a group of six experienced paddlers. It was my first run of the Upper Nanty, as well as that of, I believe, two others in our group. Everyone did well and looked comfortable on the river. I was paddling down, saw the log, and attempted to go river left, but the current took me straight to the log. Looking back, I should have tried to go river right and into the eddy and under the log, which angled at about 45 degrees from the bank into the river. I would have had plenty of clearance to go under, had I gone that route.

Kim was behind me, saw me get swept into the log, and immediately was beside me, holding me up. From what I understand, we both then were pushed by the strong current. I disappeared, and he got flushed downstream. He immediately pulled out of his boat and went to the bank to go upstream to help me, but by then I was

*not visible, so he was not sure if I had also gotten swept
downstream or was under the log. I understand that
Rob indicated to him that I was under the log, and Kim,
though exhausted, continued to make his way up to me.
I recall being under, trying to push up, trying to pop out
of my boat, and putting my hand up for a rescue before
losing consciousness. Next thing I remember was being
in the ambulance, still at the scene.*

*I know that once Rob freed me and my boat, I was
floated downstream by Kim to the bank, where CPR
was begun. I was resuscitated, taken to a local hospital
emergency department, then transported to Asheville
via ambulance. I stayed two nights, released when my
oxygen stats came up to an acceptable level without
supplemental oxygen.*

*There were many involved in the rescue, from Rob
to Kim, Ian, Terri, Sam, and everyone else who assisted.
I'm sure there were many others involved, but from what
I have heard, these were the hands-on rescuers. I am
overwhelmingly grateful to them and everybody who
played a part in my rescue.*

SERIOUS HEAD INJURY ON THE
LOWER POTOMAC AT THE FISHLADDER

ON JUNE 20, 2014, TOM McEWAN, a noted kayaking instructor and
youth leader, was taking some youngsters down the Fishladder, a
series of steep slides around the river-left side of Great Falls near
Washington, DC. The Potomac was about 4 feet, a moderate level.

According to Liam and Jacob, who were boating with Tom, he flipped in the fifth slide, hit his head, and swam. He sustained a major head injury.

Gil Rocha, surfing just downstream, saw Tom's boat and started looking for the swimmer. He spotted Tom, who was floating mostly below the surface. Gil grabbed him, pulled his head above water, and supported him as they drifted through Rocky Island rapid down toward Wet Bottom Chute. Gil finally managed to pull Tom onto the rocks at the water's edge at the head of an island above Wet Bottom. Tom was badly injured and was unable to help with his rescue.

Liam and Jacob showed great composure in assisting with the rescue. They kept a running dialogue with Tom, in addition to monitoring his vitals, until the helicopter arrived. Tom was hospitalized for several days, including a stay in the ICU. Surgery, fortunately, was not required. He returned home to face a long, and ultimately successful, recovery.

JONES FALLS RESCUE AT ROUND FALLS

JONES FALLS IS AN INNER-CITY WHITEWATER RUN through Baltimore. It has poor water quality but some of the most unique creek scenery around. Highlights include several unusual drops, including Round Falls. Despite the name, Round Falls is actually semicircular, falling over a former dam shaped like a horseshoe, with the opening facing downstream. It's been run frequently, and the drop causes occasional problems.

On October 16, 2016, Seth Burkholder encountered trouble at Round Falls. The first paddler in his group went over the center of the falls without incident. Seth followed soon afterward, landed a little sideways, flipped, was drawn into the curtain, and swam. While he was trying to swim away from the hydraulic, he was drawn to the left and got caught in a particularly strong part of it where he was pulled underwater.

Although there was no downstream safety set, his group reacted quickly by throwing ropes. One rope wrapped around Seth's leg, and he was pulled from the water unconscious and not breathing. CPR began immediately; emergency responders arrived on the scene quickly and took over caring for him. Seth was unconscious but breathing on his own when he arrived at the University of Maryland Medical Center's Shock Trauma Center. He was in critical but stable condition, kept in a medically induced coma, but recovered quickly. Several days later, he was speaking and walking and was scheduled to begin physical therapy.

NEAR DROWNING ON THE FRENCH BROAD

ON FEBRUARY 23, 2019, THE FRENCH BROAD RIVER at Asheville, North Carolina, was ripping at 14,000 cfs (average flows are in the 2,000 cfs range). In nearby Woodfin, The Ledges—a quarter- to half-mile-long set of Class II–III rapids—kicks up some fantastic surfing waves at high water. We were surfing a glassy 5-foot-tall wave at the top of the rapid, river right of Ship Rock. Eddy access is limited, but a flurry of well-timed strokes can deliver paddlers to an eddy downstream of Ship Rock. The only other option is to paddle downstream, take out, and then walk back up to the wave.

I was there with a friend who caught a long ride that lasted several minutes. He came off the wave and headed downstream. I was dropping into my surf as he was floating off the wave. I surfed for

CHARLIE'S INSIGHTS:
Staying Together

Whitewater sport is unique in the way participants watch out for each other in a dangerous environment and stand ready to help anyone who gets in trouble. Keep track of the paddler directly behind you. If you don't see them, slow down or stop. If they don't appear, you may have to land and move upstream to find out what's going on. The lead paddler sets the pace that keeps a group together, and the sweep paddler brings up the rear to make sure no one is left behind. Paddlers in peer groups seldom appoint a leader, and the lead and sweep positions often switch. Remember your responsibilities when you find yourself in this position. The incident starting on page 78 highlights the importance of staying together.

"Kim was faithful in being sweep the entire run. If he had not been behind me to hold me up when I got pinned, I would not be here."

—*kayaker rescued from the Upper Nantahala River*

5 minutes or longer and caught the eddy. I got a couple more rides before washing off the wave and paddling downstream.

I had not seen my friend for a while, but this is not unusual while surfing big water. I walked my boat back up to the wave, expecting to find him at the put-in eddy. He was not there, so I walked down the road, looking for him. As I walked up to Ledges River Park, I saw several rescue vehicles, a police car, and an ambulance. My friend was lying on the ground. He was conscious and talking to rescue personnel, but he looked like death warmed over. He was pale, his cheeks were flushed, and he was clearly exhausted.

He told me what had occurred. After he came off the wave, he got caught in a hole halfway down the rapid. He was surfed and eventually swam. The hole that got him is in the middle of the river, at least 100 yards from the shore. He was rapidly swept downstream, being forced under for long moments and being splashed in the face as he fought to keep his head up. He swam at least half a mile before managing to grab hold of a tree and work his way to shore. He thought he was going to drown. Someone saw him from the road and called 911.

He was shaken and vomiting water but uninjured. His boat and paddle were long gone.

This accident could have been prevented! We should have had a discussion about the risk of swimming in big water, but I assumed no one would swim. Being the stronger paddler; I could have waited onshore or in the eddy until he was safely out of the water. We did not think anything bad could happen on the French Broad because "it's only Class III." But flood-stage kayaking eclipses the classification system. Even in relatively easy whitewater, the consequence of swimming is exponentially greater. Flooded-out rivers are no-swim zones; you cannot come out of the boat in such waters.

If we'd had a talk about it, maybe my buddy would have elected to stay onshore. We were there with a third, highly skilled paddler, and the two of us were making it look deceptively easy. The "expert halo" was in effect. It is hard not to let others' performances cloud our personal decision-making, but we should all strive to make choices based on our abilities.

BLACK MOSHANNON SCRAMBLE

THE BLACK MOSHANNON IS A SMALL, fast-moving Class I creek in North Central Pennsylvania. The author, Alden Henrie, is an expert paddler who knows the run well. Here's what happened on November 11, 2020.

> The incident I had was with a river-wide strainer on my local run, Black Moshannon Creek. I was with four other local paddlers who also know this creek like the back of their hand: Robbie Fulton, Mark Lawrence, Aaron Roos, and David Shirey. We put in sometime around 4:20 p.m., with just under an hour of usable daylight to complete a 4-mile run. We knew there was a risk for new wood, as we had not run the Black Moshannon since early May. The strainer was about a couple hundred yards downstream of the rapid called Crack in the Rock, on the final straight stretch before Black Moshannon Creek meets with the roadside of Route 53. It was still light enough that we could easily see the strainer, but we could not easily tell how bad it was unless we got closer. Robbie

and I waited until the last possible opportunity to eddy out above the strainer on river right to see if we could possibly paddle over top of it while the others took out sooner. There was a lack of decently sized eddies to fit multiple boats in, so we all tried our best to just get to shore and climb out for the portage.

As I eddied out on the left, my helmet camera came into contact with low-lying branches. This was the catalyst for the scariest swim I have ever experienced. My head was yanked to the upstream side by the branch, catching my camera, and the next thing I knew I was upside down. I immediately went into panic mode. I tried rolling up on my right side, the upstream side, but I lacked the patience needed to nail the first attempt. I tried rolling on that side a few more times before I switched to my left side, my onside in C-1, only to keep panicking and failing to roll up. This flailing about upside down eventually brought my boat back into the main current and straight toward the strainer. I had no choice but to bail and hope for the best.

The strainer I found myself swimming into was probably around 2 feet in diameter with branches branching away from the main part of the tree. My feet were already pointed downstream, and my legs were put together, so there was no chance of being able to somehow leap up onto the strainer and crawl out on top of it. No matter what, I was going under. I kept my legs together and reached around the top, hoping that I could somehow hold myself there until the others fetched

*me a rope. My head sunk underwater and I quickly
learned that resistance was always futile. I let go, felt
my back scraping against the bottom of the strainer
and my torso scraping against the bottom of the creek.
The time between my head going under and resurfacing
downstream must have been the five longest seconds of
my life.*

*I found myself desperately scrambling to get back
to shore, and I encountered a spot that was shallow and
close enough to shore where I felt I could safely stand.
As it turned out, although I was close to shore and in
shallow water, there was nothing but moving current and
slippery rock. Gasping for air and adrenaline-fueled, I
tried standing up quickly, only to feel a sharp pain in my
right knee and immediately fall back down. I resigned
myself to crawling out of the river and testing my ability
to stand and walk onshore. My knee was crying out for
help in that moment, but I managed to deal with it while
helping to rope my boat out of the strainer.*

*During this incident, I lost my paddle, so I had a
choice: walk out, considering Route 53 was not too
far of a walk away, or hand-paddle the rest of the way.
My right knee complained enough that I decided hand-
paddling the rest of the run was probably safer than
channeling my inner mountain goat. I borrowed Robbie's
spare hand paddles and carefully navigated my way to
the takeout by instinct above all else. At this point, sunlight had all but disappeared.*

There are a few lessons I want to share:

1. Even if you are an expert paddler on a local run, the possibility that something stupid can happen is always present. Therefore, the choices we make should attempt to minimize that possibility. Yes, the five of us on Black Moshannon Creek Wednesday evening know the creek incredibly well. That being said, running it for the first time since early May with no knowledge of new wood, with just under an hour of proper sunlight to go, was pushing our luck, to say the very least. I believe my incident resulted not from one major mistake but from multiple ingredients that brewed together into a near-lethal cocktail.

2. Always try to be aware of your situation. In hindsight, the best thing I could have done would have been to swim immediately as I flipped in the eddy above the strainer. I could have kept myself and my boat and paddle from floating into the strainer had I just bailed immediately instead of panicking and flailing around upside down; it is an action that, while understandable, only gave the current the opportunity to show me whether or not a higher deity truly exists.

3. Learn from your mistakes, but do not be too harsh on yourself. If I allowed engagement in pointed critiques of myself in any fashion reminiscent of my slalom-racing days in relatively safe concrete ditches, I probably would never be able to live with myself and perhaps would never step into a boat again. Whitewater is the only thing in life I actually enjoy. I cannot allow myself to ruin the only thing I enjoy doing just because of one bad experience. I am trying my best simply to look at this whole incident in as objective a fashion as possible, learn from it, and move forward.

SUCCESSFUL RESUSCITATION ON OVERFLOW CREEK

OVERFLOW CREEK IS A SMALL, STEEP Class IV–V in the upper West Fork of the Chattooga watershed, with some big drops and beautiful scenery. Great Marginal Monster is the biggest drop on the run. This account is written as told to Adam Herzog.

On March 27, 2021, a 66-year-old man was successfully resuscitated at Overflow Creek's Great Marginal Monster. He had decades of Class V experience and had run Overflow dozens of times without incident. He was wearing an older, high-coverage fiberglass helmet. He was struck in the lower-right parietal area of his head and was knocked unconscious.

The group of three experienced, Class V boaters arrived at the Great Marginal Monster on their second lap of the day. The first two paddlers ran Marginal without incident. A second group was scouting and watched from shore as the last paddler spun out above the main drop and went over sideways. He flipped at the bottom and hit his head. They did not see him attempting to roll and ran downstream. He floated near his friend, who quickly realized he was still in his boat. He and the members of the second party pulled the victim out of the boat. He had no signs of life, no respiratory effort.

One of the rescuers, an RN with years of ER experience, immediately began CPR. Within 5–10 minutes, the victim began breathing and regained consciousness. He was initially confused and asked repetitive questions, but within 20 minutes his mental status improved.

A runner was sent downstream to call for help from a cabin. The rest of the team began a prolonged extrication effort. Their knowledge of the local egress points and trail system proved invaluable. Several more paddlers got word of the extrication and arrived to assist.

The victim was intermittently able to ambulate on his own, but at times he required assistance. He complained of shortness of breath. His breathing sounded labored and noisy. He had aspirated water.

A car was driven to the Three Forks Trail, and Rabun County EMS and search-and-rescue teams began hiking into the gorge. They had brought a rugged, lightweight titanium stretcher with a center bike wheel designed for wilderness settings. They intercepted the extrication effort, and evacuation became more efficient with the stretcher.

The patient was transported to the hospital and was discharged 36 hours later, neurologically intact (alert, walking, and speaking normally). Attending trauma physicians said his high level of fitness worked in his favor and helped speed his recovery.

The team knew how to perform CPR and knew their way around the gorge. Without their rapid response, this incident might have been fatal. All paddlers should be trained in basic first aid and CPR and have a solid understanding of trail networks and access points along the river corridor.

CLOSE CALL AT SWEETS FALLS ON THE GAULEY

SWEETS FALLS, A HIGH-VOLUME DROP over an 8-foot ledge, sees all kinds of shenanigans during Gauley releases. I have worried for years that someone would get hurt during the flips, swims, and other commotion. Fortunately, on this day, one person was paying attention. Here is his account.

On September 17, 2021, I was kayaking on the Upper Gauley River. I was approaching the end of the run and the last bigger rapid, Sweets Falls, at around 11 a.m. As I was approaching the entrance rapid above the falls, I saw a commercial raft 100 yards in front of me go over the horizon at what looked to be a sideways angle. I heard the crowd cheer, which I noted, as to me it meant I would likely find flipped boats and swimmers in the pool when I arrived. I then paddled through the entrance and over the falls myself. When I came through the rapid, I saw what I assumed was the same commercial raft (same company) with swimmers hanging on to the side of the boat and gear strewn about.

I decided to earn some river karma points and help them by collecting some paddles, as well as a shoe I found floating nearby. As I tried to enter the eddy behind the Postage Due Rock, I lost most of the gear I'd grabbed. I continued down another eddy, behind a line of boulders, collecting the loose gear. I was bringing it all to the left shore, below where the rafts were all eddied

*out, when I saw a commercial-raft guest float through a
small channel against the left shore. It was later confirmed he had fallen out of the raft; swum through The
Box, a channel to the left of the Postage Due Rock; and
then somehow gone unnoticed as he floated through and
out of the 50-foot-long eddy below, through the small
channel and into the eddy I was in. His breathing was
loud, forced, and coarse; the latter stuck in my mind, as
it seemed he had swallowed some water. I directed him to
swim left into the eddy a few feet away; he grunted and
did not attempt to swim. I then paddled over to him and
asked him to grab the back of my boat so I could pull him
to shore, assuming he was just too exhausted/scared to
swim himself. He slapped his hand onto the back of my
boat but made no attempt to hold on.*

*I then swung back around to him as the eddy was
taking him back out to the main flow. As I approached
him this time, however, I noticed he was turning blue,
and the breathing was more struggled. I asked him if
he was OK, and he did not respond. He then went limp,
floating and no longer making eye contact. I noted that
his life vest was very loose and his mouth was at water
level. I grabbed both sides of his life jacket and lifted
him so that his head was above the waterline. I began
calling for help. I noted his color turning bluer, his
breathing becoming quieter. I had the gentleman lifted
and pressed against a rock, in an attempt to keep my balance against the eddy line and keep us both from being
pulled into the current. This positioning prevented me*

from blasting my whistle as both my hands were on him, keeping him afloat and us balanced.

Finally, after what felt like a minute or so, the raft came through the same small channel against the shore, now 20–30 feet from me. I called to the raft guide that we had an emergency and I needed help. The raft guide made no indication that she understood. I called again. This time they looked at me, still smiling, not under- standing the severity of the situation. I explained that he was losing consciousness and we needed to get him out of the water "now." The guide began to understand the issue. I continued talking to the gentleman to try to get a response and encouraging him to stay awake, as his eyes looked to be drooping.

At this time, he appeared to fully lose consciousness as his eyes rolled back and his breathing got quiet. The raft was still working to cross the short distance to me. I communicated to the raft that they needed to hurry, as he had lost consciousness. It took what felt like another min- ute from this point before the guide was able to maneuver the raft close to me. As the raft approached, I directed the two guests in the front of the boat to both grab a side of the large gentleman's life jacket and to "pull hard and flop him in the boat like a fish." I then paddled around the corner to call up to the other rafters for help.

I paddled to shore, and the raft followed me. The rest of his friends in his raft were nurses and paramedics, so they began to monitor breathing. As the raft guide and I pulled the boat to shore, the gentleman began to have

*a seizure and convulse in the arms of his friends. As the
seizure ended, another raft guide who had heard my
calls for help showed up, and soon after that, the lead (I
assume) guide for the trip also arrived with the medical
kit. At this time, the victim began to regain consciousness and became responsive to the lead guide's and his
friends' medical questions and inspection. I gave my
account of what transpired prior to the raft's appearance
in the eddy, and as the situation was now in control of
medical personnel (his friends) and the lead guide, I left.*

*At takeout, I saw a company bus; they had a radio
and confirmed he was OK and that a truck was being
sent to fetch him out from Sweets Falls. I called the
company that evening to confirm that he had continued
to do well, and they said he had. But, worryingly, they
seemed to dismiss it a bit as "just a seizure," saying he
was "fine." I wanted to ensure that the company knew it
was a close call and that some lessons learned from the
incident should be applied. I was then forwarded to a lead
guide, who listened to my account but assured me that the
staff's training was adequate; that the account was fully
documented; and that private boaters should neither hit
Postage Due one after the other nor line their rafts off of
it, making it hard for commercial rafters.*

*So, my thought on this near accident is that it was
a near-drowning-induced seizure. I do not know the
gentleman's seizure history; however, he was nonresponsive, with his mouth below the waterline, which leads me
to conclude with certainty that, had I not happened upon*

him by chance, he would have been without air for at least an additional 2–3 minutes and the outcome would likely have been fatal.

My takeaways are that many times the "audience" at rapids like Pillow Rock and Sweets Falls often disregards the common practices of safety and precaution that we carry on the river. The private boaters are drinking on the shore or Postage Due Rock, and people are cheering the flips and often not looking downstream to check on the location or well-being of swimmers. The commercial boaters often seem not to work as a team to rescue swimmers in these spots and instead leave it to the raft guide that was responsible for the swims. There are video boaters but not safety kayakers. There is a "not my company/boat"; "I am private, and they are commercial" (or vice versa); or "not my group, so not my problem" mentality.

I spoke with a veteran guide back at camp about it, and he said they have always thought someone would eventually drown in The Box. Thanks to luck and nothing more, Friday the 17th was not that day.

3

PINS AND ENTRAPMENTS

MOST WHITEWATER RESCUES are low-stress, straightforward events. Pick up a swimmer. Recover loose gear. Wade out and pull a pinned boat free. But when a paddler is caught by a strainer or undercut rock, or pinned inside their boat, the pressure is on! But with the right equipment and skills, some amazing saves have been made.

DOWD CHUTES STRAINER RESCUE

TONY BARB, AN INTERMEDIATE KAYAKER, was running Colorado's Eagle River with an intermediate kayak clinic from Boulder Outdoor Center. This is his description of the near miss resulting from a very quick rescue.

> *On June 24, 1994, we were kayaking the section just*
> *downstream of Dowd Chutes on the Eagle. I was*
> *unable to roll and had to swim. Ken, my instructor,*
> *was right behind me as I worked toward the river-right*
> *shore. I shoved the kayak toward shore only 10 feet out*
> *and braced off a large rock. I dropped my legs to try to*

Paddlers in Westwater Canyon in Utah

find the bottom, and suddenly my right calf slipped into a fork in a tree that was about 4 feet underwater and quite invisible. I was instantly pinned and pushed over, with my head 8 inches below the surface. I fought and twisted, but there was absolutely no give. I was already tired from my swim and had resigned myself to drowning when suddenly my head was lifted up, high enough for a breath. There was another pull from above, and I felt a slight loosening from the log fork. I pulled hard and was free. Ken swam me ashore, where I tried to recover from shock and exhaustion. I am alive today because of Rob and Ken and have only the highest praise for these two professionals.

Ken Evans and Rob Gaffney, both instructors from the Boulder Outdoor School, had been following Tony closely during his swim. Realizing that he was pinned, they eddied out behind a rock just upstream. This is the same one from which the victim had just pushed off. Ken hopped out of his boat, reached down, and was able to grab hold of Tony's PFD and pull him free. The whole incident took about 30 seconds. Tony said his mistake was attempting to stand in what he thought was an eddy but was actually 4–5 feet of moving water. It's an error he won't make again!

OCOEE BRIDGE PILING RESCUE

JOHN NORTON OF ATLANTA, an experienced paddler who had run the Ocoee River many times, attempted to rescue his friend's canoe above Hell Hole on October 23, 1982. Misjudging his proximity to the bridge abutment as he ferried to his friend's boat, John flipped upstream, and his canoe pinned solidly on the abutment. When he attempted to bail out, one of his feet got entangled in his thigh strap. Though John had a knife, he was unable to use it to cut himself free. The current pushed him underwater, where he struggled for breath.

Onshore, professional guides from High Country Outfitters in Atlanta were setting a throw line for an upcoming trip. Though they saw the accident happen, they did not immediately realize that John was trapped in his boat.

Once they determined John was underwater, they ran to the bridge and lowered a guide, Karen Berry, 20 feet below to the pinned boat. Karen secured her footing atop the pinned boat and tied a line lowered from above to the victim's belt, allowing John's head to be raised above the water. At this point, realizing the victim was entangled in his boat, Karen called for a knife to be sent down so she could cut him free. Once John was free, he was tied in a Swiss seat and pulled upward to safety. He was evacuated by ambulance to a local hospital, treated, and released.

The victim made no serious mistakes except being in the wrong place at the wrong time. This is not an uncommon situation during rescues, so extra care is indicated at these times. The rescue, swift and well organized, was characteristic of professional guides and might be difficult for private groups to duplicate.

OPEN CANOEIST GOES UNDER SHIPWRECK ROCK ON THE UPPER GAULEY

WEST VIRGINIA'S UPPER GAULEY RIVER is a famous big-water Class IV–V run. This is close to the limit of what is possible in an open canoe. Few paddlers run it in this type of craft, and so when Chicago-area paddler John Mundt went looking for a group to run with on September 24, 1983, he had to settle for a small band of expert kayakers. This created problems, since open boats move more slowly on the river than kayaks do.

John had several swims, including long ones at Insignificant and Pillow Rock rapids. The kayakers properly suggested that he take out, but he continued. There was another swim at Lost Paddle, but the worst was yet to come. Concerned about Iron Ring, which lay below, John entered the Orange Juice Squeezer on the left side of Shipwreck Rock rapid. This drop contains a huge rock that blocks the entire left-center side of the river, forcing John to cut from left to right in very heavy water. John described his experience in the Chicago Whitewater Association's newsletter, *The Gradient*.

Shipwreck Rock is severely undercut. At the top of the rapid, I started to run right, as that looked like a good chicken route. As I began to move right, I saw Pete (another member of the party) move left. Figuring he knew something I didn't, I played "follow the leader" and moved left too. I unexpectedly dumped. Finding myself in the water above Shipwreck Rock, I moved to the stern of my boat and proceeded to casually drift down until I could find an eddy. I was not worried about the rock until someone shouted, "Get away!" At this point, I got my first view of the rock close up, too late to do anything. I was pushed against the rock, and the current took me under. From then until I lost consciousness, I struggled against the flow of water, only to be pushed deeper and deeper until my feet were kicking against trapped logs on the bottom. My last thought was that I would be there until the water was turned off.

John stayed underwater for about 5 minutes before his body was flushed out from under the rock. He appeared 30 feet downstream, where the C-2 team of Stan Chadek and George Lhota grabbed him and began mouth-to-mouth resuscitation on the spot. Onshore, kayaker Bob Gedekoh, a doctor, continued the process. When Mundt came to, he was carried by raft downstream and evacuated by ambulance. He was held overnight at Summersville Hospital, where he was pumped full of antibiotics to prevent aspiration pneumonia, a common problem in near-drowning incidents. He was able to recover his gear in the canyon the next day.

Stan, George, and Bob saved John Mundt's life. I hope that when my time comes to help someone in similar circumstances, I will do

CHARLIE'S INSIGHTS:
The Weakest Link

What do you do when a member of your group is clearly not up to the river you are running? Whether that person is a friend or a stranger, they may not be able to think clearly. While you are not responsible for their safety, you owe them whatever support you can give, and this includes an honest assessment of the situation and a forthright expression of your feelings. Here are your options:

- If you feel that there is no way the person can complete the run safely. Instead of saying, "I think you should walk out," you should say, "The group feels that you're a danger to yourself. Please get off the river; it gets much harder, and you're just not up to it." It may mean (although not in this case) that someone will have to accompany the paddler to civilization.
- If you are part of an expert party and like fast, slick trips, you may not want to expend the energy needed to help someone move downriver. And face it: it is a commitment of time and energy and an acceptance

of extra responsibility. Tell them, "You're slowing us down. We can't wait. If you try to keep going, you're going to get hurt. You said you could handle the water, and you can't. You should get off." Harsh words. But the alternative is going along on a prayer, hoping that it will turn out OK. And if it doesn't, you'll have trouble sleeping at night.

- You could also agree to give the "weak link" extra support to get down safely, including scouting, a slower pace, additional carries (with assistance from the group when needed), and actually leading that person through the drops. This must be negotiated openly. "We think we can get you down. We'll scout the big drops. You'll follow so-and-so the rest of the way. We'll set ropes for you. But if you swim again, you'll have to walk out. And if we want you to carry, you'll have to do it. OK?"

The biggest danger is when the weak link in your party assumes that you are giving them extra help when you're not: that person follows a strong paddler down a hot route thinking it's an easy one and ends up in the water in a bad place. Never follow someone to get the easiest route without first making an agreement with that person. If you are overextended, you must ask for help or walk out. The group has the responsibility to do all they can to help a paddler in trouble, but never forget: you and no one else are responsible for your safety. And walking out, while a nuisance, sure beats getting in extreme trouble on the river!

Never follow another paddler to get the easiest route without first making an agreement with that person.

as well. The use of the C-2 to begin ventilating the victim immediately is worthy of special attention and praise.

John was clearly not up to the Gauley River that day, and the party he was with did not realize the extent of his trouble and deal with it. Luck and quick thinking saved his life. If you are in a similar situation, you shouldn't count on being equally fortunate.

TANDEM FLIP ON THE SHENANDOAH STAIRCASE

SKILLED PADDLERS OFTEN FIND THEMSELVES helping novices who get in over their head on this and other runs. This happened on the Shenandoah Staircase, a popular Class II run that's not far from Washington, DC. Ed Grove tells the story:

> *At about 4 p.m. on Saturday, May 24, 1986, I was descending the Lower Staircase on the Shenandoah River with my Boy Scout troop. Out of the corner of my eye, I saw two tandem paddlers flip below the US 340 Bridge, just above the confluence with the Potomac River. They were paddling a Mohawk canoe without flotation. All the other adults in my group and all the boys (except one tandem boat behind me) were below me and nearing the end of the rapid.*
>
> *I checked the last boat of kids behind me and began to descend vigorous Class II rapids midway through the staircase in the center of the river. Suddenly, I saw a man standing near the bottom of this rapid, with a boat full of water barely discernible in front of him. He frantically*

waved for me to stop, and I did so in the eddy created by the filled canoe.

I was horrified to find the man's paddling partner pinned underneath this canoe full of water. The filled canoe was perpendicular to the flow of the current, upright and squarely on the chest of the man beneath. The pinned man (who looked about 20 years old) was on his back parallel with the flow of the current. Only his head and upper chest were visible downstream of the boat. Water was flowing over the downstream gunwale and splashing into his face.

I jumped out of my boat and attempted to help his partner move the full canoe either left or right. It would not budge. Meanwhile, the boat with two Scouts had descended just after me and bumped into the stuck boat. The Scouts jumped out and immediately pulled their boat around the filled boat.

While trying to move the boat, I worked to keep the pinned man's head above water and to prevent the water flowing over the gunwale from splashing into his face. I also talked to him to see if he was conscious. At first, there were flickers of movement and recognition, but these soon stopped. His partner and I then concluded that we had to pull the boat downstream over the pinned man's head since he had now lost consciousness and the situation was becoming desperate. This we promptly did without too much difficulty. The entire sequence of events took perhaps 2 or 3 minutes.

However, once freed, the man was now unconscious and floated on his back without movement. I immediately decided we had to get downstream—at least to a dry, flat rock. Keeping the water away from his face, I got behind the man, and we floated on our backs downstream.
He was cradled in my arms on top of me, and our feet were pointed downriver. About 50 feet downstream, we reached a dry, flat rock. We stopped there, and I partially pulled the man onto the rock.

After a few seconds, I could see he was barely breathing, so I did not start artificial respiration or CPR. At this time, I responded positively to an adult downstream on a rock who asked if the unconscious man was breathing. Another minute passed. The victim moaned and began to breathe more deeply. I pulled him farther out of the water, and he slowly regained consciousness. He rested for about 5 minutes, and I kept talking to him, asking if he hurt anywhere. He said no.

I then asked him if he felt well enough to lie down in a canoe. He was too weak at first, but after several minutes was strong enough (with assistance from his partner and me) to climb into the canoe the two Scouts had brought down with them. We put him on the flotation, facing me and on his stomach. Then we paddled to the Harper's Ferry Park a couple hundred yards downstream.

I immediately sent one of the other adults for a park ranger and propped the rescued man against a tree. Shortly thereafter, a ranger came and began talking to *the victim. The man was reasonably lucid but could not remember what happened after he came out of the boat. A second ranger with more medical knowledge arrived and asked further questions. A blanket was brought and wrapped around the man. Both the rangers and I told the man (and his canoeing partner) that a doctor should examine him immediately.*

Meanwhile, Larry Stone, who had joined our troop for the day, had taken charge of the two Scouts who had given their boat to me. Under his direction and watchful eye, they floated down the rest of the rapids in the proper safe position without incident.

My Scouts were getting tired and cold. So, seeing that the rescued man was in good hands, we left for our Sandy Hook takeout. The rangers took my name and address. Upon arriving at Sandy Hook, we saw two other men looking for the tandem boat. They were the second boat of this two-boat party but had gone downstream far ahead of their companions. I told them briefly what had happened, and they quickly went to Harper's Ferry.

I assume the man we helped fully recovered. The two Scouts who assisted in the rescue, Andrew Bowers and Stephen Foerster, should be commended.

UNEXPECTED ENTRAPMENT AT THE LEAD-IN TO WONDER FALLS

A ROUTINE RUN CAN TURN INTO AN EMERGENCY very quickly. This close call happened in April 1987.

The Lower Big Sandy in northern West Virginia is one of my all-time favorite runs—hard enough to keep your attention but not nasty enough to scare you. I'd taken out above Wonder Falls and set up my camera to photograph people running a steep chute just upstream. The left side of the chute is undercut, but no one had ever gotten in trouble there before. I photographed several people running the chute, then stopped to change lenses.

Looking up, I saw a boater heading into the chute. Her line was all wrong, and I smelled trouble! By the time I put my camera down, she had flipped and slammed head-down into the undercut left wall.

I reached over, grabbed an arm, and pulled. Her head was above water, but I couldn't lift the boat free. She was screaming for someone to get her out. I was scared to try to do it by myself because, if I dropped her, she'd be in big trouble. I yelled for help. Another guy ran up behind me. We tied a safety line to her boat in case we lost our grip, then lifted. Seconds later, she was sitting on the ledge.

She felt a lot better than I did! Reunited with her group, she ran Wonder Falls a few minutes later. I sat on a rock for 15 minutes before portaging. I never found out her name, but I do know that she was very lucky. Normally, the hardest thing in an entrapment rescue is getting to a trapped person, and in a head-down pinning, you don't have much time. Fortunately, it happened right under my nose and there were others around to help.

ROPE TRAP ON THE CHATTOOGA

THIS IS NOT A UNIQUE ACCIDENT—throw ropes can be lifesavers when properly used but deadly when abandoned. Only this paddler's resourcefulness and the quick thinking of his knife-equipped friends prevented a tragedy. Because loose ropes make potentially fatal traps, they should never be abandoned on a river. One outfitter I know tells his guides that if they lose a rope in the water, they should jump in after it! If the rope cannot be retrieved, it should be pulled out as far as possible and cut close to the place where it snagged. This article was written by David Broemel and published in the Tennessee Scenic Rivers Association's newsletter on July 31, 1989.

> *Doug Wellman, an expert kayaker who had recently won the Ocoee Whitewater Rodeo, almost drowned after becoming entangled in an abandoned throw rope. The site was Middle Crack in the Rock rapid of the Chattooga River, section IV, a popular Class IV+ run along the border of Georgia and South Carolina, a drop he had run countless times at varying water levels.*
>
> *Wellman, paddling a low-volume Jet kayak, became entangled in an abandoned throw rope at the base of the narrow drop. Desperately needing air, he bailed out. As he fought for his life, friends chased his upside-down Jet. The rope kept him from getting to the surface, but he was able, by straining against a narrow underwater ledge, to get his head above the surface for a few precious breaths of air. His friends, discovering that Wellman was not in his boat, rushed back to the base of the drop and cut him free.*

Note: Wellman's first act after getting off the river was to purchase a river knife. Every paddler should carry one—not just because of abandoned throw ropes but as a general defense against entanglement.

RACER PINNED IN TREE ON MARYLAND'S SAVAGE RIVER

THE SAVAGE RIVER IS ONE OF AMERICA'S premier wildwater race-courses. From Bloomington Dam to the Potomac River, the rapids are fast and continuous, bouncing between Class III and IV. Memorial Rock, the last drop of the steepest section, is also the most technical move on the river. Because of the stream's small size and intermittent flow, downed trees have always been a concern for race organizers. The water, released from the bottom of a lake, is extremely cold. Time is of the essence when making rescues here.

On July 2, 1990, during a practice run for the Savage River International Downriver Race, a group of American racers encountered a downed tree at Memorial Rock rapid that partially blocked the runout of the center chute. Although most of the group got by without incident, one kayaker, Kathy Bolyn, became trapped when her boat broached and wrapped around a limb. Her group responded quickly with a textbook rescue that probably saved her life.

The tree that caused the accident was a large one, with an 18-inch-diameter trunk a few feet above the water and a 5-inch-diameter limb sticking down into the river itself. This tree had been spotted and trimmed by race organizers the day before the event, but the water level was low, and the tree had not been cut back far enough. It blocked the right side of the river in the swiftwater below Memorial Rock, making the drop hazardous to wildwater racers practicing the next day.

Kathy, a nationally known racer, river runner, and instructor, was training with a group of elite wildwater racers when the accident occurred. On their first run, the group missed the tree. The danger frightened them, but the group felt they were "here to do a job" and elected to continue practicing. But they also decided to travel as a close-knit group, and several of them packed lightweight rescue gear. On the second run, the first part of the group came through fine. Kathy, leading the second wave, broached as she tried to turn in the drop. She was able to duck under the trunk, but her boat, which was equipped with vertical and lateral walls, was pushed against the subsidiary branch protruding down into the river. The kayak quickly wrapped, crushing Kathy's legs together so that she could not escape. She was left with her body facing upstream, holding on to the same branch that held her boat.

The group reacted immediately to her predicament. Jeff Huey and Paul Grabow climbed onto the tree trunk and approached Kathy from river right. As they got closer, the tree sagged, deterring them from advancing further. On river left, others in the group threw Kathy a rope. By tying it to a nearby tree branch, she was able to lean back against it and gain support. This stabilized her position for the time being.

Although well outfitted in a shorty wetsuit and drytop, Kathy was in considerable pain. Her position was stable, but she was completely helpless. She kept her cool by concentrating on other things: what still felt good and the beauty of the surrounding river. Her greatest fear was that she might pass out.

Unable to help further with the tools available to them, Mary Hipsher approached a local landowner to borrow a saw. The saw was ferried to Paul, who began to work first on the bow of her boat, then on the limb on which she was pinned. As he did this, Jeff passed a second rope to Kathy from river right. Kathy untied the first rope. When the limb gave way, she grabbed that second rope and was pulled over to safety. She was eased into a kayak and made the ferry across the fast, choppy river to the left shore. A waiting ambulance took her. She was discovered to have two torn ligaments in her right knee and minor crush and puncture wounds on both legs. She faced an extended recovery time of at least a year.

Whitewater paddling is a risky sport; part of its allure is the challenge of performing difficult moves in the face of danger. Racers must not be so distracted by the competition that they can't assess the risks and respond to mishaps. As the sport has become more competitive, pressure on the top performers has increased. Some of this pressure may have contributed to the accident.

Competitors must assume responsibility for assessing these dangers, as there is no way a championship-level course can be made risk-free. Because safety personnel cannot cover the entire run as they can in slalom, they must be prepared to rescue themselves and assist others. They must also be prepared to back off when they encounter conditions that they consider unsafe, reporting the problem to race organizers. The tree was clearly in the way; those who had cut it back earlier apparently did not realize just how far the water was going to come up.

Memorial Rock rapid has an obscure, rocky left-hand sneak route. It has been used in the past and was available for those uncomfortable with the tree's dangers. The main chute, while risky, was also negotiable. A better approach would have been to run the rapid, sneak the drop, and report the problem to race organizers.

The rescue, however, was a textbook example of effective organization and execution. The group reacted quickly, stabilizing the victim, then extricating her from the pin. The entire group must be commended for their teamwork, ingenuity, and courage. It also shows the usefulness of a saw in pinning situations.

HIGH-WATER EQUIPMENT TRAP IN WESTWATER CANYON

SLIM RAY IS AN EXPERT IN FLOOD, swiftwater, and whitewater
safety and rescue with 20 years of experience in swiftwater rescue,
including course development and instruction. Here, he describes
events that took place while he was teaching a class for the Canyon-
lands Field Institute (CFI) out of Moab, Utah.

*My rescue class got a taste of the real thing on May
23, 1991. I was teaching a course, developed by Barry
Miller, emphasizing dynamic, in-water rescue techniques for oar boats on big, continuous water. The clinic
arrived Friday at Westwater Canyon. My co-instructor
was Ron Ron, who has had extensive big-water experience in Utah and Westwater Canyon. The students were
all from S'Plore, a Salt Lake City group specializing in
trips for special populations (such as people with physical and/or mental disabilities). There were four student
boats, a student safety boat, and a safety boat from CFI.
All were oar boats, and both instructors were in student
oar boats. The Colorado River was about 8,000 cfs when
we put in, and rising.*

*Saturday night, the trip had camped at Little
Dolores, just above the rapids section of the Canyon.
After a morning classroom session on the beach, the
class did rapids swimming just below Little Dolores. By
now the river had come up to nearly 12,000 cfs, which
meant that most of the canyon was virtually one continuous big-water rapid. The class proceeded downstream,
doing safety and rescue exercises in the rapids. After a*

*boat-towing exercise, all boats from the class had eddied
out below Funnel Falls rapid. Most of the boats were
just below the rapid; however, my boatman had trouble
catching the eddies (the water was a lot pushier and
the eddies smaller than most of them were used to) and
ended up in an eddy 100 yards or so below the main
group. Ron was with the upstream group.*

*As everyone bailed, two oar rafts approached Fun-
nel Falls. The second boat flipped at the top of Funnel
Falls and began washing downstream. At the high-water
level (11,500 cfs), Westwater Gorge is virtually continuous boiling, swirling water, making rescue difficult. The
upstream CFI group saw the flip and moved into position
for a rescue. The boat accompanying the stricken boat,
however, continued through the rapid and was unable to
render assistance. The CFI student boats came alongside the upside-down raft and began a rescue attempt.
At the time, they had no idea how many victims were
involved. Only two heads were visible. One of the crew
of the overturned raft, Steve, attempted to get on top of
the boat, failed, and was picked up by one of the CFI
boats. The head of the other person (Mike Franklin) was
barely visible alongside the overturned raft. The rescuers reached him quickly but were unable to pull him
out of the water. After several long moments, it became
obvious that Franklin was hung on something. One of
the students got on top of the raft and another into the
water to try to rescue him, but both were unsuccessful.*

Meanwhile, the entire group was moving rapidly downstream toward Skull rapid, the largest rapid in the canyon (the distance between Funnel Falls and Skull is about three-quarters of a mile). Because of the power of the water, the group was unable to tow the overturned raft into an eddy. Rescue attempts continued until the group reached a point about 200 yards above Skull. The group had passed me, and I was trying to overtake them downstream, a slow process.

As Ron passed, he yelled to me that he thought we had someone entangled in a throw rope. As I approached, I could see Franklin's head surface from time to time. Ron's raft was now next to Franklin's, and Ron had Franklin by the shoulders of his life jacket. Angela was at the oars. I still had my swim fins on from the swimming exercise. After hearing Ron's shouted comments about the rope, I took off the heavy rubber gloves I was wearing and took out my folding Gerber knife (but did not open it).

As our raft approached, I saw that 1) because of the number of rafts already around Franklin's raft, I wouldn't be able to get to it quickly, and 2) somebody needed to get in the water with the victim, so I went in and swam about 50 feet to the raft. Ron and I frantically began to try to free Franklin. When it became obvious that we were all going into Skull rapid, Ron waved off the other boats to run Skull. We tried to keep contact with the victim as we did so. Ron kept hold of his life jacket, I tried to hold the boats together and keep hold of

Franklin, and Angela somehow managed to row the two boats through Skull without hitting the (very large) hole.

During the ride though Skull I got Franklin's life jacket free of the spare oar. As it turned out, the blade of the oar was pushed through the right armhole and between the top and second snaps of the his Type V life jacket. I was able to free him by unsnapping the top buckle. Ron had also had the foresight to brief everyone on how to run Skull before we left the beach for the day, and all the student boats made it through upright.

After Franklin was freed, Ron was able to get him into his raft in the tail waves of Skull rapid while Angela rowed into the eddy on river left. A quick survey showed that Franklin was breathing but unconscious. He became responsive within a few minutes and fully regained consciousness after 5–7 minutes.

A check with other members of the party revealed that two other raft passengers were missing. The overturned raft had continued downstream after Franklin's party and eddied out at Skull. Ron quickly organized a search-and-rescue party of two rafts, a CFI student boat, and the CFI safety boat, and headed off downstream in search of the missing rafters. I stayed in the eddy in Angela's raft to look after Franklin, who was in fairly serious condition.

Ron proceeded about three-quarters of a mile downstream to find the upside-down boat hung on a loop from a throw bag in swift current below Last Chance rapid (the last one in the canyon). He and Mike Smith (who was rowing the CFI safety boat) began rescue attempts and a search for survivors. They first tried unsuccessfully to bump and push the boat off with their rafts as they passed. Finally, Ron succeeded in swimming out to the raft, just in time to see a person floating away from under it. Smith picked the man up. This was Lester, one of the missing passengers. While Ron retrieved the raft and checked underneath for the second missing passenger, Smith continued around the bend. He proceeded half a mile more (the water was flat here) with the intention of stopping on a beach to warm up Lester. There he found Sarah, the other missing passenger, sitting on the beach, incoherent. Smith quickly set up a camp, changed the victims into dry clothes and sleeping bags, and gave them hot drinks.

Upstream, I decided to evacuate Franklin by raft to the Cisco takeout. We removed his wet clothes and changed him into dry ones. (Three members of Franklin's party—Gary; Sarah's husband, Rick; and Steve—had elected to remain at Skull to attempt a search upstream for Lester and Sarah. They had agreed to come out by dark if their search was unsuccessful, which they later did). From the Cisco takeout, Franklin was transported by car to the town of Cisco, then by helicopter to a hospital in Grand Junction. Sarah and Lester were rewarmed and did not require medical treatment. Franklin was diagnosed as having aspirated water in his right lung but was released from the hospital the next day.

This was a good, but in many respects lucky, rescue. The students did rescue one person without endangering themselves. It took a while to find the right combination to rescue Franklin. We were very lucky that all the student rafts made it through Skull rapid OK because we weren't in a position to help. Ron deserves credit here for briefing the Skull run beforehand. A safety kayaker, who would have been more mobile than the rafts, would have been a great help, and the student safety boat (raft) was marginal at the high-water level.

I was fortunate to have my fins on and to be able to get my gloves off prior to the rescue. I doubt whether I could have gotten to the victim as fast (or at all) without the fins. I know that I couldn't have gotten the snap undone with the gloves on. The buckle was one of the older Type V buckles that has to be pressed in the center to release. Granted, the circumstances were less than ideal, but I feel the design of the buckles makes them too hard to unsnap in an emergency. This wouldn't have happened with a zippered jacket or one with cam-lock buckles. This is not the first time we've had trouble with Type V buckles.

Evacuation time was about 2.5 hours, including air evacuation. The helicopter was nice but unnecessary; however, it would have been a godsend if we'd had to do CPR. We could also have cut evacuation time if we'd had a kayak to send out.

It was also a lesson to me to check underneath an upside-down raft for other victims. As it was, they were lucky; one went all the way though the canyon under the raft (with no wetsuit) and the other (who was underneath the rafts during the initial rescue attempt) swam most of the way. Fortunately, she got out on her own. I have no explanation as to why they both stayed under the raft: both would have been rescued instantly if they had come up. We were unable to ascertain whether they were briefed on this before starting.

It appears that Franklin was in over his head that day. It had been several years since Westwater had run that high, and many people weren't used to it. The other raft was competently piloted but was too far downstream to help. The boatman on this raft, Gary Skiles, told me that he'd tried to talk Franklin out of going down at this level but had been unable to dissuade him. Ron felt that the raft was not well rigged for big water and the possibility of a flip; the life and flip lines weren't properly rigged, and there were too many things hanging loose. An example of this was the throw line that came loose and eventually snagged the raft. Ron's comment was that "it was spooky going underneath the raft" because of all the stuff hanging off it. He also felt that there was a possibility that the spare oar was tied in incorrectly (certainly it had no quick release).

FOOT ENTRAPMENT ON THE LOCUST FORK

WE ALL KNOW THE RISKS OF STANDING UP in whitewater. The accident was caused by the victim's inexperience combined with a poor choice of footwear. His group handled the rescue extremely

well, responding quickly and effectively. This account was published
in the Birmingham Canoe Club's newsletter.

*On April 21, 1991, a 10-year-old boy almost drowned
on Alabama's Class III Locust Fork River due to a foot
entrapment. As I learned of the incident at the takeout
that Sunday afternoon (Swann Bridge), I became angry at
myself for not stopping and offering my assistance;
I had paddled right by the incident thinking it was merely
a pinned boat. OK, I admit it—I hate rubberneckers; it
seemed only natural for me and my party to continue
downstream. If others on the river that day had thought as
I did, the following story would not have a happy ending.*

*Sunday, April 21, was supposed to be warm and
sunny with temperatures in the 70s. As it turned out,
it was overcast, windy, and cool (low 60s). The water
level was great for first-timers on the river (2.9 feet
steady). Mike Callahan and his 10-year-old son, David,
were among the many on the river that day. David had
recently been given an expensive pair of hiking boots,
and to him and his father, this seemed like the perfect
time to wear them. Everything was going perfectly
until they took a spill at Double Trouble. Wet and cold
(the father tells me they had on cotton clothing), they
sat on the rocks drying off between the top and bottom
drops of Double Trouble. While watching others run
the drops, Mike spotted a party of two trying to free a
canoe that had pinned on a large boulder midstream.
This is the large rock that separates the main drop from*

a dangerous tight secondary chute at the bottom drop of Double Trouble (river right). David and his father offered assistance to the two men.

It's at this point everything started happening very fast. Mike yelled downstream to the two by the pinned canoe to throw him a rope and he'd pull from the bank upstream. When the pinned canoe didn't budge, 10-year-old David jumped in the fast water to assist them. David must have thought that he could swim or walk on the riverbed to get to the two canoeists. Instead, the current washed him into the fast, narrow chute on river right. The two canoeists watched helplessly as David struggled against the current. (Mike told me at this point that he instructed David to put his life jacket back on.) David, underestimating the river's power, tried to get his footing. Thinking he could stop against the current, he tried to stand up. Just as he entered the chute, he grabbed a large boulder on his left and yelled in terror, "DAD! DAD!" David knew his foot was stuck. His dad, who was upstream from the site, not realizing the situation, told David, "Let go. Don't hang on—go through." At this point, David either let go or lost his grip. The current pushed him facedown under a foot of fast-flowing water.

Tommy Cary (one of the rescuers) says:

I yelled for Dean to get David's head up. He did this by grabbing David's life jacket in one hand and the side of the pinned canoe in the other. I leaned out into the

*current holding Dean, who grabbed David's life vest
and pulled. We could not get his head up all the way, but
water was flowing over his head, creating a tunnel where
he could breathe. After only a few minutes of this, David's
life vest pulled off and his head went underwater again.*

*Dean grabbed the rock and worked upstream, and
I swam over and was able to stand against the rock,
just downstream in the eddy created by David's body.
We were in chest-deep water that was very swift. Dean
pulled on David's arms; got a shoulder against the boy's
body; and, using his hands, got under David's chin.
Doing this, we were able to get his head a few inches
above water—he was breathing! The two of us could
not free a hand to do anything else. Anytime we let up,
David went back underwater. I don't know how long we
held him like this, but we were getting very tired pushing
against the current and could not free his foot. Several
times, Mike jumped in from upstream in desperation and
was immediately swept by us, almost knocking us down.*

*After several minutes, two people showed up to
assist us. They threw a rope down to us, and we tied
it under David's arms. As they pulled from above, this
gave Dean and me some relief. However, we still could
not free his foot and had to maintain our position to
keep his head above the water. By now, people were
all along the bank (over a dozen boats had stopped).
Another rope was attached to David; three people pulled
from upstream, still no luck. Dean was showing signs
of exhaustion and getting cold. As I stayed in the water*

holding David's head up, someone tied a rope around his waist and went underwater to attempt to free the foot. It was this person who finally freed David's large cleated hiking boot from the rock underwater."

David's leg was immobilized with driftwood splints at the accident site. Upon examination, his leg was found to be broken, but otherwise his health was as good as any 10-year-old's can be.

QUICK RESCUE ON TENNESSEE'S PINEY RIVER

JIM BROOKS SMITH of the Tennessee Valley Canoe Club tells the story of a classic stabilization line rescue from a vertical pin.

Our group put in on Tennessee's Piney River on February 2, 1991. This is a small, technical Class IV creek falling off of the Cumberland Plateau south of Knoxville. Air temperature was to get into the 50s; water temperature was probably 50°F. The gauge at the takeout read 2.2 feet during the shuttle run. We put in between 10 and 11 a.m. The incident occurred at the rapid before the surprise ledge that accelerates the paddler across the diagonal ledge.

I was following the group when I came upon the rapid. I chose a slot to the left of a rock just left of center. I was not paddling hard enough to launch the boat, and I was not leaning back while going through the slot. I felt the bow catch, then the stern immediately dropped into a slot just past the lip of the drop. The water was flowing over my back and head. My boat was at a steep

*angle and well pinned. My first move was to wiggle my
boat with my hips, but there was no change. Breathing
was OK, but the water was flowing across my face. I
tried to stand straighter on my foot pegs, but the water
coming down on me made me feel as if I were being
driven against the boat harder. Breathing was much
more difficult in this position, causing me to swallow
more water. I was surprised, scared, and wondering
what would work to get me out of the boat. I began testing putting weight on one foot and trying to lift one knee
up above the rim of the cockpit.*

*About that time, Victor and Andy were on the left
bank, and Jim Conerly had made it to the right bank.
They quickly got a rope across and in front of my
life jacket, against my chest. Shortly afterward, the
other Jim got to the right bank, and they got the rope
secured. Looking to my left, I could see Victor and
Andy. They looked confident, and that reassured me.
I could not turn to the right because the water was
immersing me more that way. I yelled to Victor and
Andy, "What could I do next?" but they couldn't hear
me. I knew they had done all they could to give me the
opportunity to help myself. By pushing off my toes and
leaning onto the rope, I could lift my left knee a little.
The rope against my shorty life jacket constricted my
breathing. I had thrown my paddle away because I
needed both hands to push against the cockpit. The
boat felt rigid and was not turning at all, in spite of
my twisting movements. I swallowed more water doing*

this, and I would cup my hands over my mouth to keep water out of my mouth and nose. However, that kept me from using my hands to push up out of the boat.

I think, after a few unsuccessful tries, I began to quit and panic. I remembered walks with my wife and wanting to see my daughter in the science fair. I think I teared up a little bit even with all the water rushing over my face. After a few seconds, I returned with renewed efforts, determined to free myself. Somehow, I got my left knee above the rim of the cockpit. I could hear a cheer from everybody. That helped. Again I tried, slightly twisting to the right, and I got my left knee up on the cockpit rim. Quickly I pushed upright, bringing my right leg up. I knew I had to get out of there or muscle cramps would occur. I wanted to go faster and just wrench myself over the side, but I was unsure of my balance. I had been in the water awhile, my hands were numb, and I had swallowed as much water as air.

Finally, I was crouched on the cockpit rim with my feet under me. Someone threw me a line, and the line on my chest was loosened. I looked, wrapped the line under my elbow, and jumped. The water was frothy but shallow where I landed. I just held on as Jim pulled me into the eddy. He got me on a rock with my head lower than my feet, and I immediately belched out water.

Jim, Victor, and Andy were looking for my boat, which had disappeared. At that moment I knew I would be OK, but I wondered how I would get out of there and what it would mean to all of us. They tried moving

a throw rope over the place where my boat was. Later,
Andy told me they could see my boat under the water.

Andy found a large flat rock with which he and
Victor weighted down the throw rope and sunk it above
the boat. After throwing the ropes across the river to loop
the boat and pulling on them, the boat came free. Andy
caught the boat, with the stern bending up toward the
sky. He jumped up and down on the boat, which seemed
to help straighten it, and ferried it across the river to
me. Victor hung it between two rocks, and we sat on the
boat's bottom. This straightened it enough to paddle.

My spray skirt had washed off, along with an air-
bag, a throw rope, a water bottle, and my paddle. Jim
had a breakdown paddle, and Andy found my spray skirt.
We estimated that I had been in the water 12–15 minutes
and we used another hour getting the boat out, so it was
about 2 p.m. We got moving.

My paddle and throw rope were around the next
bend. I was very apprehensive and paddled conserva-
tively the rest of the way to the takeout. However, I had
a heightened sense of the beauty of this river gorge. We
took out at about 5:30 p.m.

In retrospect, I thought of other things I might have
done. I had been clumsy starting out; I should have
paddled hard and leaned back going over the ledge. I
might have used my paddle as a pole to help pry myself
out of the boat. My throw bag should have been tied in
more securely and near my grasp; then I could have
used a carabiner to hook it to the broach loop in front

of my cockpit. At one point near the end of the ordeal, I thought I had swallowed too much water, and I was weakening. I'd read it was better to use all your strength for one great attempt to free yourself. I guess that's a judgment call.

That morning I had taped a weak ankle and decided to leave my tennis shoes and breakdown paddle in Chattanooga. I had driven 340 miles and had 4 hours sleep. At my age, I cannot rebound as quickly as I used to. I let too many details slide by. I am glad I have the opportunity to paddle another day.

The other paddlers acted immediately and stabilized me. There was no wasted energy and no confusion in their efforts to rescue me. They were poised and encouraging. If you get in the wrong place at the wrong time, you had better be with the right people.

I hope this report will help warn and instruct others in some way. I am thankful I was with some competent, well-trained paddlers from Tennessee Valley Canoe Club and elsewhere to whom I owe a debt of gratitude.

BAD BROACH AT RIGHT CRACK, CHATTOOGA SECTION IV

THIS RECOUNTING OF A HARROWING COLD-WATER PIN and complicated rescue was shared to the Accident Database by Hugh Kelly of the Nantahala Outdoor Center. Note that Crack in the Rock has undergone further changes since the account was written. Visit americanwhitewater.org and search "Chattooga River Section 4" for updated information about Crack in the Rock rapid.

On October 24, 1994, Steve Yook, a Chattooga guide on his day off, was kayaking Section 4 of the Chattooga River on the Georgia–South Carolina border. The sky was clear, the river level was 1.9 feet, and the temperature was 70°F. Steve, Joy Slagle, and Bill Garrison passed a Nantahala Outdoor Center (NOC) raft trip while we ate lunch at Long Creek Falls; we reached the Five Falls sometime later.

Greg Batt, our safety boater, was running Entrance rapid when he saw Steve and Bill waving for help on the rocks to the right of Right Crack. Greg exited his boat in the right eddy below Entrance and ran down the shore, rope in hand, to Crack in the Rock. At the same time, Christopher Smith, our photo boater, paddled through Corkscrew to reach Steve and Bill. Rob Edwards, who was going to set rope on the left below Entrance, ran down the left shore to Crack. When Andrew Punsel, the trip leader, and Taz (Kevin Riggs) saw what was happening, Taz ferried his raft to the left shore and ran down to assist. Another guide, Zack Moldenhauer, followed Taz with a first aid kit.

Arriving on the scene at 1:45 p.m., we learned that 30 minutes earlier, Joy, paddling a Dancer ProLine, broached on the log in Right Crack. The kayak hit the log at her right thigh as she attempted to run to the left. It stuck there and creased at her knees as the current pushed the bow underwater and down the drop. Not only was the center of Joy's boat pinned on the log, but the bow was also up against the rocks just under the water on the left side of Right Crack. In addition to the crease, the boat's deck was compressed around Joy's knees, thighs, and hips. Her head was in the air, but the rest of her body was submerged in the 56°F water.

Steve and Bill attempted to pull Joy from the boat, but she complained that it hurt her legs, so they stopped. Next, they lifted up on the stern of her boat so it would slide down to the left of the log. Unfortunately, the plastic behind her seat creased so that even with her stern pointing straight up in the air, the rest of the boat did not move. Finally, they attached a throw bag around the boat at the seat and pulled directly from the rock upstream of Right Crack. The boat still did not budge. Bill spent most of the first 45 minutes that Joy was pinned standing on the ledge to the right of her boat, comforting her and assisting in tying and untying ropes.

When NOC arrived, Christopher and Greg went to help Steve pull on the rope, but the boat did not move. Greg relieved Bill on the ledge and stood in thigh-deep water until Joy was free. Meanwhile, Bill and Zack passed a rope around Joy's torso on the outside of her PFD to keep her head above water. This rope was held from the rock above Right Crack and could be released at any time if the boat came free of the log. During all this, Taz and Rob held throw ropes downstream, on the left shore, in case someone fell into the current below Crack.

The remaining guides on the trip, Andrew, Cathy Holcombe, and I, were waiting with the rafting guests in the middle eddy above Entrance. I walked down the left shore to find out what was happening below. When I returned, Andrew, Cathy, two Army men from Fort Bragg, and I ran a raft through Entrance and Corkscrew. We paddled over to Steve, who was on the right shore above Crack. It should be noted that we normally would not leave a raft trip unattended, but because of the urgency of the situation, we wanted to use all available manpower.

At that point, Steve was directing the rescue, and we were supplying him with equipment and bodies. When our raft arrived, Steve asked us to ferry him over to High Rock, where, with the help of Taz, Zack, and Andrew, he set up a Z-drag off of a piton. The Z-drag was attached around Joy's boat at the seat between the two creases. It was difficult to make this Z-drag work effectively because there was very little distance between the changes in direction and no room to stand on High Rock. Joy said pulling on the boat from that direction hurt her legs, so we stopped but did not dismantle the Z-drag.

By 2:30, Steve was exhausted and asked Taz to take over. Taz and Zack used the Z-drag from High Rock as a zip line, going in the raft from the left shore to the rock in between Right and Middle Cracks. Christopher volunteered to paddle out for help. After checking with Andrew, Christopher left and, with the help of Bill Coburn and the Wildwater motorboat, reached a phone by 3:05. He called

the NOC outpost and Oconee Memorial Hospital, asking
for an ambulance to wait at the takeout on Lake Tugaloo.
Also at 2:30, three other kayakers showed up and volunteered to assist in the rescue: Chris Connelly, Lee Riley,
and Will (last name unknown).

From the middle rock, Zack and Taz passed a rope
through the bow grab loop and tried pulling the boat
to the left, but Joy complained of pain, so they stopped.
Joy, who had now been in the water for an hour and a
half, became withdrawn at this point and appeared to be
losing confidence. From the left shore, Cathy sent Taz
another rope. It was tied around the boat at the seat,
at the same place that the Z-drag from High Rock was
attached. Taz sent this rope to the left shore, where it
was pulled directly and later with a Z-drag.

At 3:00, we had two ropes attached to Joy's kayak
and a heads-up line around her PFD. Her boat still had
not budged. It was time to try something else, so Taz
popped Joy's skirt and hoped it would cause the boat to
move or the hull to expand, allowing her to remove her
legs. Initially this did not seem to improve the situation.
Next we tried to cut the boat, but our Spyderco knife did
not work because the blade was too thick. [Note: A saw
would have worked.] Looking back, to free Joy from the
boat using a knife, we probably would have had to risk
cutting her legs. It was now 3:20, and even though she
was dressed in fleece and a dry top, Joy was beginning
to lose her color.

The turning point came at 3:25 when Joy rebounded and told Greg and Taz that she could move her right leg. After the remains of her spray skirt were cut away, Taz was able to reach into the bow, grab her heel, and pull her right leg from the boat. Joy's left leg was still trapped inside, so Taz retied one of the ropes to the bow security loop to counteract the water pressure on the deck. When the folks on the left shore pulled on this rope, the deck lifted and Greg and Rob were able to pull Joy from the boat and onto the dry rock.

After a primary and secondary survey, we concluded that her legs had suffered only bruises and that the only life-threatening condition was hypothermia. We exchanged Joy's clothes for relatively dry ones, gave her food, wrapped her in a blanket, and had other people lie next to her. Using the local kayakers to set throw lines, we brought our trip through the Five Falls. Then, with Joy on a backboard, we carried around Jawbone, Sock 'em Dog, and Shoulderbone and rafted her to the lake. We met Bill in the motorboat; he was carrying two more NOC guides and John Thomas, a paramedic and former Chattooga guide from Oconee Memorial Hospital. At the hospital Joy was diagnosed with leg bruises and hypothermia and was released that same night.

All of the private kayakers who assisted in the rescue were employees of Southeastern Expeditions, Wildwater, and Adventures Unlimited. Without their help, the rescue would have been much more difficult.

> *I'm convinced that Crack in the Rock changed after this summer's [1994] flood. Some say that debris stuck in the bottom of Middle Crack washed out, lowering the level of the upstream pool. Now the water washes through, as opposed to over, Right Crack. The log has become a more formidable obstacle as well; it used to be underwater at 2 feet, but now you can hang up on the log as high as 2.2 feet. After the incident, Joy said, "If you have doubts, walk it."*

MISCALCULATION IN THE WATAUGA GORGE

THIS WRITEUP OF MINE appeared in the July/August 1996 issue of *American Whitewater Journal.*

The Watauga River on the Tennessee–North Carolina border is one of the best technical river runs in the Southeast. I had run it a few times, but not since the mid-1970s. Two previous trips had been in the company of local paddlers who knew the river well. In early March 1996, the gauge was reading minus 8 inches. Half our group had run the river before, but none of us really "knew" it.

We had been proceeding carefully, scouting the big drops as they came up. We portaged Hydro and ran everything else. We arrived at a steep boulder drop (the last major rapid above Stateline Falls) that some people call Knuckles. I sat in an eddy while Ned Hughes scouted, then ran. He reported hitting a rock, so I got out and scouted the drop too. The base of the drop appeared shallow but not danger-ous. As I scouted, two other boaters went over. They tagged the rock, but it didn't slow them up.

My own run was a bit farther left than the others'. When I hit the rock, my boat stopped dead. My outfitting gave way, throwing me forward in the boat about 4 inches. I hesitated, then tried to push myself back upstream with my paddle. The paddle slipped; I lost my grip on it and watched it float away. The boat slipped to the right, then settled into the drop against a left-hand boulder. Water shot against my back and flew over my head, jamming me tightly against the front of the cockpit.

I was stuck, and in real danger. The cockpit rim was pressing hard against my hips. The deck of my C-1 was so slippery I really couldn't push myself upstream. The current was powerful enough to knock me over if I didn't brace myself upright. I was scared and called for help. Peter Hubbard, who was onshore, threw me a line. This wasn't going to work. I asked him to move behind me, then I carefully tried to slide backward, without success.

Suddenly a tag line appeared above me. Ned had paddled to the center of the river, positioned himself on a midstream rock, and thrown a line to the group on the left. I hung my arms over it and yelled for the group at river right to work upstream to put more bend in the rope. This improved their ability to support me. Peter, now joined by Kate Heisler and Cindy Otto, started to pull hard. The force pushed me against my back deck, then lifted me back a few inches. My thighs came free. I kicked my legs back and slid out of the boat. My wife was preparing to run when she heard the screaming. She saw me slip below the surface and thought I was gone, but fortunately I swam to shore about 30 yards downstream, badly shaken but otherwise OK. My full-size Hahn Munich C-1 was completely underwater and required considerable effort to pull free.

This incident was a shock. Although I have no illusions that my safety work provides any special protection, I consider myself a pretty careful paddler. At my age, I'm primarily into the scenery and not shy about carrying drops I don't like. Here are my takeaways.

1. A number of people with experience on the Watauga, including a group of local paddlers who helped recover my C-1, said that the rock had been there a long time. Except for a single prior incident involving a large man in a high-volume kayak, it had never caused trouble. I suspect that my long (13-foot) boat, carrying my 240-pound weight, dove deeper than smaller individuals in modern high-rocker designs. Or I may simply have been too far left. Either way, I did not read the water correctly.

2. It was fortunate that the remainder of my group was equipped and trained for rescue. Several of them had been in my rescue classes and performed well under the pressure. Ned, by moving into position on the opposite shore, played a key role in setting up the tag line. He routinely goes to the opposite shore in emergencies and has been instrumental in several other rescues. By setting up immediately, rather than waiting for a "leader" to give him orders, he minimized my time in the water. He was on a very small rock and held onto his end of the rope with great difficulty.

3. My reading and teaching gave me a good idea of what to expect: I knew what was coming and what to do. I did try to keep my spray skirt in place as long as possible so that water wouldn't fill the boat. Although I thought I'd released the spray skirt before exiting, in the heat of the moment I did not. I actually came out through the waistband.

4. Normally, a stabilization line, rather than a snag line, is used to recover an alert, stable victim. The trapped person holds on to the line and uses it for support as they work free. But the adrenaline was

flowing, and the group simply pulled back hard. It was a bit uncomfortable, but it lifted me enough that I could escape.

5. I was glad to be in a C-1; a kayak would have sunk much deeper, and I would have needed to work harder to get free.

To those who think that they can't get into trouble, this should serve as a wake-up call. This is a dangerous sport. Potential hazards are not always clearly visible, and anyone can make a critical mistake. If you think river rescue courses are somehow "nerdy" or impractical, this incident shows that the lessons taught can make a difference. It is sobering to think that if this had happened back in the 1970s, I could be dead. Back then, we simply didn't know what to do.

VERTICAL PIN IN GULF HAGAS, MAINE

THIS GROUP HAD TAKEN A SWIFTWATER RESCUE COURSE at Zoar Outdoor the previous year and used the techniques they learned to perform a rescue. *American Whitewater Journal* published this account, written by the victim's wife, Joan Hildreth, in its January/February 1997 issue.

> *Gulf Hagas is an incredibly beautiful stretch of the*
> *Pleasant River that carves its way through a remote*
> *section of the Maine woods. The overall gradient is 95*
> *feet per mile; the steepest section averages 255 feet per*
> *mile. It's a Class III–V run with one Class VI drop. Start-*
> *ing as a meandering quickwater stream, it drops over a*
> *series of spectacular runnable ledges. Then it narrows,*
> *dropping through a series of constricted, overhanging*

gorges. The rapids here are tight, technical, and steep. It is a river that deserves respect.

On Saturday, May 25, 1996, five expert kayakers put in on the Gulf Hagas section of the West Branch of the Pleasant River in Central Maine. The level was moderate: 1 inch below the bridge abutment platform at the put-in. The group was very familiar with Gulf Hagas, and two of the paddlers had run it 25–30 times.

When we got to Jaws, we scouted. This is a serious multistage drop (Class V) with many tight places. The final chute of Jaws is an 8- or 9-foot drop through a narrow slot between a cliff on river left and a sieve rock to the right. The chute is partly obstructed at the top left by another rock.

Bill Hildreth was having a good run, right on line. He entered the final slot in great shape, in the center after coming around the right side of the obstruction at the top. Then—boom—he hit his bow and totally disappeared. I have never seen a pin that serious, but I have been present during other emergencies and was able to perform. It was a very different story when the person trapped was my husband. I lost it and started screaming. This alerted Rich, who was still upstream, that something serious was going on. He started running down to where we were over boulders and cliffs. At some point early in the pin, a muffled voice emerged from the chute and cried, "Help" twice. It was heart-wrenching not to be able to help, but it was also a relief to know that Bill had an air pocket. He briefly stuck his paddle up through the water to let us know where he was.

Jack jumped into the chute from the rock, hoping to somehow grab hold of Bill or his boat and dislodge him. It didn't work, and Jack washed through the chute and swam into the eddy just below the drop. He tried this again, with no luck.

The previous summer, Rich, Glenn, Bill, and I had all taken an ACA river rescue course taught by Charlie Walbridge. One of the techniques we learned was vertical pin extraction. We knew what to try in order to get Bill out. We didn't have to discuss it—we knew.

While Rich was running down from upstream and Jack was attempting to get to Bill by jumping into the chute, Glenn flew out of his boat on river right and swam into an eddy on river left. He somehow managed to climb up the slippery rock face to get onto the cliff above where Bill was pinned, across from where I stood. I threw a rope to him, and the rope spanned the chute. We (mainly Glenn) scooped the rope down through the water where we thought Bill was, sweeping it from downstream to upstream. Nothing caught on the first sweep. Afterward, Bill said that he saw a flash of yellow go by. He knew what was happening and was ready to grab the rope when it came by again. The line passed through the water, with Glenn forcing it even deeper. This time Bill was able to grab it. He let go of his paddle so he could hold on with both hands. Rich arrived and took the end of the rope I'd been holding; then Jack joined Rich in holding that end of the rope. Glenn, Rich, and Jack then moved upstream and pulled the rope taut. Bill later described pulling the rope to his chest as soon as he grabbed it. As the line tightened, he let it raise his arms over his head to get leverage to lift himself out. He needed to let go of the rope with one hand so he could push off the boat with the other. As he worked into a sitting position, his spray skirt popped, and water poured into the boat. He knew he had to move quickly, before the boat destabilized.

As Bill slid partway out of the boat, his head broke the surface, and he was able to shout instructions. He told the guys to step back upstream and pull tighter. The rope slipped a little, and he was back underwater again. He worried that if the rope went slack, he would be forced forward, and because his legs were partially out of the boat, his knees could be hyperextended or his legs broken. The pull on the guys holding the rope was incredible. They were hauling with all their might, and still Bill had to use all of his strength to escape. Glenn, by himself on river left, had little room to move on the narrow, slippery shelf but somehow managed to hold on. The three maintained steady pressure on the rope, and Bill freed first one leg, then the other.

Bill later reported that when he first hit and stopped, he tried to wiggle off but could not. He tried to push off the left wall of the chute with his paddle, without success. He attempted to pry with the paddle, but nothing happened. The water on his back was forcing him *forward so he couldn't sit up. He felt there was little chance of getting out by himself. He felt that, because he was stable and had air, he should wait for help. If we didn't do something within a few minutes, he would try to get out of the boat by himself.*

Once free, Bill flushed downstream and swam into the eddy on river right. His spray skirt was gone, and his pants were inside out and around his ankles. He was OK except for a sore ankle and thigh. Seven to 10 minutes had elapsed from the moment Bill first pinned until he got out of the boat. We were all emotionally and physically drained.

After Bill was safely onshore, the next step was to free the boat. That wasn't easy. The bow was lodged on the left and the stern was wedged under a large rock to the right of the chute. It was solidly pinned, but Bill, Glenn, Rich, and Jack eventually got it out.

This incident highlights a number of important issues. It's not my intention to try to tell others what to do. The following is simply my perspective:

1. Paddle with good people. Although paddling is an individual sport, there are elements that require teamwork. I really value the friendships of my close paddling buddies, and the events of May 25 reinforced the reasons I enjoy boating with them. We have fun on rivers but are always looking out for one another. I know that Glenn, Rich, and Jack would do everything they could for a stranger. But I'm also sure that the adrenaline surge that helped them pull off the rescue was enhanced by the fact

that Bill is their buddy. I will always be grateful to them for what they did.

2. Significant others boating together add a new twist to group dynamics. If a couple are paddling together and one of them has an accident, it's bound to have a great emotional impact on their mate. I'm sure my emotional response made it more stressful for Glenn, Rich, and Jack to deal with the situation.

3. Knowledge of river rescue techniques (and practicing them) is invaluable. Some people are naturally mechanical and can come up with effective rescue techniques quickly in emergency situations. I'm not one of them and wouldn't have known what to do if I hadn't taken a river rescue course. I strongly encourage all boaters—even experts—to take one, or read books, or study a video. I believe it made the difference between life and death for Bill.

4. Carry rescue equipment and make sure it works. Fortunately, Bill's kayak was equipped with a bulkhead so that his feet didn't slip off and cause him to slip farther into the boat. It had strong walls to prevent collapse and a keyhole cockpit to allow easier exit. There was a rope available; however, it was a new rope. Had I checked it out with a practice throw, I would have found that it had been packed wrong, causing it to tangle when thrown. Fortunately, we did not need the entire length of the rope, but a tangled rope could have caused problems. Rope color might not usually be a factor, but given a choice of color I'd pick the brightest one. The yellow color of the rope we used alerted Bill to its presence.

5. We had a spare paddle (which was only needed for a brief time because Bill's paddle had conveniently eddied out on its

own not far downstream). We were considering a spare spray skirt; it could come in handy if one were badly torn. In this situation, Bill's was ripped off by the water. Our solution was to switch boats and spray skirts around. I ended up paddling the rest of the river in a full-size Freefall without a skirt. Fortunately, we were already through the hardest drops.

6. Rivers constantly change. We returned to Gulf Hagas a few weeks later at low water (8 inches below the platform) in Thrill-seekers and got a closer look at the rocks in Jaws. The left side of the final chute is formed by a cliff. The bottom portion juts out into the slot about 10 inches. There are two distinct, deep cracks at the top of the outcropping, each of which could fit the bow of a kayak. Perhaps the cliff changed, or maybe it's been that way for years. Many people have banged into the left wall and kept going. We'd never heard of a pin in the chute until this year. Another paddler was caught there a couple of weeks before Bill, but he wiggled off fairly easily.

7. It's dangerous to assume that a drop is clean just because others have run it safely. As people run steeper rapids, the risks increase. Even though Bill looked like he was on the same line as everyone else, he ended up caught in an obstruction. Perhaps he went deeper because he's a big man and weighs more than most people.

8. No matter how careful you are, things can still go wrong. We are a reasonable, cautious group of people. None of us expected a serious pin in a chute where hundreds of runs had been made without incident. No one ever thinks that something bad can happen to them, but there are no guarantees in life, and there are certainly none in whitewater!

AMAZING TAG-LINE RESCUE AT BIG NASTY

THE FOLLOWING IS A CONSOLIDATION OF SEVERAL REPORTS.

On Sunday, May 24, 1998, a group from Philadelphia was making a low-water (0.6 feet) run of West Virginia's Class III–IV Cheat Canyon. One of the participants was Conrad Grove, a *Philadelphia Inquirer* reporter who was doing a story on whitewater paddling. Paddling a Thrillseeker, a high-performance inflatable kayak, he had done well on the Lower Youghiogheny (pronounced "yocka-gain-ee") the previous day, and the group invited him to join them on the Cheat.

Big Nasty is a wide rapid studded with pour-overs. Conrad bumped a rock and fell out of his kayak partway down. He was in a good feet-first swimming position until he washed over a pour-over in the middle of the river. The water pushed his legs straight down, and his foot caught on a rock. He was stuck, but fortunately he was in the backwash of the pour-over and could stand—barely. He was almost exactly midriver and almost halfway down the rapid, the hardest possible place to reach. He had an intermittent air pocket when he was able to get his head high enough, though at one point he went head down for close to half a minute, and they thought he was gone.

Conrad describes his situation:

The irresistible force of the water was tearing at my legs. My right leg was immobilized, possibly broken. My left leg, the muscle cut loose, was flapping like a flag in the wind. The water would have been shoulder-blade-high if I were standing erect. But I was pitched forward, my upper body lying flat under the water's surface. It took all the strength in my lower back to push my head above the waterline. I

felt a sledgehammer blow; my back was wrenched. I kept
my head up, but my back was all but paralyzed.

With my right hand, I could feel the rock that snared
me. But the rock was too low, too slick, and too curved
to push off against. At best, I could find only enough
purchase for two fingers. I held that position for maybe
45 seconds, until the water beat me down again.

Submerged once more, I managed with my left
hand to retrieve and bend my dangling left leg, placing
it parallel with the right leg in the hope of pushing off
the rock. But that, too, was futile. The rock wasn't wide
enough. There was nothing for the left foot to bite into.

My strength was failing. Though I could not turn my
head, from the corner of my right eye I could see ropes
being thrown toward me. In the roar of the cascade, I
could not hear the rescuers' yells.

Then, they say, I went under for a minute, able only
to keep my right hand above the water so no one would
lose sight of me. I managed to pop my head above the
water again. By now, 5 minutes had passed. Then I went
under for what I thought was the last time.

According to a report in *The Philadelphia Inquirer,* May 31,
1998, several groups were now on the scene. They threw ropes to
him, but pulling from the sides was not working. Attempts to ferry
a line across the rapid failed. Then someone had an idea: ferry a line
across the pool above the rapid! Linking several throw bags together,
they got a line across, creating a stabilization line that they could
lower to him. They had trouble getting the rope over Conrad's head.

It kept hanging up on the back of his helmet, and he was seemingly not aware of its presence. Then he grabbed it.

Conrad describes what happened next:

The rope now spanned the river, dozens of people holding it as if in a tug-of-war. The rope drifted downstream and over my submerged head. Their plan was to tighten the slack and prop me up, creating what rescuers call a stabilization line.

All I saw, inches below the water, was a bit of yellow cord to my right. With my right hand still seeking a hold on the rock, I stretched my left hand across my body to grab the lifeline. I had strength enough only to hook it with my index finger. From there I twisted it around my wrist two times, fearing I would lack the grip to hang on. I felt the rope tighten slightly.

No one can figure how or why my leg came free. But I felt the current sweep me downstream, where Ken Sanders was in his kayak. Barely conscious, I heard him say, "You're going to make it. Grab my boat." I had been trapped for 7 minutes.

The Philadelphia Inquirer reported the following:

A Canoe Cruisers' Association group arrived, bringing Dr. Beth Koller to help out. There was a backboard strapped to a tree across the river, which would make carrying Conrad easier. Members of a hiking club who were having lunch on river right knew the trail and volunteered to help out. They sent a runner ahead to contact first responders. It took 30 people to lift Conrad, hand over hand, up a steep 50-foot embankment and a quarter mile of rocky hillside to the trail. From there he was carried to a waiting ambulance. Although the emergency-room doctor could find no broken bones, it was several days before Conrad could get out of his bed without help.

FOOT ENTRAPMENT AT FISHERMAN'S NIGHTMARE IN GORE CANYON

ROB LEROY DESCRIBES HIS PERSONAL EXPERIENCE of a leg entrapment during a raft trip in Colorado's Class V Gore Canyon. Rob has guided and kayaked in New Zealand during his 13 years as a raft guide.

> *On September 1, 2002, while working a commercial rafting trip up in Class V Gore Canyon of the Colorado River, I experienced a wicked leg entrapment. Fisherman's Nightmare (Applesauce) is the first big drop of the day. It's a one-move Class IV rapid that drops probably 5 meters [16.4 feet] over 20 meters [65.6 feet]. The move is relatively easy—charge right and straighten out for the drop. Over the past week, a seam had been developing and strengthening in the middle of the drop as the water levels continued to drop, at the bottom of the first chute, before the main drop. It had been hitting harder with the lower flows. The flow on this morning was 16 cumecs [563 cfs], the lowest we had seen it. The day before, 16.7 cumecs [590 cfs], we noticed it was hitting harder.*

As we set up for the drop, I told my clients to hold on. I was still guiding, steering, as we hit this seam and got rocked across and out the other side of the raft. My thoughts at this point were "F#@%, I'm buying tonight!" Not sure, but I think I was trapped before I surfaced. My right leg must have hit one of the rocks in the middle of the rapid and shot my foot down. My knee lodged on a large rectangular column of rock angled 35 degrees or so up from left to right, and as my momentum took me forward, my ankle was levered back upstream into a rock below and slightly upstream.

Pinned solid—my body pushed forward, my leg levered in a mostly upright position—I was completely submerged. I don't know if I had air at first, but within seconds I had positioned myself so that the stream of water passing around me created a tunnel of air extending 4–5 feet from my body. Completely unable to move my leg, I knew I had to grab the rock where my knee was and work my way upstream. Simple; the only problem was the current. It took me 30 seconds or so to reach as far as my knee against the current—an incredible amount of force, an incredible struggle. There was a moment in there where I thought, There is no way I am going to get out of this. *This wasn't a panicked thought, and I certainly took it as no reason to stop trying.*

As I reached the rock, I thought I ought to let my coworkers know where I was. I stuck a hand up through the water, two or three short waves, then went back to the real fight, pulling myself upstream. The water pressure was

*fantastic—I felt as if my leg would snap at any moment.
The strain on my thigh and calf muscles and the pull on my
ligaments and cartilage as I was hyperextended forward
and laterally were intense. I worked my arm more and
more around the rock where my knee was and got to a
place where I felt I could begin to look for some footing
with my other leg. I found some solid ground, but as I
looked for footing, my foot kept washing off. Finally, I
found a firm hold and was able to push with my leg.*

*At a minute into the event, my first view was brief,
but Billy was in the eddy below the drop, yelling and
pointing. A few seconds later, I had pushed up a little
farther and saw Billy again, enough to realize he was
telling me there was a rope at my right shoulder. At this
point, a little over a minute had passed. My right hand
was stabilizing me as best as it could, so I was able to
grab the rope with my left. Between my efforts from my
right hand, my left leg, and the rope in my left hand, I
don't think my head went under again. Tor was pulling
on the rope, and my arm was pulled back, exposing my
shoulder. His pulling wasn't going to get me out, but
he did offer some relief. He was doing what he could
at the time. A second tag line appeared before me (this
must have been 90 seconds into the event), tensioned
from shore to the eddy in front of me. They were trying
to get another rope attached to that and pull both from
upstream. That tag line also helped to stabilize my position, but the work still needed to be done by me.*

At 2-plus minutes into it, I had worked myself up enough to rotate my leg so that my knee bent around the rock, freeing my ankle. I still couldn't get my leg around the rock. I started scouting out the route I would take when I did finally come free. It was the left slot in the middle of these rocks. It looked as clean as anything there, not that I would have much to do with it, but I knew where I would go. Approximately 3 minutes into it, still trying to get my leg around the rock, I got washed down like a high jumper clearing the crossbar, backward and headfirst into the pool below.

Exhausted, I assumed the starfish position face up and floated toward the shore. My coworkers got me up onshore and began to examine my leg. Nothing was broken. The leg was limp but completely worked. After 5 minutes or so, I tried to put weight on it and decided I could certainly hobble my way out of the canyon. Had to hike an hour and a half, 3 miles, with one of the guides, until we met up with the safety kayaker who had blasted out to get the van.

I can't say I wigged out at all until possibly when I was floating limply in the pool below. I started yelling at my friends to get me the f$@% out of the river. The ropes helped me get what could be loosely called a rest, but what got me out was my knowing what needed to be done and doing it regardless of the forces around me. My training and practice, though not a conscious part of my experience, obviously played a key role in my survival. The torque on my body was tremendous, *and the fight was incredible. I ended up with some minor knee injuries (minor, though it is my knee!) and some orthopedic work to do.*

The guys I worked with were the best. Of the nine or so guides we had working up there, I don't think any had less than 10 years of experience. To have two ropes to me within a minute and a half, working on the third, is incredible.

Advice:

1. Realize the forces involved when boating, and train for the inevitable; sooner or later you will be presented with rescue issues. Ultimately, self-rescue is the best skill to have.

2. Know the skills of those boating with you, and choose your boating partners wisely.

3. Wear a soft-brimmed hat! The air pocket I had while underwater was definitely greatly increased by the brim of my hat; I had air the whole time.

4. Don't give up. It just isn't an option.

My heartfelt thanks to those who were there doing what needed to be done. My boat had a sweet line, by the way!

I had two fractures that didn't show up on the X-ray, one of the tibial plateau, and one of the head of the fibula; a torn calf muscle; a torn thigh muscle; minor tears to three ligaments (MCL, PCL, and LCL); and a sprained ankle. I was non-weight-bearing for 6 weeks while the bone healed and 11 weeks after the event, I was still working on strengthening my leg.

VERY NEAR DROWNING AT HYDROELECTRIC ROCK

THE FOLLOWING IS BASED ON Harrison Metzger's August 31, 2003, article in the Hendersonville, North Carolina, *Times-News* and conversations with Lee Belknap:

On July 20, 2003, Rod Baird was trapped in a bad sieve on Section IV of the Chattooga River. The run forms the border of Georgia and South Carolina and contains several tricky Class IV–V drops. At Jawbone rapid, the flow splits around a large undercut boulder called Hydroelectric Rock. Several boaters over the years have flushed through here, and while no one has died, all of the incidents were very scary.

Rod was paddling with five other very experienced paddlers. The group had been out all day, the water level was above the cut-off for many at 1.9, and some were tired by the time they reached Jawbone rapid. On his run through Jawbone, Rod washed too far left, swept under overhanging Decapitation Rock, and was knocked over. He rolled quickly but, without enough time to think, paddled toward some paddlers on the right, above the sieve. The paddlers were yelling to go left to safety, but there wasn't enough time for these commands to sink in, and he slammed into Hydroelectric Rock and flipped again. Before he could bail out, he and his boat were pushed into the narrow opening and wedged tightly.

Rod's friends acted quickly to rescue him. Lee Belknap, then chair of the American Whitewater Safety Committee, eddied out behind the rock and was able to give him the nose of his boat. Rod grabbed hold, but he was unable to pull his head up to the surface. He passed out, still holding on. Lee shook him loose, jumped out of his boat, and climbed up onto Hydroelectric Rock while holding on

to his own kayak with the other hand. He grabbed a rescue rope out
of his boat and let his kayak drift away. A rope was thrown from the
left bank, and he attached it to Rod's kayak, but efforts to pull him
out in that direction were in vain.

"At that point, I had people on both sides of the river yelling
to me," Lee said. "Travis Buck told me to stop everything and help
him get out to the rock. That seemed like the best plan." Travis,
a very experienced river guide, had swum around Hydroelectric
Rock at low water with a scuba mask and knew it well. Lee threw
him a rope and pulled him up on the rock. Travis then grabbed
Rod's boat and pushed it under the rock, where it floated free. He
got hold of the kayak's grab loop and tried to pull the boat to shore,
but the current was taking him toward Sock 'em Dog rapid, another
big drop. He let go of the kayak and got to shore just in time.

Rod's lifeless body came free from the kayak soon after, and
both floated down into the pool below Sock 'em Dog. The group
raced downstream and swam out to him. They pulled him ashore and
removed his life vest. About 6 minutes and 35 seconds had elapsed
since the accident. This time frame is known because Milt Aiken, a
producer of whitewater videos, recorded part of the rescue.

Baird's color was dark purple, almost black. He was completely
unresponsive, with no pulse or breathing. Terry McGhee, a doctor,
and Annette DuPont, a physical therapist, started CPR. After about
5 minutes, Terry felt a pulse. A couple of minutes later, Rod took his
first weak, rasping breath. "I thought there was no possible way he
was coming back." Travis said. "When he took his first breath, it just
energized everybody."

By this time, the group had expanded tremendously, as many
other groups had joined them in their efforts. Someone retrieved a

backboard that was stashed nearby, and the group made a pontoon boat by lashing together several kayaks. They loaded Rod on top and swam him across the river to the South Carolina side. Then they carried him a half mile downstream over extremely rough terrain with one more "pontoon" crossing until they reached Lake Tugaloo. Here they flagged down a powerboat, which took Rod 2 miles across the lake to a boat launch. Meanwhile, a member of the group had climbed a mountain ridge to get cell phone reception and called for the ambulance that was ready to transport Rod to a local hospital. There he was stabilized, then transported to another hospital in Asheville, North Carolina.

Rod went through weeks of recovery, including a medically induced coma, a respirator, and kidney dialysis. He emerged relatively unscathed. His survival, he says, is a testament to his fitness, expert medical care, and the daring and exhausting rescue by the group of friends and strangers who converged on the river that day. He and his friends will continue to paddle whitewater rivers, although he probably won't run Jawbone rapid again.

WEIRD PIN AT PIECES OF RISA ON THE NORTH FORK OF THE FEATHER RIVER

THE KAYAKER WHO SURVIVED THIS FRIGHTENING INCIDENT tells his story:

> After surviving my biggest scare in kayaking, I feel the need to make people aware of this hole so that the same thing or worse doesn't happen to somebody else. It happened on the Class IV Tobin run of the North Fork of the Feather River in California on October 25, 2006.

I was running the last rapid, Pieces of Risa, at a flow of 1,000 cubic feet per second. I ran the rapid on river right. Unexpectedly, my boat pinned vertically in a nasty hole that the river has bored into a boulder. This hole can't be seen at released flows. I had no idea it was there until I landed in it.

I was pinned for about 10 minutes before I was able to free myself from the boat. I was not able to get out of the boat because my skirt was pinned between the kayak and the rock, with the flow pushing against the back of the boat. Had it not been for my fellow kayakers, all of whom were knowledgeable in swiftwater rescue, I feel that I would not be here writing about this experience.

Four people were able to get on the rock next to me and hand a rope down to me. As I tried to get out of my boat, I realized that I was stuck in the boat. My spray skirt was holding me in and would not release. At this point, I realized that I would have to cut the skirt off to get out of the boat. My biggest problem and lesson learned here was that I did not have a knife on me. I broke one of the cardinal rules I had learned in swiftwater rescue class: always have a knife! Luckily one of my buddies on the rock above me had one and was able to attach it to the rope and pass it to me. It was very difficult, with the force of the water pushing against me, to cut through a brand-new Kevlar skirt.

After 10 minutes, I was able to finally cut through it and remove myself from the boat. The four people who were still on the rock above the boat tried dislodging the boat from the pin, unsuccessfully.

I drove back the following day to remove the boat myself after the flow had been shut off. What I saw scared the shit out of me. The boat was pinned in a perfect tube through a granite boulder. Big hole at the top, small exit hole at the bottom. A perfect sieve. Had my kayak gone in at any other angle, the situation would have been much worse. Fortunately, I was able to easily hold my head above water as the bottom of the boat deflected the current to either side of my head. The other thing I noticed was that the boat had started to fold slightly, as evidenced by the large dents on either side of it. This was my biggest fear during the pin.

I am writing about this experience for several reasons:

1. So that people who don't know about this hole won't end up here. It is not visible at higher levels.

2. To advise people who are going to run whitewater, especially hard whitewater, to take a swiftwater rescue course. The knowledge I took from the course and especially the people who assisted me saved my ass.

3. To illustrate the importance of carrying a knife! I learned this in swiftwater class but had not gotten around to buying one. Had I been in the middle of the river, especially something as wide as the Tobin section, this situation would have been a lot worse. Luckily it happened close to the side of the river, enabling people to get close enough to hand a rope and a knife to me.

CLOSE CALL AT A ROCK SIEVE IN
DEERFIELD RIVER'S LABYRINTH

THIS ACCOUNT WAS SENT TO ME BY ONE OF THE RESCUERS:

We ran the Deerfield River Dryway, a Class III–IV river in Western Massachusetts, on September 3, 2006. John's raft was the first in our group to run Dragon's Tooth, the biggest drop on the run. In spite of a quick hang-up at the entrance of the rapid, where one paddler was ejected and immediately recovered, his line was clean, and the group attained the eddy on river right, below the rapid.

We observed John's run from the river-left shore; I was approximately 20 yards downstream of the Tooth with a throw bag. Labyrinth was filled in almost completely, with the reservoir pool starting just below Sharks Fin Rock on river left. Jenn and I returned to our rafts and prepared to run. Jenn's raft went first. They ferried out from the river-left eddy above the rapid and set up to run from right of center. I lost sight of them as they entered the main rapid. My group then began its entrance into the rapid. Our line was closer to river center, resulting in a quick spin and surf in the hole above the Tooth. We passed the Tooth facing upstream, and I corrected our orientation through the wave train. Everyone stayed in the raft through the rapid, and I steered us into the eddy on river right.

Upon entering the eddy, I heard John shouting from his raft while re-coiling a throw bag. One of the paddlers from our group was stuck in the rocks on river left.

I looked downstream to see Jenn's raft on the river-right side of the reservoir pool, but I could not see anyone in the rocks. We left the eddy and paddled downstream.

Now we could see a person stuck between two rocks on river left. I stood and threw a bag from the rear of the raft. It hit her, but at that point she was underwater and not moving. We missed the turbulent eddy immediately below her entrapment but finally grounded the raft on the river-left shore downstream of Sharks Fin Rock.

John, whose boat came right behind mine, and I exited our rafts and scrambled upstream on the bank. A woman, who we later learned was Kathryn, was caught between one partially submerged rock on her right and a large boulder on her left. She was upright, but the current was forcing her torso downstream. The large boulder on her left was accessible by shore.

As John and I made our way onto it, another raft eddied out nearby. The crew was partially composed of off-duty Zoar Outdoor guides. One of the guides, Justice, got onto the rock and attempted to free Kathryn. John and I arrived at the same time. From our original position on the large boulder, we were not able to free her. Justice and John moved around the boulder and into the water upstream of her to attempt further. The other Zoar guide, Erica May, was directing some of her crew to signal danger and request help from commercial rafts making their way downstream.

After several attempts, John was able to wrest Kathryn free and, with the help of Justice and the other guides, get her to shore. I returned to the bank to assist with treatment. Erica and another guide (from Crab Apple Whitewater) had positioned her on a relatively level spot. Erica identified herself as a nurse, and I deferred direction of Kathryn's treatment to her. Erica, Justice, and I checked Kathryn's condition and found no breathing or pulse. We opened her dry suit and cut the neck and arm gaskets to facilitate CPR and rescue-breathing access. Upon confirming no pulse or breath, Erica and the other guide (who was already at Kathryn's head) started CPR under Erica's direction.

After several cycles of CPR and rescue breathing, Kathryn began to vomit and gasp irregularly for air. She was rolled over, and I cleared her airway of regurgitated water and phlegm. After a few more cycles, her pulse returned, and breathing, while labored, did too. Erica continued to monitor her condition while the evacuation was coordinated. Throughout the resuscitation process, which lasted many minutes, numerous other boaters, both commercial and private, showed up and provided assistance. Meanwhile, people were dispatched to call 911, a backboard was sent for, and efforts were made to improve Kathryn's condition and expedite her rescue.

Several minutes into the CPR and rescue breathing, Frank Mooney of Crab Apple arrived and began directing his crew to prepare for evacuation. Once Kathryn started breathing on her own, her condition slowly and steadily improved. Those by her side made every effort to keep her warm and talking as she became more conscious.

A backboard arrived, and she was carefully loaded onto it and secured. The backboard was passed hand over hand to a raft waiting in a nearby eddy. Justice, Erica, Jonathan, a few other rescuers, and I paddled her across the reservoir and took her ashore. The backboard was placed on a raft trailer as we waited for the ambulance to come. The North Adams Fire Department arrived, followed shortly thereafter by the ambulance that took Kathryn to the hospital. During the paddle to shore, her condition improved, and her level of awareness increased significantly. By the time she was loaded into the ambulance, her sentences were coherent, and her level of awareness was improving.

I followed the ambulance to the hospital with Jonathan and Erica, and we waited while the ER staff worked on Kathryn. Shortly after we arrived, a nurse gave us good news: Kathryn's condition was stable, and she was being warmed up. There seemed to be no serious physical or mental injury. At Kathryn's request, I contacted her parents and left a detailed message regarding her condition and how to contact her. Jonathan and I left after Kathryn was moved to a Critical Care Unit room for overnight monitoring.

ANOTHER GREAT SAVE ON THE POTOMAC AT HARPERS FERRY

WHEN TROUBLE STRIKES, EXPERIENCE COUNTS! Barbara Brown began paddling in the 1950s, when she joined Annavieve Abrams'

Mariner Girl Scout troop and Washington, DC's Canoe Cruisers Association. She was on the second pioneer Gauley trip in 1969, when the rapids were named—Lost Paddle was named after her paddle and her swim. Her daughters, Amy and Becky, competed in slalom and were on the Junior National team, and her son, Jonathan, jumped Great Falls regularly when he taught paddling at the Valley Mill Camp. Although she had been involved in multiple bad swims over the years (including on the Cranberry in 1970, under the same rock that claimed the life of Sally Naas, a schoolteacher and experienced paddler), she had never been directly involved in a death or near death on the river until Saturday, April 15, 2006. Here she recounts the experience:

> *The day began innocuously. I met Ron Ray at Cindy Dee's restaurant, where we connected with a Mason Dixon Canoe Club's scheduled Class II trip on the Potomac at Harpers Ferry—the Needles. This is a straightforward Class II run along the Maryland–West Virginia border. Our group was large, with perhaps 20 boats. The weather was May-like—80s, clear blue sky. The water had warmed to just below swimming temperature, perhaps 55°F–60°F. The level was medium low. To run the broken dam, the group split, with the more adventurous boaters paddling across the river to the Maryland side chutes, out of sight. The rest planned to paddle the safest and least difficult route on the West Virginia side, along the wall, to assist a newbie.*
>
> *I dropped down the next Class II riffle, planning to direct the best line to the group if needed. About 15 or*

20 minutes passed as I did small ferries to entertain myself. The group was still in the eddy near the wall, pretty much out of sight. An empty boat floated by, being rescued by a young man. I asked him if he had the paddle and looked upstream for it. About 100 yards upstream, the swimmer was in the middle of a rapid formed by a 50-foot break in the dam, standing on a rock. She seemed to be rubbing her arm, perhaps injured. Although it was not an obvious emergency, I paddled upstream, still alert to the possibility that a paddle might appear. Three boats paddled by and landed on the rocky island to my left as I continued my attainment, well downstream of the rapid, about 70 yards. As one girl was getting out, I asked her if the swimmer was injured. She said no, but that someone was behind the log. I looked upstream and saw that, along the river-right side of the break, there was a large log, 2 feet in diameter, wedged 15 feet into the river with an additional 15 feet across the shore. On the river side were the remnants of a root ball. The log arched about 1 foot above the river near the center so that you could see under it. Near the root ball, I could see about 2 feet of the bow of a boat.

I asked the girl, "Are you sure someone is in the boat?" She said yes. Alarm bells went off in my head. I shouted to the three paddlers on the island to run. They listened; they obeyed. I kept shouting to "run, run!" The slowest turned and said, "I am running." I replied, "Run faster!" It was more efficient for me to paddle up as far as possible. About 50 feet downstream of the log, I beached

CHARLIE'S INSIGHTS:
Setting the Pace

The most enjoyable groups are made up of paddlers with similar skill and fitness levels well matched to the river's difficulty, but it's not unusual for expert paddlers to hold back for the group's benefit. If you move too quickly, your group may get spread out, or a less skilled paddler may gradually work their way backward until they land in the vulnerable sweep position. On runs that have too many long, hard rapids to allow for scouting, everyone must be ready to "read and run" these challenging rapids all day. So when the group includes a weaker paddler, or someone in your group is injured or sick, be prepared to slow down.

"I kept shouting to 'run, run!' The slowest turned and said, 'I am running.' I replied, 'Run faster!'"

—Barbara Brown

the boat, got out, grabbed my throw rope from behind the seat, and hurried behind the three. When I arrived at the log, the three paddlers were waist-deep downstream of it. A fourth member of their group was straddling the log. Heroically, the paddler had been partially extricated from the kayak. The back of her head was toward me. They were shouting that she was stuck. Thinking we needed more muscle, I began screaming for other members of my group and unraveled the throw bag, asking if the rope would help. Someone was blowing a whistle. Suddenly the paddler was freed. Her head fell back. Her face was an awful shade of blue, and her lips were purple. They worked as a team to get her to shore at my feet; seated, I wasn't strong enough to pull her up the rock face out of the water. Jim Norton, from my group, appeared. I slid aside, he grabbed both shoulders of her life jacket, and pulled her 4 feet out of the water.

We worked together. Sherry, one of the members of their group, announced that she worked as a summer lifeguard and started checking her pulse. I removed her helmet, which allowed access to the carotid pulse. There was no pulse and no breathing . . . and that terrible color. We removed her life jacket and unzipped the top of her Farmer John–style wetsuit. Sherry began CPR, doing both breathing and compressions. Because one person doing both is awkward and inefficient, I leaned over and took over the breathing. I could feel that air was going in. Sherry straddled her, counting the compressions. A voice behind us (later identified as Sheila Chappelle from

our group) offered directions and suggestions. Expecting
vomit, we turned her on her side, but it was not neces-
sary, and we turned her back on her back and pulled her
up farther. With CPR alone, her color started to improve.
After only about five rescue breaths, the victim gasped
and started breathing shallowly and very weakly on
her own. We were afraid she would stop and continued
breaths. Her breathing became stronger, and somehow
we knew it would not stop. Checking, we had a pulse. It
had a count. It wasn't over.

We called her name, Dawn, over and over, telling
her it was going to be OK. She was cold to the touch.
I had a paddling top in my dry bag, and we put it over
her, and she began to get visibly warmer. Over the next
15 minutes, her breathing came in strong gasps. She
became agitated, throwing her arms around and moan-
ing. We kept talking to her, hoping her eyes would open
and she would say something back, but it never hap-
pened. She remained unconscious. We knew we needed
more help. I noticed her spray skirt was in tatters. It was
the spray skirt that had snagged, preventing the rescuers
from pulling her under the log. The leader of their trip,
Jason, had a knife and had hacked the spray skirt until it
was freed. Dawn also had abrasions along her neck, and
I was concerned she might have a neck injury, but that
was not the case.

Onshore, a fisherman had dialed 911. Sheila got
back in her boat and paddled over to the West Virginia
side to make sure the 911 call had been made accurately.

An emergency vehicle appeared on the Maryland side up the canal—over a third of a mile away. Oh no! They came to the wrong side! But before we had time to be distressed, another appeared on the West Virginia side, much closer. Would we have to move Dawn across 300 yards of river to reach it? Could we?

Jason, the leader of Dawn's group, signaled by rotating a paddle that we needed a helicopter. Sheila paddled from one side of the river to the other, trying to report Dawn's condition accurately. A motorized johnboat with EMTs appeared. They almost spilled by trying to dock upstream of the log. All available arms held ropes to help secure the boat. We used my throw rope on the bow, making sure the boat would not jerk into Dawn, whose feet were at the water's edge.

We aided the EMTs in getting Dawn strapped to a backboard. Simultaneously, the Maryland State Police helicopter appeared. They lowered a yellow guide line, then a rescue basket. They carefully placed the back-boarded Dawn into the netted basket and hauled her into the helicopter, which flew her to the hospital in Hagerstown.

Sherry, very shaken, was offered a ride to shore by the johnboat. We gave her Dawn's helmet and life jacket. Next a Zodiac appeared and told all to get in. I refused because I needed to get my kayak. Only four people were left on the island: Jason, Jim, Ron, and me. We looked downriver and saw that the helicopter had scattered most of the boats and paddles, including mine, into the river. Don of our group was patiently herding three empty boats 150 yards downstream with a strong breeze.

An hour later, we had straightened out our belongings. We learned that Ron and Jim, both graduates of the Canoe Cruisers Association's swiftwater rescue class, had remembered the girl in the river and roped her to shore. The crucial questions were: How long had Dawn been in the water? What had happened? Here is the story as I understand it.

The group was a Johns Hopkins University Outing Club. Out of the 10 boaters, three were instructors, and two were instructors-in-training. The instructors were well trained with wilderness first aid and paddling experience. Dawn Ruben was the only non-student in the group. In her late-30s, she was a doctor of veterinary medicine at Hopkins on a fellowship. She had never been in a boat before. After the first girl spilled, all the students were herded into an eddy to river right of the chute while the instructors proceeded with the rescue. One instructor chased the original swimmer's boat. Dawn, being new, didn't hold the eddy and slipped out and floated into the log. Three boats followed her down. Dawn, caught upstream of the log, was calling for help and holding on to both the log and one of the other boats. That boat slipped out of her grasp, and three boats managed to paddle safely around the log, leaving Dawn trapped in her boat. These were the boaters I had met. I feel Dawn had been underwater at least 5 minutes.

*Dawn was in a coma and in critical care for
15 hours. She woke without residual physical damage
except that she could not remember the accident. Her
recovery is nothing less than a miracle.*

QUICK THINKING SAVES A LIFE

IN EARLY JUNE 2007, A QUICK-THINKING KAYAKER made an innovative rescue of a rafting guest on Pennsylvania's popular Class III–IV Lower Youghiogheny (pronounced "yocka-gain-ee") River. The woman, who was stranded on a midstream rock, was being rescued by a guide using a throw bag when the unexpected happened. As she swung to shore on the rope, the bag end got caught between some rocks, leaving her holding on to the line in the middle. The guide let go of his end of the rope, but as the woman floated downstream, the free end of the line wrapped around her leg. She was left to dangle in the current headfirst. A guide waded out and tried to cut the rope but succeeded only in cutting himself badly.

Heather Rau, who was shooting a video for her company, saw what was happening and moved in fast. She paddled her kayak in front of the woman and told her to grab hold of the bow. By now the victim had been struggling to breathe for several minutes. Her grip was weak, and she could barely hold on. Heather paddled hard upstream, forcing the boat under her chest. This put some slack into the rope, allowing a second guide to free her. Although shaken, she was able to paddle to the takeout.

I had previously thought that this might be a useful technique, but after Heather's practical demonstration, I started teaching it in all my rescue classes.

KAYAKER SURVIVES ACCIDENT ON OH BE JOYFUL CREEK

THIS ACCOUNT IS BASED ON A JULY 20, 2011, REPORT in *The Crested Butte News.*

Oh Be Joyful is a popular Class V steep creek run near Crested Butte, Colorado. On the evening of July 18, 2011, kayakers Chris Goodnough, Ethan Passant, Chris Menges, and Paul Muirhead decided to run it. Goodnough has been paddling the run since the late 1990s and paddled in the Oh Be Joyful steep creek race. That summer he had run it four times and wanted to get one more run in before the water dropped. After scouting, they decided to run the "racecourse" section of the creek.

At Old Growth Drop, a 6-foot ledge, Menges went first and eddied out to turn and watch Goodnough. He saw him come over the top, get pinned in the falls, and disappear. Goodnough had run the drop previously without incident, but this time the nose of his boat pitoned, and the stern swung around and landed in the water perpendicular to the river. His spray skirt imploded, and he tried to bail out. His left foot got stuck in the boat, and he was pinned under the river flow.

Facing downstream with his left leg caught in the boat and water pouring over him, Goodnough pushed his upper body up, locking his elbows to create an air pocket in front of his face. Ropes were thrown, but he couldn't move to grab any of them without losing the air pocket. Even if he had grabbed a throw bag, his leg was stuck in the boat, and there was no way they would be able to pull him out.

The group set up a V-lower system, with paddlers on either side of the river belaying a rope across it. Menges and Ethan were tethered and, instead of being lowered, worked their way upstream, using the rope for support. They made several attempts to enter the drop, grab Goodnough, and pull him out.

Meanwhile, Goodenough's air pocket was shrinking, and the cold was weakening him. He held his position and waited. Another attempt to grab him proved unsuccessful. Then things got worse. The water pressure increased, and his air pocket got smaller. After 10–15 seconds, he was floating.

Finally, Menges was able to grab Goodnough and flip him over to get his head out of the water. Ethan grabbed the boat and got his leg loose. He was pulled to shore after spending roughly 25 minutes in the water. As they pulled his wet clothes off, Crested Butte Search and Rescue (CBSAR) arrived. The team was on scene within 15–20 minutes, according to CBSAR president Nicholas Kempin. They took Goodnough down the drainage and across the Slate River before transferring him to an ambulance. He was treated at Gunnison Valley Hospital and released that night, his only injury being trauma to his left calf and ankle.

Goodnough said afterward that it's important to choose your kayak partners wisely. "Chris Menges, Ethan Passant, Paul, Adam, Nick, and search and rescue all saved my life," he said. "It's that simple."

For a gripping video of the rescue, visit vimeo.com/68476394.

PIN AT KNIFE'S EDGE RAPID ON NEW YORK'S MOOSE RIVER

LONG, COMPLICATED RESCUES involving lots of people from several groups are very difficult to manage. First responders often try to sweep all paddlers from the scene, but that did not happen here. New York State Forest Rangers have been involved with a number of difficult whitewater rescues over the past three decades. They always combine strong swiftwater rescue skills with a solid appreciation for the capabilities of the paddling community. This report shows how they got everyone working together.

The Class V Moose River in Upstate New York was running at 2.8 feet on the Sunday of the Adirondack Moose Festival (Moose Fest) weekend in mid-October. It was partly cloudy and unseasonably warm, with the air temperature in the 60s and the water temperature probably in the 50s. All of us were familiar with each other's paddling skill, having run multiple sections of the Moose River at low and high flows, in addition to other rivers.

Our group of eight scouted Knife's Edge at around 2:30 p.m. The first six ran the drop and were waiting downstream in the eddy on river right. The seventh boater was on the river-right shore above the feature with a throw bag. At around 2:45 p.m. our eighth and final boater was attempting the S-turn line through the drop. He launched off the Knife's Edge late (too far river right of the intended line) and became pinned on a large rock in the middle of the rapid. His boat was completely underwater, facing upstream with the bow submerged under the rock. His upper body was above water, and he could use his arms to push against the rock, turning his back to the flow and keeping his head above water; however, he was unable to free himself.

Within 60 seconds, a member of the group was able to climb onto the large rock and reach down to the pinned boater. He tried to pull him up but was unsuccessful. He pulled two carabiners and slings from his PFD, using one biner to clip a throw rope with a sling attached to the pinned boater's PFD. He girth-hitched the other sling, attached to a biner and then to another throw rope, around one of the pinned kayak's grab loops. Both throw ropes were held by other members of our group onshore on river right, just downstream of the drop. Communication was difficult due to the noise of the water, and the group had to rely on shouting individual words and using hand signals.

Two more members of the group swam out to the large rock to assist. They tried together to pull the pinned boater up on the rock but were unable to move him. Two other downstream members of our group tried pulling on the throw rope attached to the boater. At some point during these early attempts, the pinned boat and boater shifted and sunk several inches deeper into the undercut. The boater's head was still above water, and his position seemed to be stable.

The pinned boater's spray skirt imploded (though the boat was probably already mostly filled with water). However, the neoprene spray skirt remained caught between the undercut rock and the boat's bow, limiting movement and self-rescue. The pinned boater verbalized wanting to cut the spray skirt with a rescue knife but was prevented from doing so. One of the group proceeded to pull and pry the skirt to dislodge it. Once it was dislodged, the pinned boater attempted to step out of the boat by stepping on the boat's plastic center safety pillar, without success. He soon said he was losing feeling in his lower extremities due to suspected pinching of the femoral arteries caused by the pin.

At about 2:55 p.m., member four was sent downstream to get help. The group tried to come up with some other options but ultimately decided to wait for additional support to arrive before making any more adjustments as long as the pinned boater was stable and alert. At some point, a throw rope was strung across the river that could have been used to stabilize the pinned boater in case group members one, two, and three became exhausted, but it was never used.

At around 3:15 p.m., help arrived. He informed the group that the authorities had been alerted and that he'd heard sirens on his way to Knife's Edge. Meanwhile, a group of experienced kayakers at the takeout who were packing up to head home immediately grabbed their safety equipment and headed toward Knife's Edge. One of the group waited on the nearest access road by Knife's Edge to direct first responders and experienced kayakers to the incident site.

At around 3:20 p.m., a few representatives from the local fire department arrived, and by about 3:35 p.m., a New York State Forest Ranger, members of local police and EMS, and many more experienced kayakers had arrived on scene. The ranger directed the rescue from this point forward. A rope was fastened around the pinned boater's torso (underneath his armpits) with a biner, and the rescuers tried to pull him up the slope perpendicular to the river. This greatly restricted the pinned boater's breathing and otherwise was difficult because they were pulling him directly against the flow.

The rope was repositioned downstream, and one of the experienced boaters coordinated the new approach with the ranger. Two teams of about five rescuers were lined up downstream on river right to pull on the two throw ropes that were fastened around the boater's torso and to the pinned boat's grab loop. The rope-pulling teams pulled together on the count of three, and the pinned boater was successfully yanked from the pin after just two good tugs.

The boater floated downstream and was retrieved by live-bait rescuers. At 3:45 p.m., after approximately an hour in the water, he was pulled ashore. He was responsive but hypothermic. The rescue team brought a litter (rescue basket), placed the rescued boater in the litter, and used blankets and other materials to insulate him. He was transported in the litter from the riverbank to the waiting ambulance. One member of the original group accompanied the victim to a local hospital.

A day after being treated for moderate hypothermia and traumatic rhabdomyolysis, he was in good condition with general, overall body soreness. The pinned boat was removed approximately 5 minutes after the boater was yanked from it. Two ropes were affixed to the boat's security bar/handle. One rope was pulled by at least two individuals on the downstream river-left bank. The other was pulled by multiple individuals positioned downstream on the river-right bank. All pinned paddling gear was removed from the Knife's Edge rapid.

The rescuers onshore stayed organized under the direction of the New York State Forest Ranger, and the ranger successfully utilized their abilities and recommendations to manage ropes and prepare supplies to evacuate the victim. The rescued boater and group members are all deeply grateful to everyone who responded. Many hands on and off the river contributed to the success of the rescue.

SWIM INTO A SIEVE ON WASHINGTON'S GREEN RIVER

THIS STORY IS TOLD FROM TWO PERSPECTIVES: the swimmer's and one of the rescuers'.

From the swimmer, Mary:

March 18, 2018, was a low-water day on Washington's Class III–IV Green River Gorge. Running the usual moves, I made it past the guard rocks (usually guard waves in normal levels) and was pointed to go through the Nozzle. But 5 feet from it, instead of continuing on a forward trajectory as usual, the hydraulics seemed to suck me backward and slam me against the right house-sized rock. Knowing there was a sieve down there and not feeling confident about my roll up against a rock, I panicked and swam.

There was an immediate pull of hydraulics underwater, likely through the sieve, so I could not get my head up; I was drowning. I reached up and felt a boat's bow, grabbed it, and pulled my head up with one hand, my other hand on a rock. It was my boat, and it was going under; the handhold did not last. With all my might, I smeared up on the rock, my shoulder at water level. It was difficult, strong sucking "down the toilet hole." My boat came under my feet and hesitated there, allowing me some rest. My hips were forcibly flexed along the curve of the rock, so I struggled to remain above water.

Helene and Steve were on the downstream side of the rock. The boat went through. I was going down. Helene threw a rope, which allowed me to get my chest to water level. Steve jumped up on the rock and grabbed my PFD shoulders. At first, he was unable to pull me up; the sieve was sucking my legs down and through. We waited there for a minute until a "reverse surge" released my legs and let Steve pull me out onto the rock.

From rescuer Helene:

We ran the first Class IV rapid (Mercury?) and met in the river-left eddy above the Nozzle. I had only run the river once before, and it was Steve's first time; though well within our abilities, it was not a familiar place. I knew that there was a sieve somewhere in this rapid called the

Nozzle but wasn't sure where. Mary went first, and she flipped near the entrance of the Nozzle, where you're supposed to go between two very large boulders. I was surprised to see how fast she was being pushed to the right, upstream of the right-side rock, while upside down, which didn't seem right since that rock seemed connected to the rest of the rocks onshore. There shouldn't be current going in that direction. Steve and I immediately pulled out of the eddy and headed downstream. I thought about eddying above on the right to be above the sieve, but being unfamiliar, I didn't want to end up in the sieve, too, so I decided to make the "regular" move and eddy out behind the rock. We immediately saw Mary's face above the water; she was hugging what seemed like a submerged log or a rock bridge spanning a narrow channel between that right big rock and the shore. The channel was very narrow (2–3 feet).

She was very calm and clearly said, "I need help." Still in my boat, I threw her my rope and wrapped the other side of the rope around a rock next to me since I was still in my boat and not in a stable place. I figured at least she could hang on to the rope until we got situated. Steve jumped out of his boat and stood on the rock bridge that creates the sieve and grabbed her PFD. Her boat was nowhere to be seen (I found out later she was standing on it!), but a little while later, while Steve was still hanging on to her by her PFD, the boat came popping up from underwater in the eddy below us. Shortly after, Steve was able to pull her out.

While she rested a little on the rock, I went to secure the boat. There was no place to get back in the boat in that river-right eddy, so it took some work getting her and her boat across to river left because the eddy lines were powerful. Through the whole rescue, Mary kept her cool and clearly communicated with us, so we knew how she was stuck and what was going on underwater. That made a very big difference. Thankfully, after all this, we were done with the hard rapids and got to the takeout without any more incidents.

FOOT ENTRAPMENT ON THE SOUTH AMERICAN

THIS ACCOUNT WAS POSTED IN THE ACCIDENT DATABASE by Carson Lindsay in 2017.

Over Memorial Day, I was rafting with some college friends on California's South Fork of the American River at high water. As we entered the Class II rapid above Old Scary, I looked downstream and saw a man holding a throw bag fully played out in the water. I first assumed he was in the middle of a swiftwater class, but then I noticed some raft guides standing onshore with two of their rafts tied up nearby. At the same moment, one of the guides yelled, "Help! Her foot is stuck!" I saw a woman almost completely underwater. She was about 15 feet from shore with water surging over her head.

I was born and raised on the river. My parents met working as raft guides back in the 1980s, and I've been a raft guide and kayaker for the last eight years. I've

CHARLIE'S INSIGHTS:
Key Roles in a Rescue

In every serious rescue, several key positions should be filled: The first two are the most important. Imagine a pinned boat, perhaps with a paddler stuck in it. The first person should make contact with the victim if at all possible. That person needs room to work, and you don't want to get in their way. If there is no room for a second person at the accident site, a second responder should get as close as they can, onshore or a midstream boulder; pull out their throw bag; and let the first person know they are ready to help. If there are more people, someone should set the downstream safety, in their boat or onshore. On busy rivers, send a paddler to act as the upstream lookout, to prevent other groups from blundering into your rescue; this is especially important if a rope has been deployed that blocks the river. Someone can also go to the opposite side of the stream or chute, when possible, so that if a rope is needed from that side, it will be there. Don't stand around—look for a job that's not being done, then do it!

seen a lot of things happen on the river, but I had never experienced anything like this. This past winter and spring in California, I put my years of river experience to use and began teaching swiftwater rescue classes all over the state. . . After months of instruction, I felt more comfortable and confident in my own rescue skills and decision-making on the river than ever before. But when you're practicing these scenarios, you hope the day never comes that you'll have to use your skills.

When I first saw her, I immediately thought, "This looks exactly like an entrapment scenario I would run in a swiftwater class." I had worked through a situation like this hundreds of times, and I knew I could handle this one.

In our classes, we teach the acronym LAST to apply to every rescue. This stands for Locate, Access, Stabilize, and Transport. At the same time, rescuers have to be cognizant of their surroundings because swiftwater environments are ever-changing. I had already located the victim, a middle-aged woman, as we floated by and saw I could access her by swimming and wading across the current from the shore. The only difference between a stable and unstable victim in a swiftwater environment is whether their head is above or below water. The woman had a small air pocket around her head between the surges of water, but she was mostly under. I could see her moving, meaning that she was conscious and breathing, but I didn't know how long she had been there. If I could get the woman free, I knew if I couldn't walk her to the shore or a raft, I could safely transport her downstream to my raft by swimming.

Knowing I had to act quickly, I pulled over to river right and told my friends to stay in the raft downstream in case the woman came free without me, and I ran upstream toward her. As I ran past the raft guides who were still onshore, I went through the mental checklist we teach in all our classes: I saw upstream spotters holding throw bags, knew my friends in the raft would be downstream safety, knew the guides were onshore for extra support, and I felt confident in my ability to swim and wade the 15 or so feet out to her using the eddies behind bushes and small rocks. In hindsight, I wish I had quickly told the guides my plan to get her head above water and get her to shore, but I was too worried about the woman.

I ran up the shore parallel to the woman and jumped into the river, swimming to an eddy behind some bushes. I waded the rest of the way using small eddies behind some rocks. Luckily, she was stuck next to a rock with a decent eddy behind it where I could stand about waist-deep. I immediately lifted her head out of the water and yelled to the people onshore to call 911. Her face was blue and she could hardly speak. I reached down and felt both of her legs floating free. I asked what was stuck, hoping she could respond. The only thing she could say was, "Spray skirt." I reached around and found the back of her skirt hooked on a small branch pointing back upstream. At this point, I pulled out my knife to cut the skirt but realized I couldn't hold her head out of the water and cut the skirt at the same time. I looked over to the shore and called for one of the guides to come help. Had the victim not been conscious or responsive, I was preparing myself to give the woman rescue breaths. It's imperative as river and rescue professionals that we're prepared to give air to victims in the river who are unconscious even if we cannot do CPR. Often, the hot oxygenated air from our body to theirs is all it takes to restart their respiratory system and get them breathing again.

Once the guide arrived, she held the woman's head out of the water while I pulled the skirt off the branch. The woman came free and I turned to face downstream, holding her in the eddy my body created. She was exhausted and fell limp in my arms but luckily was still conscious and breathing. As I was holding her, the guides lowered a raft down through the bushes to us. I waded over to the raft with the woman and lifted her up into the boat. One of the guides in the boat was a doctor, and she took over providing care. The ambulance met us downstream at Old Scary. I don't know how long the woman was trapped before I saw her, but it took about 30 minutes from when I arrived to get her to the ambulance.

It was incredibly fortunate that the woman had a big enough air pocket with the water flowing over her head and that we were able to act fast enough to save her. You never know when or if you, a friend, or a stranger will depend on another boater to rescue them, which is why people who play in our rivers should not only be comfortable in the water but also know how to handle a basic to intermediate rescue situation. Having the confidence to know how and when to implement tools, like wading versus a throw bag, is also critically important. Using a throw bag to access and free the woman would have been hopeless and time-consuming, whereas swimming and wading out to her was simple and fast. Taking a swiftwater class gives you different tools for your toolbox and teaches you how and when to use them. But one of the first lessons you're taught in a swiftwater course is don't attempt a rescue if you aren't sure. After assessing the victim, her position, and the water conditions and mentally going through the motions of the rescue, I knew without a doubt I could safely access the victim to stabilize her and transport her to shore.

A few weeks later, I heard from a friend and coworker that the woman had enrolled in and taken a swiftwater class with the company I work for. I haven't spoken to her, but she left a note at the local store in Coloma that read, "Thank you so very much for your rescue Saturday! My spray skirt was caught on a branch, and I was stuck there quite a while. It was like a miracle when suddenly a rescuer appeared and was able to free me. Then you guys got me into your boat and took care of me as a team. Thank you so much! You're my miracle."

To practice swiftwater rescue skills, I suggest throwing your throw bag once a day when you're on the river. Pick a target, and if you miss, keep throwing until you hit it. Find safe places to swim in the river. See how well you can swim in and out of eddies, and get to know your own personal limits.

Lastly, get comfortable walking around in the river. Most entrapments happen less than 20 feet from shore and in less than 3 feet of water. This means most of the time, walking out to the victim is a totally viable and fast option. We have a responsibility as river people to keep each other safe, so let's make good decisions, train hard, stay safe, and have fun.

4

INJURIES, RESUSCITATIONS, AND EVACUATIONS

DIFFICULT RESCUE ON A REMOTE MEXICAN RIVER

THIS ACCOUNT POINTS OUT THE DIFFICULTY of summoning medical help in remote regions of the world. There was no 911-type number to call in Mexico back then. Were it not for the man's political connections, he could have died on the river or languished in a small rural hospital. As it was, the long wait for competent care had lasting effects. The following information was compiled from an article in the *Houston Chronicle* and several phone calls.

On December 30, 1986, a pioneering trip down a remote Mexican river ended in a disabling injury. Steve Daniel, 36, a noted Texas river explorer with a passion for Class IV–V self-supported expeditions, and his companion, Victor Jones, were ahead of the group on the Río San Pedro Mezquital when Daniel attempted to run a steep, rocky drop. He hit a rock, his kayak broached and pinned, and his body disappeared from view. Victor was able to leap from the shore to the rock and recover the boat, allowing Daniel to float free. Victor

The West Virginia National Guard practices swiftwater rescue techniques on the Cheat River.

grabbed him and swam toward the side of what was now a deep gorge. In a niche in the rocks, he began mouth-to-mouth resuscitation. Fifteen minutes later, Daniel was awake and asking where he was. One leg was broken, but there appeared to be no other injuries.

The evacuation became an epic. Three kayaks were tied together to form a raft, and Daniel was ferried to a rock outcropping, where a tent was pitched. He was given pain pills, and the party split up into two groups, both seeking help. Three people went downstream in boats, and three hiked out. The hikers hitched a ride to an isolated ranch, where they were able, through personal connections, to arrange a rescue flight by a Drug Enforcement Administration helicopter several days later.

Daniel was taken to a local clinic, then to a Durango hospital. Family and friends, concerned with the level of care he was receiving, wanted to transfer him as soon as possible. But he was not released by hospital officials until his state representative guaranteed payment of a $2,000 hospital bill. Once he arrived in Houston, doctors discovered that his legs had been hyperextended during the accident, severely damaging veins, arteries, and other tissues. A double amputation above the knees was necessary.

As this narrative points out, severe injury on remote expeditions can have terrible consequences. Extra caution is needed in remote areas. Furthermore, it appears that group organization was not as tight as it should have been, with paddlers spread out over miles of river like they were on a stateside day trip. This relaxed attitude may have led to the error in judgment that caused Daniel to make the run in the first place.

The rescue by Victor was a marvel of clear thinking and effective action. Without his intervention, Daniel would have died on the spot.

BACK INJURY ON NORTH CAROLINA'S GREEN RIVER GORGE

THE DETAILS OF THIS ACCOUNT were provided by Gordon Grant and Slim Ray.

On July 15, 1991, noted paddlesports writer and rescue instructor Slim suffered a disabling back injury following a bad run of Sunshine Falls, one of the most serious drops on North Carolina's Green River Gorge.

The Green River Gorge is a stretch of Class V+ rapids in a very steep gorge. Because of regular water releases, it has been run frequently by experts. Slim was part of a strong group that included several first-timers and was led by boaters who were very familiar with the river. The group proceeded cautiously, allowing plenty of time for scouting and carrying, and arrived at Sunshine Falls without incident.

Sunshine is a technically difficult rapid generally regarded as one of the more serious drops on a section noted for its seriousness. To run it, one must dive diagonally across the lip of a 15-foot drop into a small eddy, turning immediately to run a rocky 5-foot drop. Failure to make the move results in the boat falling vertically onto a rock shelf.

The group arrived at the rapid around 3 p.m. Four of the boaters made the run without incident; four carried around the drop. Slim indicated that he'd like to make the run. He caught the eddy on river left and began his drive to the right from there. As he went over the drop, the boat lost its angle and went straight down, hitting the rock with terrific force. After pinning momentarily, the boat pitched forward and disappeared into the spray of the falls.

Slim was sucked into the hole upside down, and he intended to wait until he floated free before rolling up. Instead, he was sucked under the curtain of water until he became pinned between the falling water and the shallow rocks below. There was no specific impact responsible; rather, the tremendous pressure of the water forced his body forward until his back snapped.

After a few seconds, his paddle floated out, followed by his boat. Slim surfaced by the side of the boat as it swept over the second drop. As soon as he surfaced, he shouted. Two ropes were thrown, and Slim caught the second one. As he was being pulled to shore, he called out that he had hurt his back. The group did not bring him out of the water but kept him in the shallows while they did a primary survey. Slim reported great pain in his back but no sensation in his lower body below the waist. The time was 3:30 p.m.

The group elected to treat for spinal injury by keeping Slim immobilized in the water while sending runners for help up a very steep trail nearby. They knew that the cars of friends who had hiked in would be available to them, and they were instructed to contact rescue squads and bring them in on the same trail with a Stokes litter and backboard. The runners left at 3:50 p.m.

To keep Slim motionless, the boaters who remained with him built a supporting structure under him using foam walls removed from kayaks. As the water release ended, the water level dropped. By adding shims made of foam triangles under the walls, they were able to keep Slim's body as level as possible. By 4:50 p.m., Slim's body was clear of the water; he was covered with insulating layers and trash bags to prevent further heat loss.

At 5:15 p.m., the first of the rescue-squad volunteers arrived. The group insisted on identification of the first aid leader before Slim was turned over to them. They administered an IV and packaged Slim on a backboard and Stokes litter. They radioed for a helicopter, which miraculously landed at 5:50 p.m. a short distance downstream in the steep gorge. The group cleared a trail to a large pool, then lashed several kayaks together to float Slim out to where the helicopter was waiting on a large rock. He boarded the helicopter at around 7 p.m. and was transported to the hospital, where he underwent surgery and was placed in intensive care. His T-12 vertebrae, the lowest of the chest vertebrae, a little above the small of the back, was badly damaged, leaving him paralyzed from the waist down.

Mistakes in Class V and VI rapids carry a serious risk of injury or death. The free-fall element found in steep rapids must be respected; this is not the first instance of severe back injury from running high waterfalls. Those who make these runs must be ready to accept the risks.

The group is to be commended for their careful and conservative approach in treating Slim's back injury. There have been numerous cases of sloppy rescue and evacuation over the past few years that could have had serious consequences. Keeping Slim in the water was a good idea, given the warm water temperatures. It would not have worked in more extreme conditions. Although Slim lost the use of his legs, he continues to write and teach swiftwater rescue.

ON-RIVER EVACUATION IN WEST VIRGINIA'S CHEAT CANYON

RIVERS PASS THROUGH SOME PRETTY RUGGED COUNTRY. You can't know just *how* rugged until you're faced with the challenge of transporting someone who can't paddle. I was leading a group of first-timers on West Virginia's Cheat River in May 1992. We'd seen the group ahead of us take an unconventional route down High Falls, where one of their folks had flipped and swum.

After the run, we paddled over to them. The swimmer was banged up, cold, and scared. There were nasty bruises on one cheekbone, and her right hand was cut and swollen. She couldn't hold a paddle. The options were not good. It was late and getting cold. Three big rapids separated her from the takeout. Looking downstream at the Maze, I saw that the shores were steep and the portage options unappealing. The group couldn't decide what to do; I talked to them a bit but really couldn't offer much help, as I was responsible for the 12 inexperienced people following me. Fortunately, Chris Koll and his wife, Caron, showed up. Chris is one of the strongest kayakers I know, and he was paddling a high-volume creek boat. I asked him if he could help the woman and then continued down with my group.

Impatient with the group's indecision, Chris instructed the woman to lie on his back deck and lock her hands around his waist. Thus loaded, he proceeded down the river. At the big drops, he landed, walked the injured paddler around, then came back and ran his boat through. At his urging, the group took the empty kayak, attached the spray skirt, and tied the waistband shut. This allowed them to herd it downstream to the takeout with little effort.

The injured paddler's group was using a shuttle service with several dozen other people on board. The others didn't want to wait, so we agreed to shuttle everyone else out. Some of the paddlers in our party gathered towels and dry clothes as I sat on the bridge and waited nervously. Chris and Caron appeared first; we helped the injured paddler get dry and clothed, then one of our vehicles took her to a hospital in Morgantown, where she was treated and released. The rest of the two groups piled into the remaining cars for a crowded ride back to the put-in.

In retrospect, things worked out well. On-river evacuations, when possible, are the fastest and easiest alternatives. Had they sent for help, it could not have arrived before dusk. A night out would have been uncomfortable at best. Walking out would have taken several hours, and they would probably not have made it out before dark, either.

BROKEN NECK IN CHEAT CANYON'S PETE MORGAN RAPID

THE FOLLOWING ACCOUNT is based on the July 11, 2000, *Washington Post* article "Danger Rapidly Approaching," by Angus Phillips, and discussions with Jeff Davis.

Pete Morgan is the last major rapid in West Virginia's Cheat Canyon. There is a deceptive hazard in the runout: it looks like a clean wave train, but there is a nasty rock hidden behind the first wave. Several of my friends have been clobbered here, and on July 4, 2000, a serious injury was reported. The victim, Starr Mitchell, told Angus, "I went too far right in my kayak, flipped, and hit my head. I was going really fast. It put a front tooth right through my lip, but I was never knocked out. I came out of the boat and got shoved into an eddy. The current was trying to push me under an undercut rock. One guy tried to get me, but I couldn't reach the grab loop on his kayak. Then Jeff Davis threw me a rope, and they pulled me out."

Starr had taken a frightful hit and knew that, despite her helmet, she was badly injured. As she lay on the rocks, afraid to move, her group considered their options. Fortunately Jeff, a rescue-trained expert, took charge. He had an open boat capable of carrying her to the takeout. A kayaker volunteered flotation foam from his boat to build a stabilizing brace; Jeff cut it to fit and secured it under her life jacket with an Ace bandage and duct tape. He removed his own

CHARLIE'S INSIGHTS:
Evacuations

Once you get someone out of the water, check for injuries. Often a paddler is ready to go after a short break. If not, you need to perform first aid and plan for an evacuation if needed. Manage your own evacuation whenever you can. It may take time for someone to hike out and find cell service to call for help, and response time for first responders in remote rural areas is measured in hours, not minutes—you may end up spending the night. In most cases, it's better to get moving than to wait. Take the injured person out by river, if possible. If they can hike out, send someone with them. The one big exception to the focus on speed is spinal injuries. These require great care. Ask yourself: Is there a possibility of spinal injuries? If so, check for symptoms and immobilize the person before transporting them.

flotation and carefully laid Starr down in his canoe. He paddled her through several miles of Class II–III rapids to the takeout. It was a rough ride, but they made it.

Several hours later, they arrived at Ruby Memorial Hospital in Morgantown, where X-rays showed a broken top vertebra—an injury, she learned, that often results in paralysis or death. As it is, she was in a body cast with a halo brace for three months.

When evacuating an injured person, it's usually fastest to go by river. The trip out took about an hour. It would have taken someone an hour to paddle out and get to a phone or to climb up to find a cell signal and call 911. The Masontown Volunteer Fire Company, which responds to Lower Cheat Canyon accidents, would have needed an hour to assemble a team and 30 minutes to reach the takeout. The canyon is very rough, and bushwhacking to the site would take even more hours. Evacuation with a stretcher would take even longer. There is a good chance that she would not have been out before dark.

I met Jeff Davis afterward and complemented him on a well-executed rescue. He said he was having second thoughts; he had thought that the chance of a serious neck injury was low, but he splinted her as a precaution. If he had known for sure her neck was broken, he said he probably would have sent for help. But based on previous experience, getting outside help and evacuating would take 6 or more hours, and that has its own risks.

BROKEN NECK ON THE OCOEE

MICHAEL J. MCCORMICK, MD, A KAYAKER who was injured in 2010 on the Ocoee River, posted this account to Boatertalk, a now inactive online forum.

*My name is Michael McCormick, and I am the kayaker
who was injured on the Ocoee River on October 3. I'd
like to acknowledge the concerns and thoughts expressed
in this thread about my incident earlier this month, but
more importantly, to publicly acknowledge the heroics of
the paddlers who saved my life.*

*I am a 54-year-old emergency physician from the
Chicago area who was indulging my late-life endeavor
in whitewater kayaking with a long weekend of paddling
through the Southeast. I spent a day at the Whitewater
Center in Charlotte, followed by a day of excellent
guided instruction through the lower half of the Green
Narrows (hiking in to bypass the Big Three, which are
clearly out of my wheelhouse).*

*I hoped to find some paddlers to join at the put-in for
the Middle Ocoee for my final day of whitewater before
heading back home, as I had a great time paddling the
stretch last year and wanted to give it a shot in my new
play boat. Typical of my experiences of meeting people
on the river, I was introduced to a group of guys from
Memphis and Chattanooga; they were extremely gracious,
allowing me to join them and helping me out with the
lines. I had a rather inauspicious start, however, flipping
almost immediately at Grumpy's and a few times after that.
I found the river much bonier and the water more squir-
relly than I remembered, but my roll seemed to be working,
and I figured I'd develop a better rhythm as we proceeded.*

*As I approached Slice-and-Dice, I flipped in the hole
at the beginning. I believe that I was not injured and*

*was tucked and getting ready to roll when suddenly, the
kayak dropped. After hearing and feeling a crunch in my
neck, I was unable to feel anything below my neck, nor
was I able to move my arms or my legs. Possibly I went
over a ledge that I didn't realize was awaiting me after
the hole. Given my medical background and previous
history of cervical surgeries, I knew immediately that
I was quadriplegic from a neck injury, upside down in
rapidly flowing water, and that I was absolutely going
to die this way. I had no hope of possibly surviving this,
since I was certain that even if my newly acquired paddling companions knew I was in trouble, they could not
possibly get to me in time. With my head bouncing along
rocks, I confronted the horror of what I had just done
to my wife and children and everyone who cared about
me, wondering how long it would be before I passed out,
which I eventually did.*

*The next thing I knew, I was looking up through the
surface of the water at the face of someone who was
struggling to flip me over. I was once again conscious,
aware of my situation, and eventually cognizant of the
flurry of activity as my rescuers worked to flip me over,
hold me in calmer water, and stabilize my neck.*

*At that time, I still believed that I was permanently
quadriplegic and that I had ruined my own life and
that of everyone who cared about me, and I suggested
they let me go down the river. I was awake and lucid
enough to appreciate the extraordinary efforts my
rescuers were undertaking to keep me above water,*

maintain cervical immobilization, and orchestrate my evacuation across the river and into an ambulance. My outlook improved considerably, however, when approximately 20–25 minutes into the ordeal, I realized that I was able to move my left foot, then my right foot, and eventually my left hand. I started to regain sensation in my lower extremities.

My extraction from what was still a rather precarious spot on the river required that one of my rescuers bushwhack up the riverbank to flag down a commercial raft. After the guide emptied the raft of clients and positioned his vessel next to mine, I was lifted into the raft, still in my boat and lying along the back deck, with one of my rescuers maintaining cervical immobilization. I was ferried across the river and over another set of rapids, where paramedics had a backboard waiting for me. After being transferred to the backboard with my head taped and unable to move, I was aware only of two rows of faces on either side as they lifted me, hand over hand, up the riverbank and into an ambulance.

After a very short ride, I was transferred to a helicopter for the flight to Erlanger Medical Center in Chattanooga. My evaluation in the trauma center revealed that I had no fractures in my neck and no bleeding in my head. The injury to my spinal cord was caused by a herniated disc between the third and fourth cervical vertebrae, which pinched my cord as my neck was flexed and compressed from the impact underwater. I was later transferred by ambulance to the Rehabilitation Institute of

Chicago, and I have had nearly daily improvement in my strength, coordination, and balance ever since.

I was discharged from the hospital on October 20, able to ambulate using only a cane. My upper extremities remain more affected than my lower extremities, my right side more than my left, and I have a persistent tingling and numbness in my hands and forearms. However, numerous physicians have advised me that my prognosis is excellent and that I should continue to expect return of function for six months to a year from the incident.

But if not for the quick action and heroics of Kevin Sipe, Michael Howard, Neal Carmack, and Bryant Haley, I would have no prognosis at all. Kevin continued to go above and beyond by visiting me in the hospital, going back to shuttle my car from the takeout to Chattanooga and serving as an invaluable resource for my wife, son, and brother when they came to town.

Words are not sufficient to express my gratitude for the actions undertaken and thoughts expressed by members of this community. I hope sharing my perspective and providing some follow-up conveys at least a small portion of that appreciation.

Follow-up one year later:

On the eve of the first anniversary of the event, I thought it appropriate to post an update for so many members of this community who expressed such kind thoughts and wishes for my recovery. I have made a fairly significant recovery. Some issues with balance, fine motor coordination, stamina, and dexterity have prevented my return to work as an emergency physician, but I have had enough improvement to begin teaching in our institution's simulation center and seeing patients in a lower-volume, lower-acuity occupational health setting. I am otherwise active and independent in my activities of daily living and hope for continued improvement.

In June of this year, I had the honor of accepting a Higgins and Langley Memorial Award, recognizing excellence in the field of flood and swiftwater rescue, from Jim Coffey on behalf of my rescuers, who were unable to attend the National Association for Search and Rescue conference in Reno, Nevada. This is the first time the award has gone to recreational paddlers as opposed to an organized rescue team. I will never be able to thank them enough for what they did to give me a second chance after what should have been a fatal injury. I wish everyone in this community safe adventures as they indulge their passion for whitewater recreation.

HEART ATTACK AT LAVA FALLS

THE FOLLOWING IS BASED ON Grayson Schaffer's article "Tim Cahill's Heart-Stopping Adventure" in *Outside,* posted online on December 16, 2014.

On December 7, 2014, outdoor writer Tim Cahill suffered a heart attack after a swim at Lava Falls in Arizona's Grand Canyon. He was eventually evacuated by helicopter to a hospital in Flagstaff, Arizona.

Tim, 71, was part of a group that included 16 people in five rafts and several kayaks. His was the last raft to make the run. To run Lava Falls, the plan was to start on the right side of the river and work left to avoid a bad hole at the bottom. At the top of the rapid, the raft hit a series of curling waves. Tim and his partner were flung overboard. Tim swam hard to the right, inhaling big gulps of river water. At the bottom of the rapid, he grabbed the stern of a kayak and was pulled into an eddy where two rafts were already sitting. As he held on to one of the rafts, he saw another raft barreling toward him, so he ducked underneath the water. Unfortunately, the eddy water was coming back upstream, so when he tried to swim under the boat, he found himself swimming against the eddy current and couldn't get out.

When Tim resurfaced, Rachel Butler and Justin Kleberg pulled him aboard and rowed across the river to a beach. He was exhausted but conscious and coherent. Tim remembers getting out of the raft, stepping onto the riverbank, sitting down, and being handed a beer. At that point, he suddenly and without warning blacked out.

According to Rachel, Tim suddenly stopped breathing and turned "blue, then purple, then gray." Justin, a Wilderness EMT, and Steve Smitts, a registered nurse, began CPR, and Ralph Lee used a satellite phone to call the Park Service. Due to poor reception, he was only able to communicate their location and that they had an unresponsive person in their party.

After about 4 minutes, they checked Tim and found a weak pulse. He soon began breathing on his own and regained consciousness. Soon another satellite came into range over the canyon rim, allowing a longer connection. Upon learning more details, the Park Service quickly sent a helicopter. Forty minutes later, Tim was on his way to Flagstaff

Medical Center, where he received treatment for cardiac arrest and several cracked ribs from the CPR. He recovered completely.

BAD SWIM AND HEART ATTACK AT WOODALL SHOALS

PEOPLE WHO ARE SICK OR INJURED often try to tough it out and refuse help. Denial is not unusual! Here is one of these events, as described on Boatertalk:

Last Saturday, July 16, 2018, I was kayaking on the Chattooga River Whitewater. I had run this river over 400 times. It was a beautiful day. The river was running at a great level: 1.7 feet on the bridge gauge, a fun but intense level. Everything was runnable but very pushy. We got down to Woodall Shoals. Woodall has a Class V hole, and the rest is pretty much Class 3+. John was going far right to the cheat line. I hate the cheat line, so I decided to catch the eddy up top and run the right side of the hole. I'd probably done this line 100 times. As I got ready to go, JP was coming into the eddy. I stopped so we didn't collide. I was at the edge of the pour-over and decided just to slide over the edge. I hit a rock at the bottom of the hole and got bounced left toward the meat of it. I thought I had cleared the hole and was just fine. About that time, the hole grabbed my boat and started pulling me in. I back-paddled with all my might, only to realize I was losing the fight. So I decided I had to go into the hole.

When I was younger, we'd play Woodall at lower water levels. I know how to get out of the hole. But this wasn't a lower water level. This was a mean, nasty hole, with a backwash of probably 10 feet. So I surfed the hole to the left side, where I knew water was coming out. The front of my boat hit the wave that was going downstream, and my front spun to the right. The hole grabbed the back of my boat and pulled me back into it. The back hit the waterfall, and it stood me straight up in the air. I knew this was a good thing. I had to ride this wheelie out of the hole. I got about halfway out, turned over, and immediately rolled up. The current turned me over again. I tried to roll up again, only to get window-shaded. Now I knew I wasn't coming out of this hole in my boat; it was just too sticky.

I decided I needed to wet-exit. As I tried to grab my release handle, I couldn't reach it. Then I realized the hole had pulled me out of my boat. I popped up and thought I was out of the hole. I was facing upstream toward it. My 8-foot-long boat was between me and the pour-over, so I tried to push off of it to escape the hole, only to realize the hole was pulling me back in. I took a deep breath, unsure when I'd get a chance to breathe again. Now sucked into the hole, I was tumbling around, not knowing what was up and what was down. I just knew I'd have to go deep to catch the water going out of the hole if I was going to live.

JP and John saw that I was in trouble. They jumped out of their boat and tried to get a rope to me. According to them, they never saw me come up for air. I realized

*that I couldn't get deep because of the aerated hole
and my life jacket. So I tried to take off my life jacket
so I could get deep, without success. I was trying to get
another breath of air, but my face never cleared the surface of the water. I would just have to keep on fighting.
The hole had pulled me back in and beside the rock that
the water was pouring over. "Good, I finally know where
I am," I thought. I tried to ball up to go deep again, but
all I did was tumble. I was talking to myself and saying,
"I guess this is it." I went limp to take the rest of my
beating. About that time I felt the hole release me. I said
to myself, "You have to fight to survive." I pulled my
head up to get a breath of air.*

*Now in the main current of Woodall Shoals, I
realized that the hole had pulled my neoprene bathing
suit down to my ankles. I was about to lose my suit. So I
reached down and grabbed it with my right hand. Now
it was time to let the beating begin on all the rocks. I
tried to get into an eddy to catch my breath. No luck; I
was going downstream and the river owned me. I was
holding on to my bathing suit, buck naked and going
through the next 400 yards of Class 3+ rapids. I came to
the next deep hole and I knew I was going over, so I took
a deep breath and went deep into another hole. Luckily, I
came right out and kept going downstream. At this point
the river was getting very shallow, so I was hitting lots
of rocks. I knew I had to be very careful about standing
up or risk a foot entrapment. I tried to stand up and*

felt my foot go between two rocks. I faced downstream
to release it. The water was getting shallower. I got my
feet facing downstream. I was bouncing off all the rocks
buck naked. (There's a lot of rough moss on those rocks.)
Finally I came to a stop. The beating was over.

As I tried to catch my breath, my chest was killing
me. I was trying so hard to breathe. I had a lot of pain
in my chest. I was gasping for air with each breath. I
was having a heart attack but didn't know what a heart
attack felt like. JP had now caught up to me. He ran
up the river and crossed it in a tough current to make
sure I was OK. As he held on to me. I was still trying to
catch my breath. I assured him I was OK and told him
to go get my boat. John made it to me and told me they
were going to take care of me. I was struggling to get
my bathing suit on, but the current kept pulling it off of
me. I'd had both of my knees replaced 13 and 11 months
prior, so it was hard for me to stand up. I finally strug-
gled to my feet to put my bathing suit back on. I had to
sit down to catch my breath. As I was sitting there, I just
couldn't seem to stop hurting. I finally asked John to
help me out of the river. He walked in front of me while I
held on to his life jacket. We made it across. Immediately
I had to sit down, I was out of breath. We finally made
it to the bottom of the rapid, where my boat was. At this
point, JP informed me that I didn't have a skirt. I knew
this was where I would get out. My chest was killing me,
but I could breathe.

*I convinced the guys to go to the lake to get the
truck and come back for me. They had about 4 miles
of whitewater and 2 miles of flat water to get to the
truck. We knew that more people would be turning up
since we were the first to get on the river that day. They
paddled off to get some transportation. I was breathing
a little easier now, so I decided to walk up to the Woodall Shoals hole and see if my skirt popped out. I was
having a tough time walking but was determined to find
my spray skirt. As I was walking up, I saw a ranger. I
thought, "I should ask him to take me to the hospital."
He had a radio. He asked me if I was fine. I was embarrassed that I just swam Woodall, so I told him I was. I
was not. I now had a clot blocking flow in my heart but
was still in denial that I was having a heart attack. He
said the rafts would be here in a few minutes and they
could help me if I needed help. I made it to the hole to
look for my skirt. No sign of it. I watched the rafts run
the cheat line on the far-right side of the river and to
the end of the rapid, where they took out and carried
up to the waiting bus in the parking lot. I was thinking
I needed to ask them for help but was still too embarrassed to admit I swam Woodall.*

*I made it back to my boat. I had to lie down in the
sand. Some kayakers paddled up and immediately asked
if I was OK. I told them I swam Woodall. They said that
must have been ugly. I acknowledged that it was. Shane
offered to take my boat up to the parking lot for me. I*

said no, that my friends would be here in a minute to
help me. It had been over an hour since JP and John
left. I knew it would take them about 2 hours to get back
to me. Shane carried his friend's boat up to the parking
lot. They offered to take me to the hospital. I said I'd be
alright. Twenty minutes later, Shane returned. I told him,
"I hate to bother you, but would you carry my boat up
for me?" He was happy to help. I asked him to leave my
paddle so I would have a walking stick.

It was about a half a mile uphill to the parking lot. I
didn't think I could make it, but I had to try. I was taking
baby steps to get up the hill. I got about 100 yards and
had to sit down to catch my breath. When I got back
up and tried to continue, I began coughing, and then I
started to throw up. I knew I was in trouble. I thought,
"When I get home I need to Google 'heart attack' to see
if throwing up is a symptom." Shane made it back to me.
I asked him if I could hold on to him to get up the hill.
More kayakers were coming up the hill. They offered to
take me to the hospital. I assured them I was fine, that
my buddies would be here in a minute. I made it to the
top of the parking lot and lay down by my boat. Everyone was extremely nice to me and offered to help me. I
continued to say I was OK.

Finally, JP and John arrived and put my stuff in the
truck. We got in the truck and I started to cry. I told the
guys I didn't want to be a problem to them but would
they please take me to the hospital. We made a plan for

John to drive my car and JP would follow us to the hospital. We went to the put-in and grabbed my car. I helped the guys tie my boat onto it so we could go.

I hadn't been to the hospital in Clayton in over 20 years. Turns out they had built a new hospital and we didn't know where it was. Finally, after looking for 40 minutes, we found it. I was immediately taken back to a room and hooked up to all types of machines. JP explained to them that I almost drowned. The doctor examined me for a few minutes and then left. The nurses started to give me pain medicine. My chest was killing me. They gave me a pill to put under my tongue to dissolve. On the second pill, I asked the nurse if it was nitroglycerin. She said yes. I said, "So I'm having a heart attack." She went to get the doctor, who confirmed that I was and that they'd be flying me to Gainesville. This would be my first helicopter ride—not exactly the ride I'd had in mind. It took about 30 minutes to get me to Northeast Georgia Medical Center. They took me right to the cath lab [cardiac catheterization laboratory]. There, the cardiologist was able to remove the blockage and insert a stint. I asked him if this was the widow-maker. He said, "I don't like that term but yes, you're lucky to be alive." I am a very lucky man that God was looking after me last Saturday. I didn't listen to him sending help to me that I kept turning down. If you're going to be stupid, you have to be tough. I was pretty stupid. Enjoy every moment. We never know when it will be our last.

PADDLERS HELPING OTHERS

PADDLERS ARE OFTEN IN THE RIGHT PLACE at the right time to rescue members of the non-paddling public. It's especially rewarding to use your whitewater skills to help others.

RESCUE ON THE DELAWARE'S LAMBERTVILLE RAPID

LAMBERTVILLE RAPID ON THE DELAWARE RIVER is a Class II–III rapid on a very large, wide river. There are two wing dams protruding from the side of the river, so the flow is concentrated in the center. It makes for good play boating—and a long swim if you mess up. Mary Koeppe tells this story of a near drowning after an ill-equipped group attempted to run it.

> *On Saturday, August 8, 1987, four Wilmington Trail Club paddlers arrived at the wing dam at Lambertville rapid on the Lower Delaware River. This long Class II+ drop is a popular "practice rapid" for Philadelphia-area boaters. Water levels were moderate.*
>
> *After about 4 hours, we decided to call it a day. I noticed a small group of tiny rafts (the kind you use in*

A kayaker approaches to assist a fellow paddler who has capsized.

a swimming pool) approaching the rapids. No one was wearing PFDs. The rafts dropped into the top hole, and almost everyone was thrown out. I watched the people floating downstream and thought I noticed a head disappear. Then I heard a woman screaming and realized that the person had disappeared near a rowboat that had drifted down and become pinned during the last week. I realized that someone was trapped underwater, upstream of the boat. I sent one person to the Pennsylvania side to call for help. My husband and I jumped in our boats to aid the rescue. Both of us are certified in CPR, and I was fearful that we would have to use it.

By this time, two kayakers had gotten out of their boats and managed to work their way on top of the rowboat. They had to get in the water upstream of the boat and reach down to locate the submerged person. They began pulling but could not locate the person. Finally, they decided they could not worry about broken bones and pulled until they brought up the body. When we reached the boat, the kayakers had resuscitated the boy, who had not been breathing and was quite blue when they brought him up. We set the boy on the deck of my husband's boat and ferried him to a large, flat rock. He said his name was Drew, that he was 8 years old, and that his stomach hurt. He had bruises there and all over his back. We covered him with shirts and spray skirts to keep him warm. We sent for an open canoe and ferried him to shore, sending the kayakers who made the rescue ahead to fill in the paramedics at the waiting ambulance about his condition. Another kayaker transported the mother to shore.

Quick thinking on the part of many people and close teamwork made the difference between life and death here. The river is popular with tubers, and there are numerous near misses each year.

NEAR DROWNING CAUSED BY RAFT ROPE ENTANGLEMENT

LOOSE LINES ARE A SERIOUS HAZARD in whitewater. Several deaths and close calls have been reported because of them. Tie-downs, bowlines, and throw bags should be secured before you get on the water . . . or else!

On June 16, 2010, a 9-year-old boy survived a near drowning after his group's raft hit a boulder and capsized, trapping him underwater for about 10 minutes. The incident occurred at the upper Salmon River between Warm Springs and Peach, Idaho. The boy, Andrew Gardner, was floating the popular section of the Salmon River Monday afternoon, July 12, with his father and six others in a rental raft. The group had successfully paddled through most of the rapids when their raft broached on a midstream rock. The boat flipped and wrapped itself around the boulder. The boy's leg was caught by a rope attached to the raft, which held him underwater for about 10 minutes. After several attempts, his father, Brandon Gardner, was eventually able to cut the rope and set him free.

Andrew was wearing a helmet and life vest. He apparently hit his head against the boulder when the raft overturned. Two kayakers in a separate party, one of whom was a nurse, arrived and administered CPR for about 17 minutes. First responders were nearby and helped administer CPR. Andrew started breathing a few minutes later, and the color started returning to his face. Oxygen was administered, and he was flown by helicopter to St. Alphonsus Hospital in Boise. Doctors kept Andrew cold and induced a coma to help him recover, warming him up slowly to prevent brain damage. He later regained consciousness at the hospital and was expected to recover fully.

FLOATING CHILD ON THE SOUTH FORK OF THE AMERICAN RIVER

THE FOLLOWING IS BASED ON AN ARTICLE by Tom Stienstra that was published in the *San Francisco Chronicle* on October 3, 2010.

The South American River is a popular Class III run located in the Sierra foothills near Coloma, California. On June 16, 2010, a guided rafting trip had stopped below a rapid called First Thread for lunch when one of the guides, Alex Wolfgram, heard several guests cry out. He looked toward the river and saw a little red helmet floating down the far side.

Alex and two other guides, Nathan Fried and Jason Wasserman, jumped into a raft and gave chase. The river, running at 6,000 cubic feet per second, carried them swiftly through the next series of rapids. As they witnessed the child roll over the rocks, they thought for sure he was dead.

Finally, they caught up to him. Alex pulled him out of the water and onto his lap. The young boy's skin was totally white. Alex checked for breathing and then, when the victim started convulsing, rolled him over, held him upside down, and tried to clear his airway and get the water out of his lungs and stomach.

The boy was alive but unconscious. Nathan and Jason worked the raft into an eddy and to shore. They got the boy ashore, laid him on a rock, and removed his life jacket, shirt, and helmet. Nathan, trained as a nurse, found a weak pulse. Three kayakers suddenly appeared on the river, and the guides flagged them down. One of the kayakers rushed downstream to find help. He ran to a house, where the residents called 911. The remaining group ferried the boy by raft to a spot downriver where a helicopter could land.

The boy was going in and out of consciousness. In 15 minutes, the helicopter arrived and flew him to UC Davis Medical Center. As Alex hiked back to his group, he ran into a woman who appeared to be in shock, heading downstream in another raft. It was the boy's

CHARLIE'S INSIGHTS:
What to Do If You Witness an Accident

Whitewater rescues are not leader-driven; rather, they are initiated by the paddlers closest to the victim. The "leader" may be some distance downstream when the accident happens, and someone close by can intervene much more quickly. When someone is in trouble, you'll want to help without getting into trouble yourself. If you're not comfortable making a rescue, get as close as you can to mark the spot, and start blowing your whistle to attract the attention of more experienced people in your group and any passing boaters. You'll also be in position to help out if needed.

While commercial rafting trips have excellent safety records, attempting the same trips without training can risk lives.

mother. He told her that the little boy was alive. His name, he learned, was Joseph.

Afterward, Alex felt overwhelmed by what had happened and needed to decompress, so he went to the Chili Bar rapid, a known surf hole, to surf the river waves. There, a man arrived in a raft and identified himself as the person who had led the ill-fated trip with Joseph. He told Alex the rest of the story: Four adults and 9-year-old Joseph, none trained in whitewater rafting, had rented a raft and attempted an unguided trip. After flipping at a rapid called Maya, they all feared for their lives. One of the adults was holding Joseph, but the strength of the current pulled the boy out of their grasp. He was carried downstream for 2.5 miles. One takeaway from this rescue is that while commercial rafting trips have excellent safety records, attempting the same trips without training can risk lives.

After being airlifted out by helicopter, Joseph was stabilized and treated. He was later released and made a full recovery. Three months after the incident, the American Red Cross honored the three guides as Hometown Heroes.

NIGHTTIME RESCUE OF BOYS STUCK IN TREE IN KENTUCKY

THIS INCIDENT WAS POSTED BY STEVE RUTH ON BOATERTALK.

My phone rang at 10 p.m. tonight on May 10, 2010. It was the Elkhorn City [EC] fire chief. "Steve, there's a couple of boys hanging on a tree in the middle of the river downstream of Ratliff's Hole (the takeout for the Russell Fork River near Elkhorn City, Kentucky). We need a kayaker to get to them." I live in Elkhorn City

and am involved with a number of city projects. It's a
small place, and the EC rescue folks know me fairly
well. One of them saw the situation and thought the
only way to get to them was by kayak, so they called me,
probably as a last resort!

Now if you've run that nice little Rat Hole-to-EC
section, you're probably thinking, "Hanging on a tree in
the middle of the river? That doesn't sound right." And
you would be right . . . unless you've seen that section at
6,000 cfs, which is about what it was running this evening. Well, what can a guy do? The boat was still loaded
from the day's Grassy run, so I pulled on my dry suit,
grabbed my PFD and spray skirt, and ventured up the
road to find about seven fire trucks and rescue vehicles
blocking the road at Pool Point. The fire chief flagged
me down and said the boys were just downstream of the
train bridge; I could head over the hill there. Well, that
includes a 50-foot cliff to get to the river, so I said I'd
float down from Rat Hole.

There were six or seven more rescue vehicles down
there, with at least two aluminum-type overgrown motorized johnboats ready to launch. I got the guys' attention
and suggested maybe taking those boats downstream
beyond the bridge was a bad idea. But, if they stayed on
extreme river right, maybe they wouldn't die . . . if they
got to the right spot on river right, where they could tie
up. They were gung ho for that and even more gung ho
to tie a rope to my boat. I told them no thanks; I'd just

*follow them downstream to a place where we could get a
visual and assess the situation.*

*It all went beautifully except one small detail. The
boys weren't in a tree just downstream of the bridge,
which we were led to believe. They were actually in a
tree downstream of Meat Grinder, which is about an
eighth of a mile downstream of the train bridge. I wasn't
going to paddle down there in the dark at 6,000 cfs, and
when the johnboat rescue team heard that, they figured
they wouldn't either. We hiked downstream to find five or
six rescuers on the side of the river, shining spotlights
on the poor kids in the tree. One rescuer had managed,
hanging on to trees in the moving water, to get a rope
(tied off, mind you) to within 30 feet of the boys.*

*I was the only person wearing any type of dry (or
wet) gear. So here's me and six guys who were supposed
to know what to do standing there looking at the boys in
the tree. By this time, they'd been there over 2 hours and
were just about naked (the river had stripped them to their
underwear), miserable, and near shock. Well, the idea of
a kayak getting to them wasn't necessarily a bad idea, but
the water was really moving by them, and there were trees
all around. There really wasn't any way to safely paddle
to them and do anything at all. So I asked the guy who'd
gotten the rope sort of close how deep it was there. He
said it was chest-deep where the rope was tied off.*

*I had them attach a rope to my PFD, and I ventured
into the flow just to get a feel for what we were dealing
with. My mind is boggled that the guy got the rope to the*

spot he did. The river was pushing me hard, and it was all I could do to keep my footing. I got to the end of the rope, but it was too deep and swift to be able to throw anything to where the boys were.

I retreated to the bank, and we talked about it. The johnboat guys wanted to try to get their boat to that place and probably would have tried it if I hadn't been there. It took 5 or 10 minutes of talking to get them to give up on that idea. Thankfully, the county emergency management director had contacted the Army Corps as soon as the call came in to turn off the dam release. After half an hour or more of us standing and looking at the boys in the tree, the river started dropping. Not a lot, but about 8 inches. After three attempts, enough time for the river to drop another 6–8 inches, I was able to take a harness (attached to a rope) to the base of the tree the boys were in. I managed this by basically walking as far as I could, then lunging from tree to tree, hanging on to anything I could grab. I'd guess it took 10 minutes to cross about 50 feet of chest-deep, flowing water on the last attempt.

The boys were in pretty pitiful shape at this point. I handed the harness to the boy nearest the flow, explained how to slip it over his head and under his arms, and then talked him out of the tree. The bank crew knew to pull the harness rope when I gave a blast on my whistle. All good. So then it's me and the second boy. There wasn't any way for the guys to get the harness back, so I had to talk the kid out of the tree and convince him that I was going to hang on to him while they pulled us both in. I had him lie back on me and locked my arms under his armpits and across his chest. When the crew saw us in position, they pulled us in.

Now that I'm sitting here, I'm pretty astonished that nobody died. There was just no way to get to them. They were in a terrible spot, with too many trees around to throw ropes to them. If the river hadn't dropped—probably down to 4,000 cfs—they'd still be in that damned tree, unless they'd given out. I'm not sure how much longer they could have hung on. When I say tree, I should say very large bush, maybe 4 inches across at the base—your typical scrubby baby syca-more. The scary part is how clueless everyone involved, including me, was. The rescuers just didn't fathom the force of the flow, the coldness of the water (until they tried wading in), or the danger of ropes tied to boats, trees, etc. While I haven't had a swiftwater rescue course, I am very glad for the knowledge I'd absorbed over the years from people way smarter than me.

I'd love to grab some experts and show them the situation to see if there wasn't something we just didn't think of that would have made things easier. The first obvious thing is that everyone should have had the proper dry gear to be able to spend time in 50ish-degree water. At least they all had PFDs.

Rescue missions beat the hell out of recovery mis-sions. Be safe out there. The various rescue squads on the scene were very determined to resolve the situation. I don't mean to suggest it was a total Three Stooges scene.

These folks are determined to rescue people in trouble, and many are willing to put themselves in harm's way to succeed. It's damn frustrating when you can look right at people in trouble but can't find a solution.

Later I learned that the two boys, between the ages of 18 and 21, had found an old bass boat in town and had been floating around in it on Sunday. They didn't realize that the river was 10 or so times higher than they'd been floating on in town a couple of days before. No drugs or alcohol were involved, just youthful exuberance and daring. The quote of the night was from one of the kids, who, clinging to the tree, looked at me and said, "Don't you live next door to my mom? This is the stupidest thing I ever did!"

I'm determined at this point to get myself certified (as opposed to certifiable, which I've pretty much succeeded at) and to help the locals get the proper gear and training for such situations. It's easy, when you're very familiar with a particular environment, to toss off on people who have never experienced that environment. Those guys followed the suggestions and instructions I gave and, with a little training, would know exactly what to do and what not to do the next time.

TEEN CAUGHT IN STORM DEBRIS ON SWOLLEN PATAPSCO

THE FOLLOWING IS BASED ON AN ARTICLE by Phil Grout, published in *The Baltimore Sun* on the day the incident happened, September 7, 2011.

Three teens—David, Tyler, and Abraham—had decided to float down the Patapsco River near Ellicott City, Maryland. The river was running very high after 5–6 inches of rain. At the confluence of the Patapsco and Aspen Run, the boys' inner tubes flipped in turbulent water. All three swimmers were carried toward the south bridge, just downstream. Tyler and Abraham were swept under the bridge, but David got stuck in debris that had gathered around a pylon. He gasped, "I can't breathe," before the current pulled him partially under the surface.

Tyler and Abraham were able to swim back to their friend. Tyler grabbed hold of David and lifted his head out of the water. At about the same time, Dale Griffiths, an expert kayaker, arrived. He paddled over to the boys, and the three were able to pull 16-year-old David out. They laid his body on the kayak so he could catch his breath. Two onlookers, Ronald Markline and Craig Dell, leaned over the bridge siding and hoisted David to safety.

LONG-DISTANCE RESCUE OF THREE ON GEORGIA'S ALCOVY RIVER

MANY CALLS FOR HELP are made by people stranded midstream or on the wrong side of a river. Here's a story about how a group of experienced paddlers managed a dangerous situation. The incident was first reported by Gabriel Khouli in *The Covington News,* Covington, Georgia, July 7, 2013.

On that date, kayakers Josh Lowry, Justin Hodges, Moana Hassan, and Lee Court rescued three unidentified tubers who were stranded in Factory Shoals, a Class III rapid on Georgia's Alcovy River, about 10 miles south of Covington. The kayakers had just finished their first run when a man speeding down the road in a pickup truck stopped and said that his daughter, son-in-law, and a friend were stuck in the middle of the river. The kayakers rushed back to help.

When they arrived, they saw a woman sitting on a midstream rock and two men standing on underwater rocks, struggling to keep from being washed away. This was about 250–300 yards upstream of where the river dumps into Jackson Lake. They were in bathing suits, barefoot, with no life vests. One of the men looked fairly confident, but the other was clearly very frightened. They were struggling to stay put and not get swept over the rapid. While they talked to the woman, Josh got his throw bag and began tossing it, trying to reach the men. After several attempts he finally hit the first man with his rope. The man began wrapping the rope around his arm, but Josh yelled to him to hold on with his just his hands. (Never tie a rope to yourself—if the rope gets away from the rescuer, it could get caught on something, and then you're trapped.) He told the man to face upstream, keep his legs high, kick hard, and swim toward him whiled he pulled the rope.

Once the man was ready, Josh gave him the OK sign and moved upstream so he could pull him ashore quickly. The man crossed the current and grabbed some overhanging limbs. Other people helped pull him ashore. The second man, who seemed more confident, was able to wade close enough to allow Josh to toss the rope to him on the first try.

The third rescue was more challenging. The woman was frozen with fear and was far enough away that even two ropes tied together wouldn't reach her. Luckily Justin showed up to help. Using a tree to tie off one rope, he and Josh tied three ropes together so they reached halfway across the river. The original plan was for the woman to pull herself along the rope until she reached Justin; she made it out partway, but as the water got deeper and the current stronger, she stopped, too afraid to move.

Other people had arrived, including a police officer. Josh attached himself to the rope with a carabiner and handed it off to the men behind him, cautioning them not to let go or he could drown. He began traversing his way across the river to meet the woman.

She wrapped her right arm around Josh's shoulders, and he put his left arm around her waist, with each of them keeping one hand on the rope. Using his right hand, Josh pulled them both about 30–60 feet, with the river pounding on them and pushing his head underwater. He kept on for what, he says, seemed like a mile, until finally reaching the shore for a successful rescue.

TUBER STUCK IN SUCK HOLE ON ARKANSAS'S OUACHITA RIVER

ON OCTOBER 19, 2016, A TUBER GOT SEPARATED from her party and floated into a bad hydraulic in the middle of the Ouachita River at Rockport Ledge. The hydraulic, known to locals as the Suck Hole, is shallow and very sticky. Paddlers typically avoid playing here. The tuber was not wearing a life jacket when she dropped into the hole and started being recirculated.

Fortunately, a group of experienced whitewater paddlers were surfing about 30 yards away. They immediately recognized the danger and ferried over. Two experienced boaters, a kayaker and open-boater, attempted to surf across the hydraulic and grab the victim, who was recirculated more than 10 times. They had great difficulty predicting when she would surface. Because the hole is in the middle of the river, it was difficult to reach with a rope. Other paddlers in the area prepared to help once the victim left the hydraulic.

The woman lost consciousness and became limp. The kayaker paddled to the nearest eddy and called for help to perform a live-bait rescue. The paddler in the open boat managed to time the victim's recirculation properly and pushed her clear of the hydraulic. She was beginning to turn blue. The paddlers got her to shore quickly, giving rescue breaths as they paddled. Onshore, she initially had no pulse, but after 20 seconds of CPR, she slowly came to.

This rescue was a "right time, right place" rescue. Had she not been tubing on a busy weekend for Rockport Ledge, she could have easily perished. Nearly every paddler on the water helped with the recovery. Paddlers should always keep an eye on Suck Hole and have a rope handy.

CHAIN SAW REQUIRED FOR A RESCUE ON ALASKA'S EAGLE RIVER

THE INCIDENT SUMMARIZED BELOW was reported by Michelle Theriault Boot in the *Anchorage Daily News* on September 16, 2012.

An unidentified kayaker pinned in Alaska's Eagle River was pulled from the high water on Sunday, September 16, 2012. His boat was pinned under a partially submerged log just across from the Eagle River Campground. Someone onshore saw him struggling and called for help, and an off-duty Anchorage police officer stayed with the man, offering encouragement until rescuers arrived.

An Anchorage Fire Department jet boat got to him quickly. The man could barely hold his head above water and told rescuers that he was getting really tired. The boaters ended up having to use a chain saw to cut the log into pieces. The log was under so much pressure from the current that it had to be kicked out of the way. Captain Bayless grabbed the man by his life jacket and pulled him to safety. He was hypothermic but began to show improvement on the way to the hospital.

DARING RESCUE ON ALASKA'S SIXMILE RIVER

JAMES BENNETT, A FREELANCE WRITER who was present for this incident, first reported it in the *Anchorage Daily News* on August 15, 2017.

Sixmile River is one of the Alaska's most popular Class IV runs. August 12, 2017, was race day of the Six-Mile Creek Whitewater and Bluegrass Festival. Daniel Hartung, 64, was paddling a recreational kayak. He wasn't racing but had decided to run the river on a day when lots of other people were around. He was wearing a PFD, a bike helmet, and chest waders. In the third rapid of the first canyon, he broached on a rock, flipped, and swam. He washed into a log about 10 feet from shore and was pinned against it. "I was draped over the log like a C," Daniel said later.

A number of experienced kayakers were nearby. James alerted them that a swimmer was pinned, and kayaker Obadiah Jenkins grabbed a throw rope. He downclimbed to where Daniel was pinned and lowered him a rope. This helped Daniel keep his torso vertical, with his head in an air pocket formed by the falling water.

A group of 30-plus racers were conducting a safety briefing 200 yards upstream when they heard calls for help. They moved quickly and found Daniel in desperate trouble. He had been in the river more than 5 minutes, and the cold water was taking a toll. "The more I struggled, the more my head went lower," he said. "At first I could keep my head up and breathe, but then it became really difficult to catch a breath."

Suddenly Daniel lost his hold of the rope and was pushed underwater. Obadiah reacted, moving upstream, grabbing a second rope, and lowering himself down toward the log. He grabbed hold of Daniel, trying to free his leg. Suddenly they were both shoved underwater before washing free several seconds later. A log, probably the one that pinned Daniel, floated out behind them.

Daniel was unconscious. A crew of kayakers got him ashore and began CPR. After two rounds of chest compressions, he regained consciousness and started breathing on his own. One of the rescuers had a satellite phone and used it to call for help. Using a deflated packraft as a gurney, they carried him out of the canyon to the road. An ambulance took him to a nearby hospital, where he was treated and released.

AWARD-WINNING RESCUE ABOVE OHIOPYLE FALLS

THE TWO RESCUERS IN THIS INCIDENT RECEIVED the Carnegie Hero Award for their actions. The following is a condensed version of Scott Patton's nomination letter.

> *On June 26, 2017, two kayakers, Patrick McCarty and Eric Martin, put their lives at risk to rescue two women whose raft capsized in turbulent whitewater on the Youghiogheny River at Ohiopyle, Pennsylvania. The incident and rescue occurred during a period of unusually high water generated by several days of heavy rainfall. The*

rescue occurred just 200 yards above the approximately 20-foot-high Ohiopyle Falls. The falls are dangerous at "normal" river levels, and being washed over them during periods of high water is nearly always fatal.

On that Monday, Raecyne Bechtold, 45, and Arnetta Johnson, 55, traveled to Ohiopyle State Park to go white-water rafting. They rented a raft, paddles, and life jackets from one of the river outfitters in Ohiopyle and received instructions on the basic procedures and safety rules.

The Youghiogheny was unusually high that day due to recent rainstorms. On a typical summer day, the water-level gauge reading at Ohiopyle is generally between 1.5 and 2 feet. On this day, however, it was close to 6 feet.

Johnson and Bechtold paddled the 8-mile section of the Middle Yough. The day of rafting was without incident until the last rapid before the designated take-out. The roller-coaster action of the waves in that rapid caused the raft to capsize, tossing both paddlers into the swift-moving river. The upside-down raft and the two women were quickly carried downstream by the current. Fortunately, they were able to grab the raft's perimeter line, and Bechtold managed to climb up onto the raft. Johnson remained in the water throughout the ordeal. From on top of the raft, Bechtold was able to grasp the strap of Johnson's life jacket and keep her from being swept away from the raft.

The current carried the two women past the take-out. About 100 yards farther downstream, in clear view of many tourists, they floated under the PA 381 bridge and toward the waterfall, which was about 300 yards farther downstream. The women were frightened by their predicament but didn't realize how incredibly dangerous their situation had become. They had no idea that they were approaching a waterfall.

Multiple 911 calls were made to the Fayette County Emergency Dispatch, which immediately notified Ohio-pyle State Park and the Ohiopyle-Stewart Volunteer Fire Department. The state park immediately dispatched an emergency response vehicle with two rangers to the scene, and the fire department sounded its alarm siren to beckon any available volunteers to assist.

A bike/pedestrian bridge, supported by several midstream piers, crosses the river just 200 feet down-stream of the highway bridge. Fortunately, the raft washed up against one of those piers and was held there by the push of the current. The raft was further kept in place by Bechtold and Johnson, who had grasped the narrow upstream edge of the pier and held on. One of the witnesses was Dee Reddick, an experienced white-water boater. She rushed out onto the pedestrian bridge to a point where she was directly above the women. Reddick shouted lifesaving instructions to them and used her words to strengthen and encourage them: "Hold on! Do not let go of that raft! Do not let go of the pier! You are doing great! Stay strong! Help is on the way! Do not let go! Help will be here soon!" She repeated these and similar instructions and words of encouragement over and over.

Other onlookers also began to shout directions to the victims; Reddick knew that some of their well-intentioned directives were incorrect and downright contrary to the resolution of the situation, so she confidently took charge, shouting, "Folks! We need just one voice here! Please! I will handle this!" Because Johnson, who was still in the 60°F water, would be tiring and would also be experiencing the effects of cold water, Reddick recognized that time was of the essence, but she didn't allow her anxiousness to show through in her words to the two women. She didn't want them to panic. She just kept up a steady stream of reassurance that help would arrive soon.

Patrick McCarty of Laurel Highlands River Tours, one of the whitewater rafting outfitters in Ohiopyle, has been a whitewater guide since he was 16 and is an emergency response instructor/trainer. His office happens to be within 300 yards of the emergency scene. Fortunately, he was there at the time and heard the siren, as did other employees. McCarty heard one of them exclaim, "Something is going on above the falls!" McCarty grabbed his helmet and life jacket and ran toward the river to see if he could help.

Within a minute or two, he was at the river shore and saw the raft pinned on the bridge pier with Bechtold on top of it. He immediately recognized that, considering the high water level and the short distance downstream to the falls, the situation was life-threatening;

only moments stood between a rescue and an impending drowning. Looking upstream to the highway bridge, he could see the park's emergency vehicle and two rangers. He also could see Eric Martin on the bridge, unloading a kayak from the roof of a stopped car. In Martin he saw a partner in the rescue and immediately ran the 100 feet up to the bridge to team up with him.

Martin is the owner of Wilderness Voyageurs, another whitewater rafting outfitter in Ohiopyle. Like McCarty, he is an expert kayaker and has worked this river as a guide and operations manager his entire adult life. His company's headquarters is near the river, and Martin's office has a small balcony with a direct line of sight to the highway bridge. Upon hearing the siren, he went out onto the deck and shouted to the rangers, "Hey! Do you need help?" The rangers shouted back, "Yes!" and made vigorous "come on" arm motions.

Like McCarty, Martin also knew that an on-river situation, downstream of the highway bridge at this high water level, could very well be life-threatening. He grabbed his helmet and life jacket and ran toward the scene, shouting along the way to his employees to grab kayaks and paddles and to follow him as quickly as they could. In about a minute, he was on the highway bridge and could see the pinned raft with Bechtold on top, but he couldn't see Johnson clinging to the far side of it. How long had the raft been there? How much longer could it stay there before breaking free and continuing to float toward the falls? Martin concluded, as McCarty had, that there wasn't time to investigate those answers. If the raft broke free of the pier, which could happen at any moment, there would be no possibility of a rescue by kayak and an infinitesimally small chance of a shoreline rope-throw rescue. He needed to initiate this rescue now. When he saw McCarty running his way, he knew that there would be two highly competent whitewater rescuers available.

The rescue:

Martin's employees were running toward the bridge with a kayak and related gear and would be there in moments. Coincidentally, a random car with a kayak on its roof happened to be crossing the bridge at that moment. Martin didn't hesitate; he held up his hands in a "stop" signal. The car stopped. Martin shouted, "This is an emergency—I need your boat!" and started to undo the straps holding the boat down. The driver was Dylan Isaacs—a competent kayaker himself. Isaacs recognized Martin and immediately pitched in to help. Just as Martin took the kayak and related gear and rushed for the water, McCarty arrived on the bridge and Martin's employees arrived with a second kayak and paddle. McCarty was then right behind Martin, rushing to the river with the second kayak. They ran to the water's edge. They did not take the extra time to attach the spray skirts, though they knew that if either of them capsized without one, they would very likely, in a flooded kayak, be swept downriver and over the falls themselves. They entered the kayaks with their street clothes on, paddled into the swift current, and made their way to the pinned raft—a distance of about 150 feet. The sprint across the water took only seconds. Martin arrived first, and it was only then that he realized there were two victims.

Martin approached the woman who was in the water (Johnson) and told her to grab the rope loop that was on the stern of his kayak and to hold on for all her worth. Instead, in her panic, she grabbed the cockpit rim of the kayak and almost tipped it over. Also in her panic, she tried to climb up onto the deck of the kayak. Martin firmly instructed her not to try to climb but to just hold on and he would tow her to safety. She understood and complied. With Johnson clinging to his kayak, Martin paddled toward the right-hand shore, where the two rangers and several river guides were rushing to assist. But the kayak was being pushed by the current downstream of the shoreline helpers. They threw a rope line out in an effort to assist, but it fell short. Martin and Johnson were being carried downstream toward the falls.

Martin, however, spotted a flat rock ledge that protruded about 6 inches above the water, and he was able to pull his kayak and Johnson into an eddy on the downstream side of it. That protruding ledge turned out to be a lifesaver. The water's force was split around the ledge, and Martin was able to hold his position there in the calm water of the eddy. He prodded with his paddle and found that the water was only about 3 feet deep. He told Johnson to get to her feet and to steady herself on the back side of the rock ledge while he exited the kayak.

Once out of the kayak, he slid it up onto the exposed ledge and then stood in the water next to Johnson, put his arm around her waist, and steadied her. He and Johnson were now somewhat secure but were still about 40 feet from the shore, and the current between the eddy and the shore was swift. He decided it was best to wait in that eddy for further help. While waiting, the victim was able to catch her breath and gather herself while Martin reassured her.

McCarty was right behind Martin in arriving at the pinned raft. When Johnson let go of her grip on the bridge pier and grabbed onto Martin's kayak, the raft, with Bechtold still on top, floated free from the pier and started downstream toward the falls. McCarty used his kayak like a tugboat to push against the raft. This was a tricky maneuver: he had to push upriver from the downstream side of the raft because if he allowed it to get downstream of him, it would pick up speed and be unstoppable. McCarty paddled with all his strength to push the raft and its occupant against the current, at an angle toward the right-hand side of the river. Slowly but surely, he got the raft in close to the riverbank, where another rescuer was able to grab its safety line and pull it and Bechtold to safety.

But Martin and Johnson were still out in the eddy, about 40 feet from shore. For the moment, they were safe in their position, but with Johnson holding on to the side of his kayak, Martin would not be able to safely paddle across the current to get to the shore. Seeing that, McCarty headed back out onto the river. McCarty paddled out into the current and then maneuvered into the eddy, joining Martin and Johnson. Like Martin had before him, he got out of his kayak and parked it up on the rock ledge. Behind that ledge to the right-hand shore, the current was threateningly swift, but the water was only about 30 inches deep. Together McCarty and Martin could stand, though somewhat unsteadily, on the solid-rock bottom of the river. With one on each side of the victim, they planned to assist Johnson in the unsteady walk/shuffle across that last 40 feet to the shore.

One of the shoreline rescuers, river guide CJ Revtai, threw a rope to McCarty, who was wearing a rescue life jacket with a quick-release attachment ring. McCarty secured the rope to the ring and looped it behind himself and Martin, who were facing upstream with Johnson between them. With their arms around Johnson's waist, they cautiously waded/shuffled out of the eddy and into the current. With CJ anchoring the rope from upstream on the shore, it provided the critical stability that supported the final walk across that last swiftwater channel. Moments later, Johnson was safely onshore.

Once the victims were again together and safe, they were driven to a nearby parking lot, where an ambulance and EMT soon arrived. Both women recovered completely and were able to drive themselves home within an hour.

This rescue simply would not have happened—and tragedy most likely would have resulted—were it not for McCarty and Martin. Both of these rescuers were

CHARLIE'S INSIGHTS:
The Stress Factor

Understand the effects of stress and pressure on you when you're responding to an emergency. Stress and fear release adrenaline, and this can put the primitive brain in charge, causing you to act out of instinct rather than logic. That's why athletes choke and people panic. Some people freeze up under pressure, but knowledge and training will help you react with confidence. Stress also tends to narrow a rescuer's "sphere of awareness." When responding to an emergency, consciously widen your sphere of awareness by looking around—take in your surroundings and the people nearby. You may spot something that's helpful or avoid a dangerous problem. Adrenaline often causes rescuers to respond too quickly, at speeds beyond their skill. Consciously slow down; chances are you'll still be moving faster than usual. Remember that river shorelines are almost always rugged and uneven, so move deliberately and watch your feet when you're on the move to avoid a jarring fall.

available by coincidence but became directly involved by choice when they recognized the gravity of the situation. They both reacted immediately to the pressing need of this rescue without a moment of hesitation. They took calculated risks to accomplish this rescue, but they had confidence in their knowledge of the river and in their skills, and they completed without further incident this tricky and dangerous rescue in which time was so crucial.

MIDNIGHT MIRACLE AT KANAWHA FALLS

THIS IS QUITE SIMPLY THE MOST AMAZING RESCUE STORY I've encountered in 50 years of paddling! On the afternoon of September 20, 2020, a kayaker, paddling solo, missed the High Flow line on Kanawha [pronounced ka-naw] Falls, just below the mouth of West Virginia's Gauley River, and ended up trapped behind the curtain of the falls. His boat flushed out and was discovered floating in the pool below the falls. Thanks to social media and a strong sense of community, a group rallied late in the evening to make a truly remarkable rescue. Felicia Conyer was the among the first to sound the alarm upon spotting the victim's empty kayak. She posted this account on Facebook.

Yesterday, on our way back from Fayetteville, Victor and I stopped at Kanawha Falls to fish—it was approximately 6:25 p.m. As soon as we got there, we saw a red kayak floating in the water upside down. I called 911 a few minutes later and was told that they had already received a call, and that West Virginia Division of Natural Resources (DNR) personnel were on their way.

The kayak was circling in the water but staying in the general area.

Thinking that perhaps the kayak had just gotten away from someone, I posted two pics on the Kayak WV Facebook group with a message that basically said, "If you're looking for this kayak, it's here." Almost an hour went by, and we were getting ready to leave. Being the investigative-type person that I am, I noticed a van in the parking lot (there were only a couple of vehicles left) that belonged to a kayaker—it had a kayak license plate from Tennessee. As I started taking pictures of the van, I noticed a note on his window [from someone who had shot video and wanted to send it to him.]

I called the number on the note, and Brandon Richmond answered. I asked him if the video he captured was of a kayaker in a red kayak. He said yes. I explained the situation, and he was in disbelief, stating that the kayaker had been by himself and that he had last seen him just before 6:30 p.m. headed for the horseshoe area. I hung up and called 911 again, stating that I was now pretty sure there was someone in the water who needed help. The dispatcher told me that someone had been dispatched earlier and, seeing a kayak tied to a tree, had assumed everyone was OK. I told her that the kayak was still in the water floating in the same area and that I would stay there until help arrived so I could point it out.

A Fayette County officer arrived at about the same time a fishing boat was coming to shore. Vic ran down to the fisherman, who we later learned was Robbie

Thaxton, and asked him if he could help retrieve the
boat. Afraid that the kayaker was still in the kayak, Vic
went with him to help. They came back a short time later
with the empty boat. I took a picture of it and sent it to
Brandon, who confirmed that it was the same kayak. He
sent me a picture from the video he had taken. We were
sick, fearing that the kayaker was not OK!

Brandon told me exactly where he had last seen him.
He later sent me a picture of the falls and, after talking
to his boss, who was also an experienced kayaker, sent
me a picture of where the kayaker could possibly be
trapped. I texted that picture to the officer on the scene.

I also received a private message from a girl from
Tennessee, who stated she believed she knew this kay-
aker and asked me to describe the van. Sure enough, it
was her friend Sam.

Another kayaker, Stephen Wright, also described the rescue
on Facebook:

Early evening, I started seeing posts online about a boat
seen floating below Kanawha Falls. For those who don't
know the area, this is just downstream of the confluence
of the New and Gauley Rivers near Gauley Bridge, West
Virginia. A boat below Kanawha could have come from
a swimmer on either of these rivers or from someone
running the falls. It wasn't until 9:30 or 10 p.m. that I
got the message from Corey Lilly that there was also
an unattended boater's van with Tennessee plates in the

parking lot. He was trying to identify the now seemingly missing paddler. The rescue squad was there, as were a few other local boaters. Corey, Paul Griffin, and I loaded up in Paul's truck and drove down to help out.

We knew of a spot that would be hard to access or see for non-kayaking rescue personnel but would be the most likely spot for an accident on the falls: the river-right undercut wall and "cave" next to the landing of the High Flow (main drop) line at Kanawha. Kanawha Falls is a high-volume waterfall around 15 feet tall. The river-right half of the outflow pushes into the undercut right wall. There is a cave or crack in the river-right upstream corner, where there is usually a calmer spot of approximately 20 square feet. Many people who swim out of the wall wash back upstream into that cave, where they can be rescued by a raft or other kayakers. This is the spot where we hoped to find the missing kayaker, but in all honesty, we were not hopeful that a person who had been missing for several hours, likely in the water, would be able to be rescued.

After coordinating phone contacts with two other friends/kayakers onshore, we and another local boater paddled out to the island next to the falls to begin looking. I was last to the island and heard the other guys yelling, "He's here! He's alive!" At the flows of last night (close to 9,000 cfs), there was water pouring over the entire lip all the way into the cave/crack. This completely blocked it from our line of sight, but we could hear Sam yelling for help over the roar of the falls. We

texted our contacts onshore to let them know he was
alive and that we could use more help.

　We desperately wanted to communicate with Sam
to assess his situation and assure him that we would get
him out. We were sure he was freaking out. With just
four of us out there, we first tried to establish contact
with Sam via tethered wading out to a high point on the
lip of the falls, where we hoped to be able to look down
and see him and talk with him. After a few attempts,
this proved to be impossible. We also knew that at these
flows, it would be impossible to get a raft or motorized
rescue inflatable to where he was—there was just WAY
too much current flowing in the undercut wall.

　Our best bet to communicate was determined to be
either a kayaker with a phone who could seal-launch the
calmest part of the falls into a very small "calmer" eddy
next to the cave, or a kayaker running the smallest part
of the falls, which landed next to it. It was dark, and we
only had two headlamps. Corey volunteered to run the
drop, as he had run this line before at these flows. He
would take his headlamp and phone, leaving me onshore
with the other headlamp and phone to manage things
from above. His goal was to make contact with Sam
without creating another victim. He successfully ran
the falls into the eddy, but due to the mist; wind; dark,
swirly, and powerful currents; and his contact lenses
creating issues, he was prevented from seeing Sam or
communicating with him. He quickly peeled back out
and paddled around the undercut wall to regroup.

At this point, we had been there for about an hour, and there were many more rescue vehicles and others onshore. Sam was still yelling and alive, but we had to assume that his situation was unstable due to hypothermia and the environment. The three options for evacuation would be a 15- to 20-foot vertical extraction up the crack and onto the island; sending down a kayak for him to paddle himself out (with the help of others); or waiting for the water to drop from the Gauley River upstream until a raft rescue would be possible. We determined that the best option would be to lower a rope through the curtain of the falls into the crack and pull him vertically out, but we needed more than four of us to do it. Corey and I paddled back to shore to gather more volunteers, leaving Paul and the local boater to maintain contact with Sam (which was limited to garbled yelling due to the roar of the river).

On arrival, we found nearly 30 vehicles there with a ton of rescue personnel and a few motorized inflatables. Matt Jackson (our contact onshore) had also managed to mobilize the paddling community, and many private rafters and kayakers had arrived. I told them all that we needed at least 10 bodies on the island to lift Sam up and out. Several rafters, kayakers, and a few rescue personnel came out quickly with us to attempt extraction. This was around midnight.

Once we established our pulling zone and got organized, I set up our largest-diameter Spectra throw rope with a locking carabiner to lower through the falls into the crack for Sam. I attached my headlamp to the carabiner to help him see it. Had he not been able to see or grab the rope, we likely would have had to lower a rescuer on the rope, which would have added another level of complication and danger. Fortunately, Sam grabbed the rope almost immediately. We couldn't talk to him over the roar of the river, so it took a number of tries pulling before he understood that we wanted him to clip in to the rope with his rescue PFD. On the fourth or fifth try of us pulling on the rope, he was clipped in and being lifted.

As our group pulled on the rope over the edge of rock, we regularly heard yells from him, which we interpreted to mean that he was stuck on the rock wall. After a few stop-and-goes, I saw one arm and the top of his head come up through the curtain of falls in the corner of the crack. Slowly, he managed to climb, wiggle, and be pulled up and over the lip. What a relief!

After cheering, hugging, and doing our best to quickly warm him up a little, a few rescuers helped him walk down to the powered rescue boat, which took him back to shore and to an ambulance. Even from the island, we could hear the roar of the crowd that had assembled onshore cheering for his safe return. By this time, it was around 1 a.m. I can no longer remember the names and faces of all the incredible people who came out to the island and lifted him to safety in the dark, but you are all heroes.

A few takeaways (meaning no criticism or disrespect to Sam—I've seen these things many times before now):

1. Kanawha Falls' High Flow line is not a beginner waterfall. Anyone who runs it should know that they are risking going under the right wall, and they need to have safety set up to deal with that. Unless the levels are butt-low, a person who breaks a paddle, drops a paddle, misses a few rolls, or blows a skirt will likely go under the wall. I've run far harder whitewater and bigger drops all over the world, and I won't mess around with this drop. I consider the consequences seriously every time I run it.

2. In many situations, self-rescue is impossible. Had this not been a solo paddler, he likely would have been rescued almost immediately after the incident. As kayakers, we need to stop glorifying solo boating—and those who do it should stop talking about it.

3. There are many places we go that professional rescue personnel will not know how to access or navigate safely. These people want to help, but they simply don't have the whitewater experience of most kayakers or rafters. We need to be ready to help out or lead in whitewater rescues. We need to remember that a missing boater (even one who's been missing in the water for 7 or more hours) may still be alive and waiting for rescue. Our best safety standards should involve local paddling experts and professional rescuers working together.

4. The water at Kanawha Falls comes from the New and Gauley Rivers. During Gauley release days, the water at Kanawha will rise dramatically in the late afternoon/early evening. The water yesterday likely rose from 6,500 cfs to 9,000 cfs as Sam was paddling.

Thanks to all who helped with this rescue. We're all grateful that Sam is safe and OK. Ours is a great community of helpful people. We live or die together in the power and beauty of the river. Take a swiftwater rescue class if you haven't already. You could save my life someday. Keep each other safe, and I hope to see you all on the river.

ALERT PADDLER RESCUES TWO VICTIMS IN MATHER GORGE

BELOW GREAT FALLS, THE POTOMAC RIVER enters a sheer-walled 3-mile stretch known as Mather Gorge, which contains several Class III rapids. It is close to Washington, DC, and is very popular with local paddlers. The entire area is protected as a national park and draws a number of hikers and climbers from the city. On July 10, 2021, Michael Graham participated in the rescue of a 7-year-old boy and a second victim in his 30s. At the time of the incident, the water level was about 3.1 feet and running at 3,400 cfs. It was a warm, mostly sunny day, with a water temperature of 86°F. Here is Graham's account.

At about 11:15 a.m., John Alden, Rich Schneider, Bill Collier, and I were in the river-right eddy below Rocky Island rapid, preparing to attain the rapid. Rock climbers on the Virginia-side cliffs overlooking the Potomac and upstream of the Rocky Island rapid called to us to alert us of a person in the water. We saw the boy on river left, about 5 feet off the Rocky Island shore and about 20 yards upstream of the Rocky Island rapid. The boy was very low in the water and did not appear to be getting a breath or trying to swim. We all quickly ferried to river left to try to intercept him. I was able to navigate toward the boy as he entered the rapid, but he disappeared underwater at the first wave. As I started to paddle up to where I last saw him, I noticed him floating listlessly about 1 foot below my boat and was able to quickly grab his shirt before he sank lower.

When I pulled him onto the deck of my kayak, he was nonresponsive (did not speak or try to hold on) but did start gasping and then breathing. I could not release the boy and paddle without him falling back in. My fellow kayakers quickly and without direction surrounded me and helped hold the boy out of the water. We calmly reassured the boy that he was safe. Within about 2 minutes, he started becoming responsive. We asked his name and used his name, Anish, to continue to calmly assure him he was safe. Rich took off his own PFD and loosely secured it to the boy. Rich and John steadied my boat and moved the boy to its rear deck. At this point, we were about halfway to Wet Bottom rapid and moving into the large eddy behind Rocky Island. I paddled to the Maryland shore because it was closer.

Once onshore, the boy became adamant that he needed to get to the Virginia shore to reconnect with his parents. He did not know the phone number for either parent, so I called 911 (thinking that, if the parents called 911, the operator could let them know their son was safe). The 911 call was placed at 11:39 a.m.

We decided we could safely transport the boy to the Virginia side. Rich secured the PFD to Anish very well, and we had him lie on the back deck while holding my waist. John went ahead to find the parents. Rich and Bill flanked me as we ferried back without incident.

We got the boy to the shore just as John returned with the parents.

Discussion:

I am a current L4 swiftwater rescue (SWR) instructor, an L4 whitewater kayaker with wilderness first aid (WFA) certification. I credit this training with my being calm during the rescue. We were all paddling well within our abilities in the water where we rescued the child, and at no point were we ever in danger of becoming part of the problem. I have second-guessed myself about returning the child to the Virginia side of the river, but once we had the PFD secured to him, I am absolutely confident that no one was placed in danger by crossing the river to return the child to his parents. It was because of the experience, training, and kayaking skill of the other kayakers that the rescue went so well. Looking back, it felt like everything went very smoothly. No one yelled or got in the way. Everyone picked a task and did it.

I noted that there were at least 20 people observing the drowning boy before they could have seen us. None of these bystanders jumped in to help the child. It may be that, unless there was an expert swimmer among them, if any of them had jumped in, they may have become another victim. Still, it surprised me, and it drove home the point that the boy would have died if we had not been there exactly at that time.

After reuniting the child with his parents, I continued up above Rocky Island rapid with the hope of

*reaching Portage rapid. However, just above Rocky
Island rapid, I discovered a man (about age 30) on a
rock just off the Virginia shore at a location from which
it did not seem possible to climb out. He asked if the boy
was OK. I said yes. The man said he was free climbing
the rocks and the boy was doing the same above him (the
man did not know the boy). The boy fell and knocked
him off the cliff and into the river. The man said he tried
to save the boy but was only able to save himself and
was now trapped on the rock. After a brief discussion,
I had him grab the strap on the stern of my boat, and I
took him to the trail below Rocky Island rapid.*

*After I dropped off the man, I continued down-
stream. Virginia and Maryland Search and Rescue
arrived in motorized inflatables, and I gave them an
incident report. While Search and Rescue did arrive
very quickly, I am certain the boy would have been
dead because he was certainly seconds from passing
out and filling his lungs with water when we got him
out of the water.*

*The water in this stretch of the Potomac is very
swirly, and it is hard to get to shore because of the eddy
waves. The fact that a fit man in his 30s fell in with the
child and only managed to save himself drives home how
dangerous those waters are without a PFD.*

For his actions that day, Michael Graham received the 2021
Uncommon Service Award from the George Washington Memorial
Parkway branch of the National Park Service.

PLAY BOATERS RESCUE SWIMMER AT COLUMBUS WAVE

THIS RESCUE OCCURRED at the Columbus Whitewater Park on the Chattahoochee River near Columbus, Georgia. This stretch of river was recovered when several dams were decommissioned and developed as a whitewater park. The high flows, outstanding features, and warm temperatures have made this the preferred winter training site for many serious play boaters. Clay Wright is a well-known freestyle competitor and a Jackson Kayak representative. He posted the following on Facebook on April 4, 2022.

> *We went to surf Ambush when this man appears, bouncing over the rocks in the middle, clutching a bag. He's in jeans, boots, and a winter jacket, despite the 70°F weather, and disappears in the eddy below. Haley McKee and I ferry out, and he yells, "Help! I can't swim." But he's in that boily middle eddy and goes under again as we get there. I can see the tan jacket and white bag waving around under my boat but can't reach down far enough to grab on, and soon the bubbles cloud him from view. We drift down, following his path, hoping he'll surface before the big seam below. Then I see Haley bending over her bow struggling to stay upright—she snagged him! As she held him up from the seam, I bulldozed them out of the current, and we got him onto a rock in the middle of the river. Rachel Scheffe ran back to call it in, and 20 minutes later she was guiding an EMS raft crew down and transferring him to shore. I tried surfing again, but we decided a cocktail might be a nice reward instead. You never know what the day will bring in Columbus.*

6

WORKING WITH FIRST RESPONDERS

RESCUERS ARRESTED: HOW IT HAPPENED AND WHAT WE CAN LEARN

OVER THE YEARS, I'VE FOUND MANY EXAMPLES of strong cooperation between paddlers and first responders. Building this relationship takes time. Outfitters and paddling clubs who have a solid relationship with EMS have usually worked on it *before* an emergency. Some paddlers and guides join rescue squads, and some outfitters schedule joint training to develop a formal or informal relationship with local teams. In places like the Nantahala and New Rivers, rescue squads typically depend on outfitters to manage the in-water portion of the rescue. Once the victim is onshore, the rescue squad takes over. Then the greatest strengths of EMS professionals—advanced medical care and fast transportation—come into play.

Swiftwater rescue training for first responders has come a long way since the mid-1970s, when most of them were untrained in swiftwater rescue. This article I wrote for the May–June 2011 issue

Yellowstone National Park rangers participate in swiftwater rescue training.

of the *American Whitewater Journal* explains some of the issues that get in the way of better cooperation nowadays.

Experienced whitewater paddlers know how to deal with anything from a routine swim to a life-threatening pin. Despite this, very few of them are prepared to work with emergency responders. When police, fire, and rescue personnel arrive, the situation changes. They are, to use a legal phrase, the designated state authority. This means that they can take over a situation and arrest anyone who disobeys their lawful orders.

In most cases, first responders are better trained to handle emergencies than the average person. In swiftwater situations, however, expert whitewater paddlers have superior in-water skills—better than most top-notch search-and-rescue professionals. But while these paddlers want to help, they're not always welcome.

Clear Creek, which runs along on I-70 and US 6 in Colorado's Front Range, has sections ranging in difficulty from Class II to Class V. It's a popular after-work run for many Denver-area boaters. But there are risks: six paddlers have died here in the last 20 years, along with a number of swimmers and fishermen. This past summer, two raft guides were arrested while trying to rescue one of their guests. The story has useful lessons for paddlers, outfitters, and first responders.

It was a very high-water day on June 10, 2010, when an Arkansas Valley Adventures (AVA) raft missed an eddy at the end of their beginner trip and floated into the advanced section just downstream. They flipped, tossing everyone in the water. The adults got to shore, but a 13-year-old girl washed downstream through several miles of serious Class IV–V rapids.

Ryan Snodgrass is a 10-year veteran guide and a Class V kayaker who is certified in swiftwater rescue and first aid. He works as trip leader, guide trainer, and safety kayaker for the company. He'd just finished a trip on the intermediate section when his manager told him what happened. Grabbing his gear, he and several other AVA guides began a wild drive downriver. Just below a tunnel they stopped and listened. They heard a girl screaming. They ran to the guardrail and spotted the girl on the far shore. Her back was against a cliff, so she couldn't move up- or downstream.

Someone, probably a passing motorist, had seen what happened and dialed 911. The Clear Creek County Sheriff's Dive Rescue Team responded. Many rescue squads deal with fast-moving water only once every four to six years, and their training is spotty at best. This team is different. Set up in 1984 and trained by Dive Rescue Specialists and Rescue 3 International, they are in the river year-round managing auto wrecks and searching for missing persons, as well as responding to the usual swimming and boating accidents. They have a strong reputation in Colorado and are often called on to assist with searches and recoveries elsewhere.

Two strong teams, highly trained and confident, converged on the scene. Both felt a responsibility to perform the rescue. Adrenaline was flowing and everyone was keyed up. It's not easy for two groups who don't know each other to team up for a rescue under ideal conditions. This meeting was more like a collision. Several Dive Rescue Team members wearing civilian clothes shouted at the AVA guides not to intervene. This would later escalate to cursing, name-calling, and shoving on both sides. But the guides were intent on doing their job and paid them no mind.

Several AVA guides planned to reach the girl so they could check her for injuries and offer support. They went downstream to a calm stretch and set up safety so Ryan could swim across the river. He described the swim as "a simple jump from a rock at the bank and a swim ferry into a well-defined eddy." He moved quickly upstream and made contact. Finding her unhurt, he began scouting for a place to catch a throw bag to pendulum her over to the near shore. That's when a uniformed rescuer shouted that he was in charge and ordered Ryan not to move the girl.

After several attempts, a Dive Rescue Team swimmer (most rescue squads don't even have a rescue swimmer) made it across the river. The AVA guide stepped back as the swimmer checked the victim over and the rest of his team set up a system to bring a boat over and back. It took about 45 minutes to get the system up and the girl across. Ryan was then ordered to cross the river using the same system. When he reached the near shore, he was arrested, handcuffed, and taken to jail. A second AVA guide, Justin Lariscy, was also arrested. They were both charged with obstructing a rescue and obstructing a government operation.

Analysis: First Responders vs. Expert Paddlers

Why such a serious conflict between two very competent groups? It starts with a real difference in training and philosophy between whitewater paddlers and emergency responders. Swiftwater rescues are just one type of emergency that first responders train for. By contrast, river guides and whitewater paddlers are totally focused on the river; many of them paddle more than 100 days per year, and rescuing swimmers, unpinning boats, and picking off stranded paddlers are all in a day's work.

Their varying backgrounds result in very different rescue styles. Guides and paddlers have limited resources and are presented with evolving situations that demand immediate action. They respond individually or in small ad hoc groups with fast-moving, in-water techniques that are considered reckless, even dangerous, by search-and-rescue professionals. First responders bring lots of gear and people but take more time to get to the scene. Most situations they encounter are stable, though as yet unresolved. They are trained to work as a team, with a well-defined chain of command. They handle these low-urgency, high-risk situations in the safest possible manner. Although this approach is seen as slow-moving and awkward by whitewater paddlers, first responders would counter that rescuing a member of the general public, rather than other paddlers, demands extra caution.

Furthermore, the groups each had unflattering stereotypes about the other. Emergency responders as well trained as the Clear Creek Dive Rescue Team are rare, and paddlers are more familiar with many bungled rescues made by other "professional" search-and-rescue units. For most first responders, emergencies requiring moving-water skills are quite unusual, and training resources are therefore limited. Even a rescuer who has six days of swiftwater rescue training and takes four days of practice per year has less time on the river than the average intermediate kayaker or rookie raft guide. So, naturally, they work differently than true whitewater experts.

Rescue squads also deal with the most inexperienced and irresponsible whitewater paddlers. They do body searches and help out clueless river runners stranded on islands or midstream boulders. Not surprisingly, they often think of paddlers as beer-drinking fools who don't wear PFDs or cold-weather gear, take stupid risks, and generally don't take care of themselves. Trained whitewater paddlers and guides, by contrast, handle their own mishaps and rarely call for outside help. So the two seldom meet.

Emergency responders are rightfully wary of accepting help even from skilled bystanders. Imagine, as the incident commander (IC) of a rescue team, being approached by someone who says they're a whitewater paddler trained in swiftwater rescue and want to help. You don't really know if that person is who they say they are, but you do know that when someone gets hurt, you'll be held responsible. You, your crew, and the government could be sued for damages. One professional put it bluntly: "The world is full of idiots and wannabes, and we don't have time to weed out the idiots and pick the good guys. We go with people we know." They are required to secure the scene, and this means keeping people who aren't part of the team away from the action.

In swiftwater rescue classes, I discuss what paddlers should do if they encounter another group of paddlers with a rescue in progress. Put simply, you have to work with the people who are already there. Maybe those folks will accept your input. If not, you can help out on their terms or move on. Sometimes a hotshot boater who jumps into a rescue without talking to those involved screws everything up. I still remember a fellow who came upon a pinned open canoe I was trying to release. He barged in, and a few minutes later broke the boat in half, insulted the boat owner, and left us with a mess. Months later, he still felt he had performed a useful service. Only the actual risk of death or serious injury justifies starting an argument or interfering with a rescue in progress. Even then, you should think twice. There's no question that either the Clear Creek Dive Rescue Team or the AVA guides could have rescued the young girl safely.

This story had a reasonably happy ending. Duke Bradford, owner of AVA, stood firmly behind his guides. The guides' arrest received wide publicity throughout the region and drew hundreds of comments in chat rooms. The sheriff received a torrent of critical emails and phone calls. Although the public was clearly sympathetic to the guides, cooler heads recognized that the Dive Rescue Team had a point too. There was plenty of blame to go around. Eventually

CHARLIE'S INSIGHTS:
False Alarms

Cell phone usage creates additional challenges. Nowadays, 911 operators often receive calls from passersby. On roadside rivers, these calls often involve problems that experienced paddlers can manage themselves. False alarms occur regularly. On one roadside stretch of the Potomac near Harpers Ferry, West Virginia, 911 operators hear not only from drivers but also from livery customers who lose their boats or tubes and call for help. One outfitter told me that he often encounters rescue squads when picking up stranded customers or recovering pinned boats. Sometimes there are arguments about who is in charge, and a simple situation turns more complex. He described one incident where two paddlers sunbathing on a midstream rock were reported by a passing motorist as "stranded." This set in motion a huge response involving two fire companies, a major bridge closure, and a helicopter! It's pretty difficult for 911 operators to know what's going on, and everyone probably overreacts in the interest of safety. The AVA guides who were searching Clear

Creek never called for outside help, and the Dive Rescue Team was not told that there was a team of skilled professional guides on the scene.

One other concern with overreaction, aside from the wasted resources, is that rescuers have occasionally tried to help people who don't want or need assistance. This has been an issue in the mountains when relatives of overdue climbers notify authorities. For skilled climbers, waiting out a bad storm for several days is not only possible; it's prudent. Some years ago, a young man named Scott Mason got lost in Mount Washington's Great Gulf in winter. Although he was several days overdue, he was tough and self-reliant. He was walking out on his own when the "rescuers" found him. Later he got a $10,000 bill from the state that was only withdrawn after an extended legal and political fight. You can decline help politely but firmly and should do so when it's appropriate. AVA, if given the opportunity, would have probably done this.

the sheriff, district attorney, and guides had a sit-down. The guides wrote a letter of apology, and the charges were dropped. We expect that this is the beginning of real cooperation, or at least mutual respect, between AVA and the county dive team.

CHEAT NARROWS HELICOPTER RESCUE

ON SATURDAY, JUNE 6, 1981, a commercial rafting trip entered the Class III Narrows of the Cheat River at Rowlesburg, West Virginia, after having canceled the usual Canyon run due to high water. Unbeknownst to the trip leader, the river level, already uncommonly high for June, was rising to unprecedented levels. Several rafts came to grief a few miles into the trip, and one customer was marooned on a rock. The guides could not extricate him easily and were hampered in their efforts by a local civil defense squad who closed the river and took over the site. The victim was eventually removed by helicopter.

The Cheat River is the largest free-flowing river in the East, with no dams of any significance on its headwaters. Because of its large drainage area, it can rise or fall quickly for no apparent local reason. The Canyon, from Albright to Jenkinsburg Bridge, is a classic whitewater run that is used frequently by many commercial outfitters during the spring season. The Narrows, upstream between Rowlesburg to a point several miles downstream along WV 7, is easier and more accessible and is frequently used as an alternate run when the river is too high to attempt the Canyon safely. Between the Canyon cutoff of 5 feet and the maximum sane level (in the author's opinion) of 10 feet, the Narrows is broad, fast, and uncomplicated, with huge waves and boiling eddy lines. There are few dangers, and rescue is generally quick and easy. The outfitter is one of the oldest and most experienced on the river and has never had a river-related fatality in over a decade of operation. This report is based on interviews with their river manager and other guides who were at the scene.

The Cheat River on the weekend of June 6 was rising rapidly, even for a high-water year like 1981. On Friday morning, it was just under 2.5 feet; by 11 p.m. it was at 4.5 feet and coming up fast. At 6 a.m. Saturday, the river had reached 6 feet; by 8 a.m., with the river running close to 8 feet, a decision was made to transfer the trips to the Narrows.

The river was still coming up, but no one expected it to continue to the point where trips would be endangered. The Cheat seldom got over 8 feet in the early season, much less in the spring and summer, when growing vegetation slows and absorbs the runoff. The company had successfully handled the river at levels up to 12 feet; the river was to crest at over 14 feet later that day, and the fast rise was to draw considerable debris into its swift waters.

When the company arrived at the put-in, it was evident that the Cheat was still on the rise. Quantities of debris, including whole uprooted trees, were floating down the river. A raft, which was originally placed near the shore, soon became awash in the surging current. Soon after the first trip launched, a raft collided with a floating log, puncturing a raft tube and banging up one of the guides. These people were swiftly recovered by the rest of the party.

At this time, the second trip, moving hard on the heels of the first in the quickening current, capsized a raft in a series of huge waves. All hands were picked up except for one person, who found himself marooned on a midstream rock. (This rock is found on the shoreline at normal flows!) By this time the outfitter, having observed the rising gauge at Albright and witnessing the problems on the river, had driven up to the put-in and canceled all further trips.

The problem was now to remove the person from the rock. River manager John Lichter maneuvered his kayak into the eddy below the victim and did not like what he saw. The river was continuing to rise, and as this happened, the safety zone was shrinking. Just downstream was a massive logjam that would make any approach by raft extremely difficult. In addition, a bunch of snakes trapped in the area were also clinging to the rock, and the presence of these creatures (who were too preoccupied with survival to be very hostile) was nerve-wracking, to say the least!

By this time, too, the Rowlesburg Civil Defense Squad, which serves as a rescue squad for the Narrows, had closed the river down and mobilized its members. Any action by the trip guides would have been in defiance of this local authority. A helicopter was in the area and was called by the rescue squad. Shouting across the water, they discussed with John the alternatives. The victim was banged up and badly shaken. The approach to the rock was treacherous even for an expert kayaker, much less the raft, which would have been required to remove the victim. The chopper was the best alternative. Deftly piloted by two local men, it came in and landed as John peeled out and headed downstream. The pilot, a Vietnam veteran, placed one skid on the rock and hovered as the victim entered. Minutes later, they landed safely at nearby Camp Dawson, a National Guard training area.

This sequence of events leading up to this incident shows how even experienced paddlers can be caught off guard when a river flashes. The Cheat seldom gets over 8 feet, much less to a level where it is unsafe to run the Narrows. However, 1981 was a high-water

CHARLIE'S INSIGHTS:
The Hazards of Floating Debris

Sudden surges of high water can cause the river to pick up debris, even uprooting marginal trees and carrying them downstream. Many of the problems associated with this rescue were the result of debris, and the first capsizing was a direct result of it. When large quantities of trash are afloat in a river, it is a sure sign of danger, even for experts. Everyone, regardless of ability, is advised to wait until the water's crest has passed unless they must get on the water to save a life. Debris-laden water is too unpredictable to offer good sport.

Just downstream was a massive logjam that would make any approach by raft extremely difficult. In addition, a bunch of snakes were also clinging to the rock, and the presence of these creatures was nerve-wracking, to say the least!

year in northern West Virginia, and although the guides were accustomed to these above-average flows, they clearly did not realize how quickly the water was rising to unreasonably dangerous levels.

Although the rescue turned out well, there was little cooperation between the rescue squad and the outfitter. This might have caused serious problems in other circumstances, particularly if the helicopter had not been available. Jurisdictional and technical squabbles are best resolved beforehand by both parties meeting in an atmosphere of minimal pressure and mutual respect. Most rescue squads are not familiar with modern whitewater techniques and are unaware that local outfitters can be a valuable resource for them. Outfitters are also likely to be less knowledgeable about the lay of the land, access, and other possibilities well-known to locals. River outfitters owe it to themselves to arrange a meeting with the local authorities. You never know when they'll need each other.

This accident had a happy ending. Hindsight tells us that certain actions might have prevented it; however, that is not the point. We must learn from it so that similar miscalculations by experts do not have more serious results.

RANGER TO THE RESCUE ON ARKANSAS'S BUFFALO NATIONAL RIVER

THIS INCIDENT WAS INCLUDED in the National Park Service *Morning Report*.

> *During the afternoon of Saturday, April 30, 1983, a rapid and unexpected rise in the river level produced swift currents, treacherous eddies, and other hazardous conditions for inexperienced floaters. Park Technician Richard*

Brown initiated a canoe patrol to warn floaters about these conditions. While on this patrol, Brown observed two occupants thrown out of a canoe. The canoe and its occupants were being swept toward another capsized canoe. In attempting to help his female companion, the male victim became pinned between the two canoes. The tremendous force of high water pressed the canoe against both of his legs, causing excruciating pain.

After pulling the female victim to safety, Brown single-handedly prevented the upstream canoe from crushing the man or forcing his head and torso backward and underwater. Brown removed his own life jacket and put it on the man, keeping the man's head above water during periods when he lost consciousness. Only with the aid of eight volunteers and a 15-minute struggle was Brown able to free the man from the canoe. As the canoe was released, Brown and a volunteer were swept away in the swift current. Brown grabbed the volunteer and caught hold of a willow branch until both could regain their balance and be helped to safety. Despite being wet and cold, Brown directed the evacuation of the victim 2 miles overland by Stokes litter.

Brown's conduct was exemplary throughout this rescue; however, had it not been for his initial actions, which can only be described as a selfless act of courage, it is probable that Buffalo National River would have recorded its first canoeing fatality. For his courage, Brown was granted the Valor Award by the Department of the Interior.

CHARLIE'S INSIGHTS:
Working with a Rescue Squad

Working with other paddlers on the scene of a serious accident can be challenging. Differences of opinion are not uncommon, and you can waste a lot of time arguing. If you encounter a rescue squad working on a river rescue and think you can help, ask to speak to the incident commander (IC). Ask, "What's the situation?" and "How can we help?" Make your case calmly and respectfully. You may still get turned down; the IC is under a lot of pressure and may be abrupt with you.

Rescue squads vary in how open they are to outside help; some have written policies against it, while others leave it to the IC's discretion. Remember that even a rescue that you don't think is ideal is often good enough. Be patient. It's also perfectly OK to stand back or keep going downstream if a situation seems under control.

If a rescue squad comes across an incident that you're working, send someone who can serve as trip leader to talk. Explain what's happening and ask for whatever help you need. In one incident, Adirondack Park rangers were called to the scene of a fatality where the victim's group was working hard to recover her body. They set up their system, then approached the paddlers and asked if they could attempt the recovery. They were, in fact, successful, and their sensitivity brought them a great deal of respect from the whitewater community.

Bottom line: Don't get into a conflict unless it's a matter of life and death.

Emergency responders are rightfully wary of accepting help even from skilled bystanders. They don't really know if a person is who they say they are, but they do know that when someone gets hurt, they'll be held responsible.

THREE KAYAKERS RESCUED FROM VALLECITO CREEK GORGE IN SEPARATE INCIDENTS

THE FIRST INCIDENT DESCRIBED BELOW was reported in *The Durango Herald* by Garrett Andrews on May 28, 2009. The second was reported by Ann Butler and Shane Benjamin in the same publication. The third incident appeared in the *Herald* on April 23, 2019, reported by Jonathan Romeo.

Colorado's Class V Vallecito Creek runs through sheer-walled gorge. According to American Whitewater, the creek is "remote and hazardous. The gorge is committing, and escape is not easy." All of these accidents occurred in Trash Can rapid, partway down the run.

Don Smith, 42, was an expert kayaker with more than 10 runs down the creek. On this day, he got spun around in Trash Can rapid and flipped. As he bailed out, his leg got caught in his kayak and broke. He swam to the right side of the river. Members of Don's party splinted his leg and were making a plan to get him out of the 100-foot-deep gorge without contacting rescue authorities.

Several other groups of kayakers offered to help. One kayaker paddled downstream, hiked out to a phone, and called 911. Another party that included two medical professionals—Eric Parker, an ER nurse, and Dan Steaves, an EMT—advised against attempting to self-evacuate. At 3:06 p.m., the call was received by the Upper Pine Creek Technical Rescue Team. They reached Don at 4:27 p.m., set up a hauling system near the top of the gorge, and had him back to the trailhead by 7:45 p.m.

On June 20, 2016, an unidentified kayaker was lifted out of the sheer-walled gorge after a swim in Trash Can rapid. When he tried to climb out of the gorge, he fell, seriously injuring his leg. Rescuers received the call at 2:15 p.m., and he was on his way to the hospital 6 hours later.

At 3 p.m. on April 23, 2019, the Upper Pine River Fire Protection District got a call that an unidentified kayaker was stranded in Vallecito Creek gorge. Although the man was a skilled kayaker, he injured his shoulder while tangling with a strainer in Trash Can rapid. Once the injured kayaker got to shore, his partner paddled downstream to an area with cell phone service and called for help. Rescue crews arrived at the trailhead by 4 p.m. They made contact with the injured man and set up the rigging system required to lift him up 100 vertical feet to the top of the canyon. By 6 p.m., the injured kayaker was at the top of the canyon and able to hike out. Drone footage showing this rescue can be found at tinyurl.com/vallecitorescue.

KAYAKERS ASSIST VEHICLE RESCUE IN LOGAN CANYON

ON MAY 30, 2020, A TOYOTA MINIVAN carrying a mother and four children went off the road into the Logan River in Logan Canyon, Utah. The vehicle was stable and aligned with the current in the midst of a long Class III rapid. Rescue squads arrived around 2:15 p.m., but they were having trouble reaching the vehicle. About this time, a group of experienced kayakers were shuttling along the road. One of them, Marc Nelson, was also an experienced rock climber. The rest of the group members were trained in swiftwater rescue, and one of them was a swiftwater trainer who had worked with fire companies.

Marc approached the incident commander (IC) and offered his help; he was told to stand by. As time passed, he continued discussions. The biggest problem was getting a rope across the river. Marc assured the IC that his group could do this. The rope would need to be anchored; Marc was familiar with the anchor the firefighters wanted, and he demonstrated it. After being given the go-ahead from the IC, the kayakers ferried the rope across the river and anchored it on the far shore.

After setting up the line, the group provided downstream rescue backup for several hours. It was very fortunate they had the time and that the victim's car was perfectly aligned in the current to maintain stability. All five victims were brought ashore using the rope. Battalion Chief Joshua Francis said later, "One of the cool things is we just had some people come downcanyon who actually were kayakers and certified in swiftwater rescue as well."

Firefighter-led rescues of inexperienced, poorly equipped civilians move much more slowly than experienced paddlers are used to, and Marc's respectful, patient approach was vital to the kayakers' success.

TROTLINE SNAG CAUSES LEGAL WOES

A TROTLINE IS A FISHING LINE WITH MULTIPLE HOOKS set in the water. This incident inspired a still-ongoing effort to change Tennessee law that allows a trotline to be set all the way across a river. Kayaking instructor Robin Pope posted the incident to the Accident Database.

> *On May 30, 2021, I helped teach a kayak instructor course on the lower Nolichucky River in Tennessee. During the course, one of the instructor candidates (who happens to be my son) ran into a line set across the river. In the process of disengaging from the line, he discovered that it was actually a fishing line with multiple suspended hooks.*

Our group examined the line. It was secured across the river and had no tag or label that would help identify an owner. The line was dark-colored against a dark background, making it difficult to see until it couldn't be avoided. It was suspended at a height that would strike a canoe, kayak, or raft paddler (or an inner tube rider) anywhere from just above water level to neck and head level, and a stand-up paddler at ankle to thigh level. It extended at a downward angle from shore well out into the current before actually entering the water. Its position could cause a paddler to capsize or fall overboard. To make matters worse, the line was set at an angle to the current, so that if someone fell overboard or capsized, they would flush underwater into the fishing hooks.

The lower Nolichucky is heavily traveled by private boaters and commercial groups, including rafts, tubes, and stand-up paddleboards. The line was untended and created a clear, imminent threat. It obviously impeded safe navigation, and there were several large novice groups upstream of us. It had no identifying information on it. If we'd been doing a waterway cleanup, there's no question it would have been taken down. If I had deliberately wanted to hurt a paddler, I'm not sure I could have set it any more effectively. Given all that, we removed it. Unfortunately, the owners showed up as we prepared to leave and later confronted us at the takeout.

Law enforcement was called (by our group, because the owners of the line had arrived and become

> *threatening), the Tennessee Wildlife Resources Agency*
> *(TWRA) did a brief investigation over the next few days,*
> *and the local district attorney reportedly said something*
> *to the effect of "I'd have done the same thing in your*
> *shoes." Unfortunately, he later changed his mind, sub-*
> *mitted the evidence to a grand jury (for a misdemeanor*
> *charge of interfering with fishing), and Scott Fisher, the*
> *owner of the school running the class, was charged.*
>
> *Fisher is the owner of Nolichucky Outdoor Learning*
> *Institute (NOLI), an American Canoe Association level 3*
> *swiftwater rescue IT (with paperwork in place for level*
> *5 swiftwater rescue IT and level 4 river-kayak IT), and*
> *a former Army Ranger officer. Through NOLI, he offers*
> *a variety of discounted programs for the community,*
> *including school and other youth groups, and is deeply*
> *involved with Team River Runner. In essence, a former*
> *Army officer has been charged for removing trash from*
> *the river, the day before Memorial Day, to prevent others*
> *from being injured by it.*

Several months later, the case was dismissed. The fight to make cross-river trotlines illegal is ongoing.

7

ACCIDENTS AT WATERFALLS

WATERFALL RUNNING IS RELATIVELY NEW. I remember the first "big ledges" we ran in the early 1970s. Fifteen to 20 feet was considered high, and low flows were mandatory. But the sport has progressed. By the early 21st century, waterfalls of 50–70 feet were being run routinely, and drops of more than 100 feet have been run a number of times. While skilled paddlers make running high drops look easy, the forces released dropping over a big waterfall are really impressive. Although there are recognized techniques for making successful runs, serious injuries result when things go wrong. Here are a few examples.

BAD LAUNCH CAUSES BROKEN BACK

KAYAKER CHRISTIAN COOK describes his close call running the falls of Colorado's Crystal Gorge.

> *I spent most of two months in the summer of 2007 creeking in Colorado. It was my first season out there, and I had really gotten into the whole creeking thing. After paddling almost every day for two months, I was feeling pretty good and started running some harder stuff. After*

Kayaker Eric Deguil runs a waterfall in Voss, Norway, for Ekstremsportveko, an extreme sports festival.

some real good days on Vallecito Creek and Big South, the water levels started to drop, leaving only a couple of runs open, one of them being the Crystal Gorge. When I got a few days off from work, me and a buddy decided to go for it and headed out on July 9. We got to the takeout and waited for the third member of our party.

While we were waiting, a group paddled up to the takeout. We asked how their run went, and they said it was good minus one person's piton off of Zute Chute (his boat certainly didn't look good). Finally, the third member of our group got there and we headed to the put-in. When we arrived, Tommy Hilleke made sure to give me the jitters by continuously talking about how nervous he was, while Nick Wigston was simultaneously puking in the background (in usual Nick Wigston fashion). Nervously, we finally put on.

The top section of the Crystal was really awesome, with bluish-green water, perfectly crisp boofs, and very clean, quality rapids. When we got down to the inner Crystal Gorge, I was feeling good and paddling well, as were Nick and Tommy (go figure). We hopped out to have a look from the rim before we committed. After checking out the rest of the gorge, we came back to our boats and scouted Zute Chute, the 40-foot entrance falls.

Zute Chute is a tricky waterfall that starts off with the first 15 feet being at 75 degrees and the last 25 feet free-falling. You have to start 2 feet from the left bank and work to the center of the drop before it goes into a complete free fall. If the landing was deep, it probably would be considerably safer, but unfortunately it's only about 5 feet deep, and that's if you hit the right spot. This last detail was on my mind when we were scouting. After analyzing the drop, we all decided to drop into the inner Crystal and headed back to our boats to give it a go.

Nick and Tommy went first in minute intervals, and both had good lines. When it was my turn to go, I got prepared, took some deep breaths, and focused on my line. I was scared but ready to step up. I peeled out and dropped the 5-foot entrance. I was now completely committed to the gorge. As I floated to the lip of the big one, the 200-foot vertical granite walls looming in the background completely removed my focus. Horizon lines always look bigger from the lip. As I hit the slide part, I was leaning far forward and moved to just where I wanted to be, giving a slight boof stroke when I started to free-fall. As I was falling, I felt like I was coming in a little flat and pushed my feet down to try to change my angle.

SLAM. My whole body went numb, and my paddle was gone. Then I looked down and saw my paddle gripped firmly in my hands. This is when I realized I couldn't feel my entire body. I was staring down at one of the hardest sections of whitewater in Colorado and could barely move my arms or breathe as I desperately tried to paddle into the nearest eddy. I missed the first eddy and was able to catch the next one at the lip of the first rapid on river left. I knew something was wrong, *as feeling crept slowly back into my body but breathing remained difficult.*

Tommy paddled over to the eddy where Nick and I were to check if I was alright, and as he had figured by my face, I was not. There was no way I was going to be able to paddle out of the gorge. This is where I got lucky. The eddy I had caught was at a cliff wall that was only 50 feet tall (by far the smallest of the entire gorge). If I had missed that eddy, I probably would have had to run the gorge. Tommy free-climbed up the cliff and dropped down a rope for me to climb with ascenders. When I made it to the top, the only thing left to do was hike out about a mile and then paddle a half mile of Class II and finish off crossing the lake at the end. That mile-long hike was the most painful thing I've ever been through. Breathing was a chore, and I later found out why.

When I got to the hospital, the doctors told me I had a 50% burst fracture [an injury in which the vertebrae break in multiple directions]. It was the vertebrae directly behind my diaphragm, and with every breath I took on that hike, I pressured the fragments of my vertebrae. I got lucky. I owe Tommy and Nick a big one for their help. What I learned: Rather than leaning forward on the first part of that drop, I should have had a neutral position so that when I was free-falling, I could have leaned forward and pushed my bow down. When I tried to push my bow down the way I did, it only moved my body position back.

LOW WATER LEVEL KILLS APPROACH, CAUSES BAD LANDING

RUSH STURGES POSTED THIS EXPERIENCE on his *River Roots* blog (no longer online).

> *Our group arrived at Bonito Falls in Argentina for the second time on December 14, 2009. On a previous visit, Ian Garcia and Tyler Bradt had paddled to the lip but determined that the water was too low and did not run. Three weeks later, we returned to identical water levels. With only five more days in the country, I was anxious to bag this drop. Our crew was Steve Fisher, Evan Garcia, Ian Garcia, Anton Imler, and myself. We made the decision to run it.*
>
> *From a distance, this drop looks good to go, but when you get to the lip, you realize how difficult the entrance is: a diagonal lateral feeding to the right, then current moving back to the left, before finally falling around 60 feet to the pool at the bottom. You don't want to be on the river-left side of the drop, as there is a big flake that could send you flat. We decided Ian and I would go first while the rest of the crew filmed and photographed from the bluffs. We were both nervous and excited to get it over with.*
>
> *Honestly, one of the sketchiest parts of this drop is scouting it. To get to the lip, we tied a rope off to a rock and then waded through the fast-moving current. One slip into the rushing river could send you over the falls. I hate this kind of thing and took my time getting to the scouting*

*zone. After some thought and speculation, Ian decided
to run and began hiking up to the lip. I watched from the
top of the drop as he vanished into the snakelike entrance
over the lip of the drop. Fisher came through on the
radio; Ian's spray skirt had imploded, but he was fine.*

*I was stoked to get my huck on. I climbed into my
kayak, hit record on my head camera, and paddled
toward the falls. The entrance was smooth as butter. A
sweet boof from the left side, up against the right wall,
back to the left, and then momentum back right. This is
where I made my mistake. In an attempt to be farther
right, I angled my boat just slightly farther right than it
needed to be. My last thoughts as I went off the lip were,
"I am going to stomp the hell out of this thing!" Then,
right as I hit the lip, the flake grabbed my right edge and
immediately tossed me flat and sideways. In one last desperate attempt, I threw my weight back and forward to
try to get the bow down, to no avail. I landed sideways,
flat, and sitting upright.*

*Basically, a flat landing on a big drop is every
kayaker's nightmare. (For any future or current waterfall hucker reading this, remember: it is always better to
land flat, tucking forward, than sitting upright.) Had I
landed flat and tucked forward, I might not have broken
my back. There was hardly any aeration, and I had a
lot of momentum at the bottom. The water was too low,
and even with a perfect line, this bad boy will hurt you.
The next part of the incident was not very much fun. I
couldn't breathe for about 30 seconds, and all I could do*

was gargle muffled wheezing. It sounds like I'm dying on the video.

After some time, Ian got me out of my boat and laid me in the water. I was in shock but after a while was able to stand. My muscles were all twitching, and it was pretty clear something was not right. I had full mobility, and the pain wasn't actually that bad. The next step was getting me out of the canyon. There are vertical walls on both sides and really the only way out besides paddling would be via helicopter. Not wanting to go that route, I opted to paddle out the remaining 300 meters [about 0.2 mile] of Class III+. Steve Fisher belayed me so I could pull myself the 300 feet of brushy steepness to the road. We then got to the truck and drove about 1.5 hours to a hospital in Bariloche. Thank God for Ian's fluent Spanish at the hospital.

After my X-rays, it was clear I had compressed and broken a piece off of my L2 vertebra [in the lower back]. It didn't seem to be that bad of a fracture. It sucked, but I thought I could make a full recovery with good rehab. After some negotiations, we convinced the hospital to let me go and stay at a friend's house in Bariloche. Special thanks to Frederico Medina and all his friends for letting us stay in their home.

I'd already mentally prepared myself for an injury at some stage in my kayaking career. If you continue to step it up in any sport, it's unlikely that you will go unscathed. I'm just really thankful it wasn't worse. Luckily for us kayakers, we don't have to deal with these things as much

*as our pro snowboarder or biker friends. Kayaking is a
fairly forgiving sport. Look at other kayakers: Jason Hale,
Ben Brown, and James Bebbington, and they are all as fit
and savage as ever.*

NEAR DROWNING AT A 10-FOOT LEDGE IN CHILE

HERE, A HIGH-LEVEL KAYAK INSTRUCTOR describes an awful
swim at the base of a 10-foot waterfall.

*It is with a humbled heart that I describe my own
near-drowning incident on December 12, 2010. It had
been raining in Pucón, Chile, for about three days, and
our kayak academy group was looking for the right
run. The Río Turbio is the closest run to our base, just a
3-minute drive to a bridge overlooking the river's gauge.
Many of the small rivers were on their way back down,
and the Turbio had dropped to an optimal level. While
the upper stretch has serious Class V drops, there are
some beautiful Class II–IV slides on the lower part of
this section. The run is a young basalt flow, making this
the most hikable and portageable river in the area. We
planned to hike this gorgeous run with the option to run
the Class II–IV slides and rapids. No Class V drops would
be permitted.*

*It was a gorgeous day after the rain, with the sun
clearing the clouds. As we scouted the portages, a
professional group of kayakers known as the Demshitz,
which many of our students look up to, passed us. We
dropped our kayaks some distance below the normal*

Class V beautiful slides and cascading put-in and hiked up to watch the big boys. Students were excited to watch them run a 40-foot waterfall and then two Class V slides. We hiked back to our kayaks, ran a Class III rapid, and then portaged another 400 yards of rapids. In this section we again saw the big boys on a Class V drop.

We eventually put on and ran our first Class IV, eddied out, and began to get into a groove. Students were in groups of three, hopping eddies. Everyone got into a flow and rhythm. The day was sunny and photogenic. I was happy for the kids to see this unique river. Near the end of the run, we arrived at a large eddy above a 10-foot waterfall to scout. While I had made a rule for the students not to run any Class V drops, I chose to run this drop myself.

I ran a left-side boof flat that landed, and immediately I flipped. There was a strong bubbly boil or frothy current line that pulled me back into the waterfall curtain, not allowing anything close to a roll. I swam out of the kayak and after a few seconds resurfaced briefly about 6 feet downstream of the waterfall. I glimpsed a rope and quickly went under as I began my recirculation pattern. I would not have the luxury of resurfacing for another 60–90 seconds. Under the water, I attempted several exit maneuvers, but ultimately the waterfall froth kept me just under the surface. Eventually, I swam down to the bottom of the river with the waterfall current to try to flush out of the hydraulic from the downstream side. Swimming down to the bottom with the current was the last thing I recall during my struggle that is vivid in my mind.

Witnesses said I rose to the surface unconscious and face down and floated out of the back of the recirculation zone. Three students pulled me to the bank. They cut my PFD straps and the neck gasket and neck of my dry top to get to my body and performed CPR for 2 minutes until I regained consciousness.

I walked out, with help from the students at first; I was later able to move more quickly unassisted. Nearby residents drove me 200 meters [about 0.1 mile] to their home and placed me in a warm shower as I undressed. They called the Pucón hospital emergency room. After warming, warm clothes, and wrapping in a blanket, we drove 10 minutes to the hospital, which immediately accepted me based on the previous phone call. My vitals were checked, and I was given oxygen. The doctor stated I had an inflamed lung but would be fine. An anti-inflammatory and an antibiotic were prescribed.

I was embarrassed, humbled, and upset with myself. No student ran anything more than a Class IV drop, and they acted swiftly to perform the rescue that ultimately saved my life. Today we discussed the incident and the reason why coaches have continually made students walk serious rapids. Last night I was sleepless as I, too, have learned and contemplated deeper lessons throughout the night. This morning I felt like I had a hangover. Now I am feeling much better. I will not paddle this week.

RESUSCITATION OF EXPERT KAYAKER IN MEXICO

THE FOLLOWING ACCOUNT IS BASED ON an interview that appeared in the November 2013 issue of *Outside*.

The Río Tulijá is a remote whitewater river in the rainforest of southern Mexico. Often called Agua Azul because of its clear blue color, it features a series of five waterfalls ranging from 40 to 70 feet tall. On March 13, 2013, a team of four world-class kayakers—Evan Garcia, Rafa Ortiz, Gerd Serrasolses, and Rush Sturges—attempted to run them.

They'd made a first descent of the five waterfalls on the Río Santo Domingo the previous day. The group was tired, having driven 7 hours from the Santo Domingo the night before. They had scouted and run the falls the previous week and knew their routes. Their plan was to meet a helicopter to get some aerial shots.

Evan ran the drop first, followed by Rush. They had good runs, then got out of their boats and waited on a ledge about 25 feet from the base of the falls. Gerd ran next, got buried at the base of the falls, missed several hand rolls, and was pulled underwater for a minute and a half. Then Rush and Evan spotted Gerd floating face down 100 yards away. Another waterfall was just downstream. They got in their boats, chased him down, brought him to shore, and started CPR.

Gerd's eyes were open a little, but he showed no sign of life. His skin was a mixture of white, purple, and black. Working as a team, the group started CPR. They pulled off his life jacket and loosened the neck gasket on his dry top. They slapped him and called out his name. After 4 minutes of CPR on what seemed like a dead body, he took a breath, then started vomiting mucus and blood.

The group signaled their helicopter, which came down and hovered over the middle of the river. They carried Gerd out to it. He was breathing a bit but still convulsing and coughing up water. Rafa got in the chopper with him, and they were flown to a hospital in Palenque, where Gerd recovered.

EPIC NIGHTTIME WATERFALL RESCUE IN NEW ZEALAND

THE FOLLOWING IS BASED ON Jeff Moag's accounts, published in *Men's Journal* online on December 3, 2019.

On February 3, 2017, Ryan Lucas and Mike Roy hiked 6 miles to 70-foot Tauranga-Taupo Falls on New Zealand's North Island. It's a beautiful falls, runnable but hard to catch up. That day, the river was running high due to recent rains and was at a perfect level of 900 cfs. A shuttle driver dropped them off at 3:30 p.m.; she was to wait at a bridge 5 miles downstream.

They scouted carefully. Everything looked OK. Ryan ran the falls first. There's a nasty Class V rapid in the gorge just above the falls that terminates in the pool just above the big drop, creating an ugly boil about 30 feet from the lip. Ryan planned to ferry across the boil, then turn sharply downstream to run the falls on the left side. Using a rope, he climbed down a steep embankment. Mike lowered his boat, then went downstream to set safety below the falls.

At the landing zone, the falls created a boil of aerated water that piled into the overhanging left wall before washing around a rocky island. Mike waited on the island with his kayak and a throw bag. He was ready. He blew his whistle. Ryan whistled back and began his run. As he launched off the lip, Ryan struggled to bring the nose of his kayak down for a smooth entry. He threw his body weight forward but still landed flat. He hit his head on the rim of his cockpit and was knocked unconscious. He surfaced upside down in the boil and was pushed toward the overhanging left wall.

Mike jumped into his boat and started paddling toward him. He managed to fight his way up the wall where Ryan's boat was bobbing upside down. There was no sign of movement. When he reached the kayak, he attempted a Hand of God rescue, grabbing the kayak and twisting it upright. When that failed, he released the spray skirt and pulled Ryan out of the kayak. Ryan was turning blue. Mike clipped the tether on his rescue PFD to Ryan's life vest and paddled him to the island.

The time code on Ryan's GoPro showed that he had been underwater for 3 minutes. Mike, a Wilderness First Responder, began CPR. When Ryan started to vomit water, foam, and blood, Mike turned him on his side. After 2 minutes of CPR, Ryan's eyes opened, and Mike started slapping him to get him to wake up.

Evacuating Ryan from here was going to be very difficult. There was no cell service in the canyon, the road was miles away up a steep trail, and there were 5 miles of Class III–IV rapids downstream. Ryan could walk only a few steps at a time, and Mike didn't want to leave him alone. The temperature that night would be in the low 50s, and Ryan, though wrapped in a Mylar space blanket, was already showing signs of hypothermia.

With sunset about an hour away, they decided to try to run the river. Neither paddler knew the river well, and it was getting dark fast. Ryan was struggling, and his lips were turning blue. Mike decided to stop to build a fire to rewarm him. By about 9 p.m., it was completely dark, with no moonlight. Ryan rested in an emergency blanket next to the fire while Mike talked to him to keep him awake.

They tried again to walk, but Ryan was struggling for breath. At 11 p.m., Ryan told Mike to leave him to get help.

Mike gathered a big pile of firewood for Ryan to use, then began hiking through the bush on river left toward a road that paralleled the river. He found a rough forest road, marked the spot with crossed branches, and began to run. After about 2 miles, he got cell service and dialed 111, the emergency-services number in New Zealand.

Using the cell signal to approximate Mike's location, search-and-rescue mobilized, and a helicopter was dispatched. Mike could hear sirens, but the rescuers were having trouble finding him. Moving down the road to a locked gate, he found two policemen and a search-and-rescue volunteer. The gate was unlocked, and they drove down the road. The helicopter had spotted Ryan using an infrared camera and was hovering nearby, and Mike used its location to lead the rescue team to Ryan. The search-and-rescue volunteers agreed that because of the severity of Ryan's condition, a night hoist was warranted. The helicopter had only 20–30 feet of clearance between its rotor and the canyon walls. The pilot flew as low as he dared and lowered a rescue cable 60 feet. The ground team got Ryan into a harness and clipped him to the cable. Moments later he was headed for Taupo Hospital, arriving at 4 a.m. Mike pulled the kayaks to high ground, grabbed his dry bag, and led the search team out of the canyon. Then he got a ride to the hospital to check on Ryan.

A week after the accident, Ryan was still struggling to breathe. He had water in his lungs, a concussion, and torn cartilage in his chest. But there were no broken bones, and doctors predicted a full recovery. Ryan said afterward, "I still love kayaking, and I'm thinking about getting back in my boat step by step, just seeing how I feel and getting strong and healthy. I'll see about running hard stuff as it comes."

PREPARATION FACILITATES A KANAWHA FALLS RESCUE

ONE OF THE EMERGING ISSUES IN WATERFALL RUNNING is that
the bases of some drops have dangerous undercut features. The far-
right side of Kanawha (pronounced ka-naw) Falls is one of these
places. The falls is run frequently, and after several close calls, hardware was installed in 2021 to facilitate rescue. It was put to use the
very next year. A report by Tyler Thornton in the Accident Database
reads as follows:

> On September 19, 2022, a group of three kayakers ran
> the falls in the early afternoon. The first person to run
> was a safety; the second was me leading a first-timer
> and setting safety after I dropped. The newbie flipped,
> swam, and was pushed to the right into the dangerous
> "pocket," which was the scene of a miraculous night
> rescue in the fall of 2020 [see page 238]. Fortunately,
> Carson Wright had installed several bolts and a chain
> there to facilitate rescue. The swimmer was able to grab
> hold and wait for help.
>
> After one or two attempts to ferry her out on the
> back of my boat, we decided we would need to lift her
> out. I sent the other safety kayaker up top to help set up a
> Z-drag while I stayed with the swimmer. Our first priority
> was to get her out of the water. The water was low that
> day; the ledge was a foot or so above the waterline, and
> the bottom of the chain was barely in the water. It was
> impossible for her to get up onto the ledge by herself. A
> Z-drag was set up top using the anchors, but we felt we
> didn't have enough equipment to safely get her out.

I decided it would be a better idea to clip to the working end of the chain and use it as a step to get the swimmer out of the water and onto the ledge. Someone made a trip to the parking lot to get river-rescue gear and a climbing harness. We set up a Z-drag and a separate belay rope to catch a fall. Two people held on to each line, with another man belayed off the tip of the rock with the two anchors close together. I could see and talk to him, so everyone was on the same page.

The climb out was pretty difficult. She slipped at least two to three times and was caught by the rope, and just as many times, the Z-drag was used to pull her up a few feet to get a good hold on the rock. An issue we ran into was that the rope and knot kept getting stuck in a notch at the top of the rock. We remedied this by adding a vector from the rope to the one guy rappelling out on the edge of the rock. We finally got her over the top of the drop.

Getting the boat out was much more difficult than helping the swimmer. I struggled a lot trying to unpin the boat and get it hooked to the rope. It probably took longer to do that than to get the swimmer out.

BEHIND THE CURTAIN OF MEXICO'S AGUA AZUL FALLS

CURTIS MAY HAD A VERY CLOSE CALL at the Agua Azul waterfalls in Chiapas, Mexico, on December 18, 2022. He posted a video of the rescue on YouTube (tinyurl.com/trapped-behind-curtain), with the following description:

The climax of this section consists of five waterfalls
called the Five Kings. At the third "King," my approach
was too far right and I dried out at the lip in about
3 inches of water. I lost my speed and dropped behind
the curtain of the waterfall. For the next 75 minutes, I
made multiple attempts to escape and repeatedly blew
my whistle in an attempt to let my friends know that I
was still alive. My friends acted swiftly to begin rescue
operations. I was the last of us to run the drop, so the
other five boats were all downstream of this waterfall
and a 60-footer below it.

There is no access to the river between the 35-foot
drop and the 60-foot drop, so Issac and Wesley hiked their
boats back upstream and ran the 35-footer again to get
into position. I could not see or hear anything beyond the
curtain of the waterfall, and they could not see or hear
me. Isaac and Wesley made many attempts to gain access
behind the curtain, both with ropes and their bodies.
After about 60 minutes with no success and sunset fast
approaching, Wesley decided to try to paddle behind the
curtain through a small gap on river right. Both Wesley
and Issac were able to get behind the curtain and stash
their boats before launching a heroic live-bait rescue
behind the curtain. It wasn't until Wesley was about
30 feet from me that we were finally able to hear each
other. This was their first indication that I was still alive.

After over an hour of failed attempts to escape and
zero contact with anyone, I was beginning to lose hope.
When I first heard another voice and knew my friends

were still working to get me out, we couldn't see each other because there was a rock wall between us. I had no idea that he was just around the corner from me until I saw him while making another attempt to paddle through the curtain. When I saw Wesley floating there, I felt a level of relief and joy that I had never experienced in my life.

At this point, it had been well over an hour, and I was exhausted. Every attempt to paddle through the curtain zapped my energy, and it took a few minutes to recharge between attempts. I retreated back to my point of safety and gathered my strength for a moment to make the ferry around the corner to where Wesley was waiting. When Wesley reached me, he gave three blasts on his whistle, and Issac started pulling us both along the undercut wall back to safety. They saved my life on this day, and I will forever be grateful.

8

STAYING OUT OF TROUBLE IN WHITEWATER

READING ALL THESE NEAR-MISS REPORTS can be pretty scary!
But whitewater paddling is remarkably safe when you take the right
precautions. Here are some things to think about:

- **Wear a life vest.** A PFD would have prevented at least
  25% of all moving-water deaths reported to American
  Whitewater in the last 20 years.

- **Avoid alcohol and drugs** while on the river, and moderate your consumption the night before so that you are
  well rested and at your best on the day of your trip.

- **Don't paddle alone and avoid one-boat trips.** You will
  need help from time to time in whitewater. Make sure
  there are at least two boats in your party (three is better). If
  a single boat carrying two or more people flips, you have
  no backup and are at the mercy of the current.

- **Be prepared for the challenges of high, cold water.**
  Cold water requires wetsuits or drysuits to avoid hypothermia; high water requires expert paddling skills

A guided trip with a professional outfitter is a wise choice for first-timers.

because there is little margin for error. (See Appendix A, page 301, for more gear suggestions.)

- **Know before you go.** Find out how difficult the rapids are before your trip. Avoid known danger spots like strainers and low-head dams.

A FEW OTHER USEFUL GUIDELINES

- **First-timers should go with experienced people.** Canoe Clubs are a great place to start; kayak schools and commercial outfitters get you on the water quickly and safely.

- **Know the phone number for emergency services,** especially in countries outside the United States. Tell someone where you are going and when you expect to be back.

- **Good spacing is important,** as collisions between paddlers can cause serious injury. Don't crowd anyone. Generally speaking, the downstream paddler has the right-of-way, but if you are in an eddy, don't eddy out in front of an oncoming paddler. Always look upstream before surfing a wave or hole. Regardless of these guidelines, do all you can to avoid running into someone.

- **If you need to leave the group** for any reason, even to answer the call of nature, be sure to tell someone so the whole group doesn't have to stop and search for you.

- **Consider your skills and experience** and how they match up to the river you plan to run, especially when the river difficulty approaches the limits of your skill. Take into account factors that reduce performance, like a recent illness, lack of sleep, or a hangover. Consider the remoteness of the river and access in case of an emergency; you'll need to be more careful on wilderness runs than on rivers that are close to civilization.

- **Beware of starting runs late in the day.** Night runs are trouble! Know how much daylight is left, and allow extra time to deal with mishaps.

- **Do a gear check before getting on the water.** Experienced paddlers usually have the right gear, but is it in good shape? A cracked boat or a leaky spray skirt or drysuit can cause real problems! Safety gear like throw ropes, first aid supplies, and rescue hardware are seldom used but are essential when needed. Extra gear for cold weather and long runs makes sense.

- **Be especially cautious when trying new gear.** A boat or spray skirt that doesn't fit right may be an entrapment risk.

- **Work to develop your paddling skills.** Decked boaters should develop a bombproof roll. Practice using a throw bag. Swiftwater rescue and first aid training will give you an edge in emergencies.

- **Don't underestimate the importance of encouragement** in any rescue. A pin or bad swim can be exhausting and frightening. Encourage the victim by reassuring them that help is on the way.

- **If you have to swim a rapid,** roll over on your back and assume a feet-first position. If you are being pummeled, relax and trust your PFD to pull you to the surface. Be prepared to swim into an eddy at the first opportunity.

APPENDIX A:
RECOMMENDED GEAR

HERE'S A SHORT LIST OF ESSENTIAL GEAR for whitewater paddlers. Most of us have a large duffel bag to keep everything together on trips.

- **Life vest** (PFD)

- **Helmet**

- **Knife** attached to an accessible part of your PFD

- **Whistle**

- **Protective footwear** Sandals are OK if they protect the toes. Wetsuit boots are needed in cold weather.

- **Appropriate clothing** Quick-drying clothes for warm weather; wetsuits or drysuits for the cold; waterproof paddle jackets and pants as needed

- **Spray skirt** for decked boats

- **Flotation bags** sized to fit your boat

- **Throw bag**

- **Spare paddle** (takedown-style, in case a paddle is lost; one per group)

- **Carabiners and slings** for rescues or steep portages

- **Fire-starting supplies** (waterproof matches or lighter)

- **First aid kit** Simple for day trips; expanded for long trips (one per group)

- **Dry bag** to carry loose items, food, and other essentials

APPENDIX B:
USEFUL TERMS

Boil An upwelling of water caused when current pours over or around a rock or other obstruction. It looks like boiling water.

Boof A technique used to keep a kayak or canoe straight and flat while going over a drop.

Brace Paddle stroke used to prevent the boat from flipping over.

C-boat Any decked canoe. There are one-person (C-1) and two-person (C-2) C-boats.

Carabiner A D-shaped clip used to secure ropes and other items.

Chock stone A stone onto which water flowing over a falls lands.

Chute A channel between obstructions that has faster current than the surrounding water.

Curler A wave with a top that curls over onto the face of the wave.

Deadfall Trees or brush that has fallen into a stream, totally or partially obstructing it.

Decked boat A kayak (usually) or canoe that is completely enclosed and fitted with a spray skirt that keeps the hull from filling with water.

Downstream V A river feature that often marks the best route through obstacles; the point of the V faces downstream. It's formed by the eddy lines resulting from two obstacles bracketing a faster channel of water, or by turbulent water bracketing a smooth tongue.

Drop-and-pool A river on which rapids are separated with long, placid stretches. The rapids act as natural dams that still the current preceding the drop.

Eddy An area behind an obstruction where the current has been diverted by the obstruction. A good place to rest and regroup.

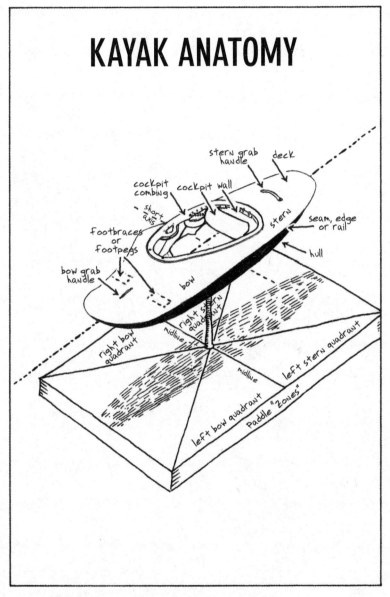

KAYAK ANATOMY

William Nealy, from *Kayak: The New Frontier* (Menasha Ridge Press, 2007)

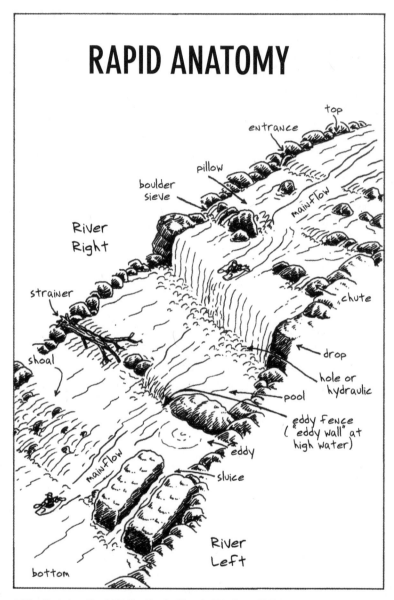

RAPID ANATOMY

top

entrance

pillow

boulder sieve

mainflow

River Right

strainer

chute

shoal

drop

hole or hydraulic

pool

eddy fence ("eddy wall" at high water)

mainflow

eddy

sluice

River Left

bottom

William Nealy, from *Kayak: The New Frontier* (Menasha Ridge Press, 2007)

Eddy out To exit the downstream current into an eddy.

Ferry To move laterally across a stream, facing up- or downstream.

Gradient Altitude change over a fixed distance, usually expressed in feet per mile.

Hand of God rescue A technique used by a paddler to flip a second, capsized kayaker upright.

Hole/hydraulic A spot where water drops over a rock and curls back into itself, creating a frothy water cycle. A large hole can recirculate (hold and tumble) a boat or person.

K-1 A kayak.

Line A route through a rapid; may be hard, easy, or dangerous.

Live-bait rescue A swimming rescue made by a paddler wearing a quick-release harness. A rope is attached to the harness and is managed by a rope handler, or belayer.

Low-head dam A structure built across a river from bank to bank and designed to divert water. As water flows over the crest, a hydraulic jump forms downstream, producing a reverse current that can trap boaters.

PFD Personal flotation device (life jacket)

Portage To carry your boat and gear over land to avoid a rapid.

Pin When a boat or paddler is held in place by the current against a rock or other obstruction.

Window-shaded Flipped multiple times in a hole.

Wrap When boat pinned against an obstruction is held there, being pushed by the current, until it is deformed.

Z-drag A rope-and-pulley system used in rescue situations to make moving heavy objects or people easier; creates a three-to-one mechanical advantage.

APPENDIX C:
SAFETY CODE OF AMERICAN WHITEWATER

Charlie Walbridge, Safety Chairman | Mark Singleton, Executive Director
© 1999–2016 American Whitewater, PO Box 1540, Cullowhee, NC 28723;
866-BOAT-4-AW; info@amwhitewater.org.

INTRODUCTION

This code has been prepared using the best available information and has been reviewed by a broad cross section of whitewater experts. The code, however, is only a collection of guidelines; attempts to minimize risks should be flexible, not constrained by a rigid set of rules. Varying conditions and group goals may combine with unpredictable circumstances to require alternate procedures. This code is not intended to serve as a standard of care for commercial outfitters or guides.

I. PERSONAL PREPAREDNESS AND RESPONSIBILITY

1. Be a competent swimmer, with the ability to handle yourself underwater.

2. Wear a life jacket. A snugly fitting vest-type life preserver offers back and shoulder protection as well as the flotation needed to swim safely in whitewater.

3. Wear a solid, correctly fitted helmet when upsets are likely. This is essential in kayaks or covered canoes, and recommended for open canoeists using thigh straps and rafters running steep drops.

4. Do not boat out of control. Your skills should be sufficient to stop or reach shore before reaching danger. Do not enter a rapid unless you are reasonably sure that you can run it safely or swim it without injury.

5. Whitewater rivers contain many hazards that are not always easily recognized. The following are the most frequent killers:

A. High water. The river's speed and power increase tremendously as the flow increases, raising the difficulty of most rapids. Rescue becomes progressively harder as the water rises, adding to the danger. Floating debris and strainers make even an easy rapid quite hazardous. It is often misleading to judge the river level at the put-in, since a small rise in a wide, shallow place will be multiplied many times where the river narrows. Use reliable gauge information whenever possible, and be aware that sun on snowpack, hard rain, and upstream dam releases may greatly increase the flow.

B. Cold. Cold drains your strength and robs you of the ability to make sound decisions on matters affecting your survival. Cold-water immersion, because of the initial shock and the rapid heat loss that follows, is especially dangerous. Dress appropriately for bad weather or sudden immersion in the water. When the water temperature is less than 50°F, a wetsuit or drysuit is essential for protection if you swim. Next best is wool or pile clothing under a waterproof shell. In this case, you should also carry waterproof matches and a change of clothing in a waterproof bag. If, after prolonged exposure, a person experiences uncontrollable shaking, loss of coordination, or difficulty speaking, he or she is hypothermic and needs your assistance.

C. Strainers. Brush, fallen trees, bridge pilings, undercut rocks, or anything else that allows river current to sweep through can pin boats and boaters against the obstacle. Water pressure on anything trapped this way can be overwhelming. Rescue is often extremely difficult. Pinning may occur in fast current, with little or no whitewater to warn of the danger.

D. Dams, weirs, ledges, reversals, holes, and hydraulics. When water drops over an obstacle, it curls back on itself, forming a strong upstream current that may be capable of holding a boat or swimmer. Some holes make for excellent sport; others are proven killers. Paddlers who cannot recognize the difference should avoid all but the smallest holes. Hydraulics around man-made dams must be treated with utmost respect regardless of their height or the level of the river.

Despite their seemingly benign appearance, they can create an almost escape-proof trap. The swimmer's only exit from the "drowning machine" is to dive below the surface when the downstream current is flowing beneath the reversal.

E. Broaching. When a boat is pushed sideways against a rock by strong current, it may collapse and wrap. This is especially dangerous to kayak and decked-canoe paddlers; these boats will collapse, and the combination of indestructible hulls and tight outfitting may create a deadly trap. Even without entrapment, releasing pinned boats can be extremely time-consuming and dangerous. To avoid pinning, throw your weight downstream toward the rock. This allows the current to slide harmlessly underneath the hull.

6. Boating alone is discouraged. The minimum party is three people or two craft.

7. Have a frank knowledge of your boating ability, and don't attempt rivers or rapids that lie beyond that ability.

8. Be in good physical and mental condition, consistent with the difficulties that may be expected. Make adjustments for loss of skills due to age, health, fitness. Any health limitations must be explained to your fellow paddlers prior to starting the trip.

9. Be practiced in self-rescue, including escape from an overturned craft. The Eskimo roll is strongly recommended for decked boaters who run rapids Class IV or greater, or who paddle in cold environmental conditions.

10. Be trained in rescue skills, CPR, and first aid, with special emphasis on recognizing and treating hypothermia. It may save your friend's life.

11. Carry equipment needed for unexpected emergencies, including footwear that will protect your feet when walking out, a throw rope, knife, whistle, and waterproof matches. If you wear eyeglasses, tie them on and carry a spare pair on long trips. Bring cloth repair tape on short runs and a full repair kit on isolated rivers. Do not wear bulky jackets, ponchos, heavy boots, or anything else that could reduce your ability to survive a swim.

12. Despite the mutually supportive group structure described in this code, individual paddlers are ultimately responsible for their own safety and must assume sole responsibility for the following decisions:

A. The decision to participate on any trip. This includes an evaluation of the expected difficulty of the rapids under the conditions existing at the time of the put-in.

B. The selection of appropriate equipment, including a boat design suited to their skills and the appropriate rescue and survival gear.

C. The decision to scout any rapid, and to run or portage according to their best judgment. Other members of the group may offer advice, but paddlers should resist pressure from anyone to paddle beyond their skills. It is also their responsibility to decide whether to pass up any walkout or takeout opportunity.

D. All trip participants should consistently evaluate their own and their group's safety, voicing their concerns when appropriate and following what they believe to be the best course of action. Paddlers are encouraged to speak with anyone whose actions on the water are dangerous, whether they are a part of your group or not.

II. BOAT AND EQUIPMENT PREPAREDNESS

1. Test new and different equipment under familiar conditions before relying on it for difficult runs. This is especially true when adopting a new boat design or outfitting system. Low-volume craft may present additional hazards to inexperienced or poorly conditioned paddlers.

2. Be sure your boat and gear are in good repair before starting a trip. The more isolated and difficult the run, the more rigorous this inspection should be.

3. Install flotation bags in non-inflatable craft, securely fixed in each end and designed to displace as much water as possible. Inflatable boats should have multiple air chambers and be test-inflated before launching.

4. Have strong, properly sized paddles or oars for controlling your craft. Carry sufficient spares for the length and difficulty of the trip.

5. Outfit your boat safely. The ability to exit your boat quickly is an essential component of safety in rapids. It is your responsibility to see that there is absolutely nothing to cause entrapment when coming free of an upset craft, such as the following:

A. Spray covers that won't release reliably or that release prematurely.

B. Boat outfitting too tight to allow a fast exit, especially in low-volume kayaks or decked canoes. This includes low-hung thwarts in canoes lacking adequate clearance for your feet and kayak footbraces which fail or allow your feet to become wedged under them.

C. Inadequately supported decks that collapse on a paddler's legs when a decked boat is pinned by water pressure. Inadequate clearance with the deck because of your size or build.

D. Loose ropes that cause entanglement. Beware of any length of loose line attached to a whitewater boat. All items must be tied tightly and excess line eliminated; painters, throw lines, and safety-rope systems must be completely and effectively stored. Do not knot the end of a rope, as it can get caught in cracks between rocks.

6. Provide ropes that permit you to hold on to your craft so that it may be rescued. The following methods are recommended:

A. Kayaks and covered canoes should have grab loops of ¼-inch-plus rope or equivalent webbing sized to admit a normal-sized hand. Stern painters are permissible if properly secured.

B. Open canoes should have securely anchored bow and stern painters consisting of 8–10 feet of ¼-inch-plus line. These must be secured in such a way that they are readily accessible but cannot come loose accidentally. Grab loops are acceptable but are more difficult to reach after an upset.

C. Rafts and dories may have taut perimeter lines threaded through the loops provided.

Footholds should be designed so that a paddler's feet cannot be forced through them, causing entrapment. Flip lines should be carefully and reliably stowed.

7. Know your craft's carrying capacity and how added loads affect boat handling in whitewater. Most rafts have a minimum crew size that can be added to on day trips or in easy rapids. Carrying more than two paddlers in an open canoe when running rapids is not recommended.

8. Car-top racks must be strong and attach positively to the vehicle. Lash your boat to each crossbar, then tie the ends of the boats directly to the bumpers for added security. This arrangement should survive all but the most violent vehicle accident.

III . GROUP PREPAREDNESS AND RESPONSIBILITY

1. Organization. A river trip should be regarded as a common adventure by all participants, except on instructional or commercially guided trips as defined below. Participants share the responsibility for the conduct of the trip, and each participant is individually responsible for judging his or her own capabilities and for his or her own safety as the trip progresses. Participants are encouraged (but are not obligated) to offer advice and guidance for the independent consideration and judgment of others.

2. River conditions. The group should have a reasonable knowledge of the difficulty of the run. Participants should evaluate this information and adjust their plans accordingly. Maps and guidebooks, if available, should be examined if the run is exploratory or no one is familiar with the river. The group should secure accurate flow information; the more difficult the run, the more important this will be. Be aware of possible changes in river level and how this will affect the difficulty of the run. If the trip involves tidal stretches, secure appropriate information on tides.

3. Group equipment should be suited to the difficulty of the river. The group should always have a throw line available, and one line per boat is recommended on difficult runs. The list may include: carabiners, prussic loops, first-aid kit, flashlight, folding saw, fire starter, guidebooks, maps, food, extra clothing, and any other rescue or survival items suggested by conditions. Each item is not required on every run, and this list is not meant to be a substitute for good judgment.

4. Keep the group compact, but maintain sufficient spacing to avoid collisions. If the group is large, consider dividing into smaller groups or using the "buddy system" as an additional safeguard. Space yourselves closely enough to permit good communication, but not so close as to interfere with one another in rapids.

A. A point paddler sets the pace. When in front, do not get in over your head. Never run drops when you cannot see a clear route to the bottom or, for advanced paddlers, a sure route to the next eddy. When in doubt, stop and scout.

B. Keep track of all group members. Each boat keeps the one behind it in sight, stopping if necessary. Know how many people are in your group, and take head counts regularly. No one should paddle ahead or walk out without first informing the group. Paddlers requiring additional support should stay at the center of a group and not allow themselves to lag behind in the more difficult rapids. If the group is large and contains a wide range of abilities, a "sweep boat" may be designated to bring up the rear.

C. Courtesy. On heavily used rivers, do not cut in front of a boater running a drop. Always look upstream before leaving eddies to run or play. Never enter a crowded drop or eddy when no room for you exists. Passing other groups in a rapid may be hazardous: it's often safer to wait upstream until the group ahead has passed.

5. Float plan. If the trip is into a wilderness area or for an extended period, plans should be filed with a responsible person who will contact the authorities if you are overdue. It may be wise to establish checkpoints along the way where civilization could be contacted if necessary. Knowing the location of possible help and preplanning escape routes can speed rescue.

6. Drugs. The use of alcohol or mind-altering drugs before or during river trips is not recommended. These substances dull reflexes, reduce decision-making ability, and may interfere with important survival reflexes.

7. Instructional or commercially guided trips. In contrast to the common adventure-trip format, these trip formats involve a boating instructor or commercial guide who assumes some of the responsibilities normally exercised by the group as a whole, as appropriate under the circumstances. These formats recognize that instructional or commercially guided trips may involve participants who lack significant experience in whitewater. However, as a participant acquires experience, he or she takes on increasing responsibility for his or her own safety, in accordance with what he or she knows or should know as a result of that increased experience. Also, as in all trip formats, every participant must realize and assume the risks associated with the serious hazards of whitewater rivers. It is advisable for instructors and commercial guides or their employers to acquire trip or personal liability insurance:

> **A. An "instructional trip"** is characterized by a clear teacher–pupil relationship, where the primary purpose of the trip is to teach boating skills, and which is conducted for a fee.

> **B. A "commercially guided trip"** is characterized by a licensed, professional guide conducting trips for a fee.

IV. GUIDELINES FOR RIVER RESCUE

1. Recover from an upset with an Eskimo roll whenever possible. Evacuate your boat immediately if there is imminent danger of being trapped against rocks, brush, or any other kind of strainer.

2. If you swim, hold on to your boat. It has much flotation and is easy for rescuers to spot. Get to the upstream end so that you cannot be crushed between a rock and your boat by the force of the current. Persons with good balance may be able to climb on top of a swamped kayak or flipped raft and paddle to shore.

3. Release your craft if this will improve your chances, especially if the water is cold or dangerous rapids lie ahead. Actively attempt self-rescue whenever possible by swimming for safety. Be prepared to assist others who may come to your aid.

A. When swimming in shallow or obstructed rapids, lie on your back with feet held high and pointed downstream. Do not attempt to stand in fast-moving water; if your foot wedges on the bottom, fast water will push you under and keep you there. Get to slow or very shallow water before attempting to stand or walk. Look ahead! Avoid possible pinning situations, including undercut rocks, strainers, downed trees, holes, and other dangers, by swimming away from them.

B. If the rapids are deep and powerful, roll over onto your stomach and swim aggressively for shore. Watch for eddies and slackwater, and use them to get out of the current. Strong swimmers can effect a powerful upstream ferry and get to shore fast. If the shores are obstructed with strainers or undercut rocks, however, it is safer to "ride the rapid out" until a safer escape can be found.

4. If others spill and swim, go after the boaters first. Rescue boats and equipment only if this can be done safely. While participants are encouraged (but not obligated) to assist one another to the best of their ability, they should do so only if they can, in their judgment, do so safely. The first duty of a rescuer is not to compound the problem by becoming another victim.

5. The use of rescue lines requires training; uninformed use may cause injury. Never tie yourself into either end of a line without a reliable quick-release system. Have a knife handy to deal with unexpected entanglement. Learn to place set lines effectively, to throw accurately, to belay effectively, and to properly handle a rope thrown to you.

6. When reviving a drowning victim, be aware that cold water may greatly extend survival time under water. Victims of hypothermia may have depressed vital signs, causing them to look and feel dead. Don't give up; continue CPR for as long as possible without compromising safety.

V. UNIVERSAL RIVER SIGNALS

These signals may be substituted with an alternate set of signals agreed upon by the group.

STOP: Potential hazard ahead. Wait for the "all clear" signal before proceeding, or scout ahead. Form a horizontal bar with your outstretched arms. Those seeing the signal should pass it back to others in the party.

HELP: Emergency. Assist the signaler as quickly as possible. Give three long blasts on a police whistle while waving a paddle, helmet, or life vest over your head. If a whistle is not available, use the visual signal alone. A whistle is best carried on a lanyard attached to your life vest.

ALL CLEAR: Come ahead. In the absence of other directions, proceed down the center. Form a vertical bar with your paddle or one arm held high above your head (see left). Paddle blade should be turned flat for maximum visibility. To signal direction or a preferred course through a rapid around an

obstruction, lower the previously vertical "all clear" by 45 degrees toward the side of the river with the preferred route (see left). Never point toward the obstacle you wish to avoid.

I'M OK: I'm not hurt. While holding an elbow outward toward your side, repeatedly pat the top of your head.

VI . INTERNATIONAL SCALE OF RIVER DIFFICULTY

This is the American version of a rating system used to compare river difficulty throughout the world. This system is not exact: rivers do not always fit easily into one category, and regional or individual interpretations may cause misunderstandings. It is no substitute for a guidebook or accurate first-hand descriptions of a run. Paddlers attempting difficult runs in unfamiliar areas should act cautiously until they get a feel for the way the scale is interpreted locally. River difficulty may change each year due to fluctuations in water level, downed trees, recent floods, geological disturbances, or bad weather. Stay alert for unexpected problems! As river difficulty increases, the danger to swimming paddlers becomes more severe. As rapids become longer and more continuous, the challenge increases. There is a difference between running an occasional Class IV rapid and dealing with an entire river of this category. Allow an extra margin of safety between skills and river ratings when the water is cold or if the river itself is remote and inaccessible.

Examples of commonly run rapids that fit each of the classifications are presented in the document "International Scale of River Difficulty: Standard Rated Rapids." This document is available online at tinyurl.com/awriverdifficultyscale. Rapids of a difficulty similar to a rapids on this list are rated the same. Rivers are also rated using this scale. A river rating should take into account many factors including the difficulty of individual rapids, remoteness, hazards, etc.

THE SIX DIFFICULTY CLASSES

CLASS I: Easy. Fast-moving water with riffles and small waves. Few obstructions, all obvious and easily missed with little training. Risk to swimmers is slight; self-rescue is easy.

CLASS II: Novice. Straightforward rapids with wide, clear channels that are evident without scouting. Occasional maneuvering may be required, but rocks and medium-sized waves are easily missed by trained paddlers. Swimmers are seldom injured, and group assistance, while helpful, is seldom needed. Rapids that are at the upper end of this difficulty range are designated "Class II+."

CLASS III: Intermediate. Rapids with moderate, irregular waves that may be difficult to avoid and can swamp an open canoe. Complex maneuvers in fast current and good boat control in tight passages or around ledges are often required; large waves or strainers may be present but are easily avoided. Strong eddies and powerful current effects can be found, particularly on large-volume rivers. Scouting is advisable for inexperienced parties. Injuries while swimming are rare; self-rescue is usually easy, but group assistance may be required to avoid long swims.

Rapids that are at the lower or upper end of this difficulty range are designated "Class III-" or "Class III+," respectively.

CLASS IV: Advanced. Intense, powerful, but predictable rapids requiring precise boat handling in turbulent water. Depending on the character of the river, it may feature large, unavoidable waves and holes or constricted passages demanding fast maneuvers under pressure. A fast, reliable eddy turn may be needed to initiate maneuvers, scout rapids, or rest. Rapids may require "must" moves above dangerous hazards. Scouting may be necessary the first time down. Risk of injury to swimmers is moderate to high, and water conditions may make self-rescue difficult. Group assistance for rescue is often essential but requires practiced skills. A strong Eskimo roll is highly recommended. Rapids that are at the upper end of this difficulty range are designated "Class IV-" or "Class IV+," respectively.

CLASS V: Expert. Extremely long, obstructed, or very violent rapids that expose a paddler to added risk. Drops may contain large, unavoidable waves and holes or steep, congested chutes with complex, demanding routes. Rapids may continue for long distances between pools, demanding a high level of fitness. What eddies exist may be small, turbulent, or difficult to reach. At the high end of the scale, several of these factors may be combined. Scouting is recommended but may be difficult. Swims are dangerous, and rescue is often difficult even for experts. A very reliable Eskimo roll, proper equipment, extensive experience, and practiced rescue skills are essential. Because of the large range of difficulty that exists beyond Class IV, Class 5 is an open-ended, multiple-level scale designated by 5.0, 5.1, 5.2, etc. Each of these levels is an order of magnitude more difficult than the last. Example: increasing difficulty from Class 5.0 to Class 5.1

is a similar order of magnitude as increasing from Class IV to Class 5.0.

CLASS VI: Extreme and exploratory. These runs have almost never been attempted and often exemplify extremes of difficulty, unpredictability, and danger. The consequences of errors are very severe, and rescue may be impossible. For teams of experts only, at favorable water levels, after close personal inspection and taking all precautions. After a Class VI rapid has been run many times, its rating may be changed to an appropriate Class 5.x rating.

INDEX

S *(continued)*
swiftwater rescue classes/training,
253–254
cooperation at rescue scene, 259
LAST acronym, 181
swims, how to handle, 41. *See also* bad
swims

T
tag-line rescue
on Cheat River, WV, 146–149
in Gore Canyon, CO, 149–153
in Watauga Gorge, NC, 137
tandem flip, at Shenandoah Staircase,
107–110
Tauranga-Taupo Falls (New Zealand),
289–291
Tennessee Valley Canoe Club paddlers,
126–130
Tennessee Wildlife Resources Agency
(TWRA), 274
The Ledges, NC, 84, 86–87
Thomas, John, 135
Thornton, Tyler, report/account by,
292–293
throw bag, 52, 67, 119, 184, 223–225
Trap Rock, WV, 25–27
Trash Can rapid, CO, 270–271
Tri-Town Ambulance & Rescue
Association, 21
trotlines, 172–174
tubing/tuber rescues
on Alcovy River, GA, 223–225
on Ouachita River, AR, 225–226
on Patapsco River, MD, 222–223

U
Uncommon Service Award, 249
Upper Nantahala River, NC, 78–82
Upper Pine Creek/River rescue teams,
270, 271

Upper Salmon River, ID, 213–214
Upper Watauga River, NC, flooded, 44–49

V
V-lower system, setting up, 171–172
Vallecito Creek Gorge, CO, 270–271
Valor Award, 267
vehicle rescue, from Logan River, UT,
271–272
vertebral injury, 280–281, 283, 284
vertical pin/pinnings, 11–19, 27–32
at Gulf Hagas, Maine, 139–145
rescue techniques, 126–130

W
Wasserman, Jason, 214–215, 217
Watauga Gorge, NC, 136–137
waterfalls
accidents/injuries at, 31, 277–295
curtain entrapments, 83–84, 94,
190–191, 238–246, 293–295
Wellman, Doug, 111–112
Westwater Canyon/Gorge, UT, 116–122
Wilderness Voyageurs (rafting outfitter),
232
Wolgram, Alex, 214–215, 217
Wonder Falls, WV, 110–111
Woodall Shoals, SC, 203–209
Wright, Clay, report/account by, 250
Wright, Stephen, report/account by,
240–246

Y
Yanowski, Tom, 10
Youghiogheny River, PA, incidents on,
42–43, 55–57, 170
Young, Fred, report/account by, 62–63

Z
Z-drag, 133, 134, 292–293
Zoar Outdoor, 139, 160
Zute Chute, Crystal Gorge, CO, 279–281

The Story of AdventureKEEN

We are an independent nature and outdoor activity publisher. Our founding dates back more than 40 years, guided then and now by our love of being in the woods and on the water, by our passion for reading and books, and by the sense of wonder and discovery made possible by spending time recreating outdoors in beautiful places.

It is our mission to share that wonder and fun with our readers, especially with those who haven't yet experienced all the physical and mental health benefits that nature and outdoor activity can bring.

In addition, we strive to teach about responsible recreation so that the natural resources and habitats we cherish and rely upon will be available for future generations.

We are a small team deeply rooted in the places where we live and work. We have been shaped by our communities of origin—primarily Birmingham, Alabama; Cincinnati, Ohio; and the northern suburbs of Minneapolis, Minnesota. Drawing on the decades of experience of our staff and our awareness of the industry, the marketplace, and the world at large, we have shaped a unique vision and mission for a company that serves our readers and authors.

We hope to meet you out on the trail someday.

#bewellbeoutdoors

ABOUT THE AUTHOR

CHARLIE WALBRIDGE IS A NATIONALLY KNOWN WHITEWATER safety expert with more than 50 years of river-running experience.

He began paddling whitewater seriously in 1967 while attending college. He has paddled rivers throughout the US and Canada and made several first descents. He was an A-ranked C-1 slalom and wildwater racer in the mid-1970s and worked part-time as a river guide until the mid-1980s. He has collected and published reports of US whitewater fatalities for more than 40 years and has written books and articles on whitewater safety, including *The American Canoe Association's Knots for Paddlers* (Menasha Ridge Press, 1995) and *The American Canoe Association's River Safety Anthology* (Menasha Ridge Press, 1996). He has served as an expert witness in many wrongful death cases and is quoted often in newspapers and magazines.

Charlie has been active in both the American Canoe Association (ACA) and American Whitewater (AW). He held the position of safety chairman for both organizations and now serves on the AW board of directors. As a member of the ACA Instruction Committee, he helped develop programs in whitewater canoeing and swiftwater rescue, and he trains students and instructors in swiftwater rescue.